Jesus
and His
Adversaries

Jesus and His Adversaries

The Form and Function of the Conflict Stories in the Synoptic Tradition

ARLAND J. HULTGREN

AUGSBURG Publishing House • Minneapolis

JESUS AND HIS ADVERSARIES

Copyright © 1979 Augsburg Publishing House

Library of Congress Catalog Card No. 79-50093

International Standard Book No. 0-8066-1717-9

Scripture quotations unless otherwise noted are from the Revised Standard Version of the Bible, copyright 1946, 1952, and 1971 by the Division of Christian Education of the National Council of Churches.

MANUFACTURED IN THE UNITED STATES OF AMERICA

To
Carole

Contents

PART TWO: STUDIES IN THE FORMATION OF THE SYNOPTIC CONFLICT STORIES

Foreword

Form criticism is better known in the English speaking world than it used to be. But since it was the late Dr. Vincent Taylor who was largely responsible for introducing it, we have for a long time followed his nomenclature for the English equivalents to the German form-critical classifications. This means among other things that most English speaking writers have operated with the broad classification of stories about Jesus culminating in a significant saying as "pronouncement stories." Not many writers in English have followed Bultmann, who broke down these stories (which he called "apophthegms") into three subdivisions: "scholastic dialogues," "conflict stories" and "biographical apophthegms." Nor has there been any agreed translation of these three terminologies. A further point: the only monograph devoted exclusively to the second of these categories, the conflict stories, is that written by M. Albertz right at the beginning of form criticism, namely his work, *Die synoptischen Streitgespräche* (1921). Since then there has been no full-length treatment of these stories. Consequently the English speaking world has been hardly aware of them. The time for such a treatment is thus long overdue. Not only was Albertz' work not very satisfactory, but since his day form critical methods have been sharpened, and redaction criticism has entered the field. As the late Norman Perrin once remarked, it is necessary today to write a complete history of the tradition of any given pericope. This is the task of *Traditionsgeschichte,* which puts together all the previously developed methods, i.e., sources, form- and redaction criticism.

This is precisely what Arland Hultgren has done. His work thus fills a long-standing void in Gospel criticism, and should be welcomed by the scholarly community and by all who are interested in the study of the Gospels, in Christian origins, in the quest of the historical Jesus, and in the history of early Christian thought. What I particularly like about Professor Hultgren's work is its judiciously discriminating character. Much New Testament work nowadays is done on the one hand by those who assume without question that the gospel reports of the sayings and doings of Jesus are historical as they stand, while others feel that the only way to do redactio-critical work is to assign the entire story to the creativity of the particular evangelist. A more judicious way would seek wherever possible to establish an original "authentic" nucleus behind the tradition and then to trace its constant reapplication to the needs of the church in successive stages. Sometimes, of course, we have to draw a negative verdict on the question of authenticity, but sometimes it is possible to trace the nucleus of a particular tradition all the way back to Jesus. This is precisely what happens with the conflict stories in the hands of Professor Hultgren. And for me at any rate, this is a model of what such work ought to be.

REGINALD H. FULLER
Virginia Theological Seminary
Alexandria, Virginia

Preface

This study of the conflict stories in the synoptic tradition culminates an interest of mine which has extended over many years. It is based partially on work submitted as a doctoral dissertation at Union Theological Seminary, New York, and further work which has resulted in articles published in journals. But it is not a replication or even a revision of earlier works. It is addressed to a broader audience, written for this occasion, and it takes account of books and articles related to the theme which have appeared over the years since my earlier studies in this area.

Various persons deserve an expression of thanks. These include persons who served on the original dissertation committee, especially Reginald H. Fuller (now a professor at the Episcopal Theological Seminary in Virginia), who served as chairman at that time, and who has graciously accepted the invitation to write a foreword for the present volume. His insights and suggestions have always been helpful, and his kindness and interest in present and former students remain a source of joy. Others who offered assistance and critique in the earlier work at Union include J. Louis Martyn, Walter Wink, and George Landes. Of course the present volume represents my own work and perspectives which have developed since the days of the original dissertation, and none of these persons is responsible for any weaknesses which may exist. Mary C. Strug, a student at Luther-Northwestern Seminaries, has given valuable assistance in proofreading and work on the indexes, for which I am grateful.

Finally, it is fitting that I record gratitude to my wife Carole, who has made this work possible in many ways, not least of all by her abiding interest and encouragement. To her it is affectionately dedicated.

ARLAND J. HULTGREN
Luther-Northwestern Theological Seminaries
St. Paul, Minnesota

Abbreviations

I. General Works Cited

M. Albertz, *Streitgespräche* — Martin Albertz, *Die synoptischen Streitgespräche* (Berlin: Trowitzsch, 1921)

Babylonian Talmud (I. Epstein) — The Babylonian Talmud, ed. Isidore Epstein (34 vols.; London: Soncino, 1935-1948)

F. W. Beare, *Earliest Records* — Francis W. Beare, *The Earliest Records of Jesus* (Nashville: Abingdon, 1962)

K. Berger, *Die Gesetzesauslegung Jesu* — Klaus Berger, *Die Gesetzesauslegung Jesu: Ihr historischer Hintergrund im Judentum und im Alten Testament*, Part I (WMANT 40; Neukirchen-Vluyn: Neukirchener, 1972)

G. Bornkamm, *Jesus* — Günther Bornkamm, *Jesus of Nazareth* (New York: Harper, 1960)

R. Bultmann, *Synoptic Tradition* — Rudolf Bultmann, *The History of the Synoptic Tradition* (2nd ed.; New York: Harper, 1968)

M. Dibelius, *Tradition* — Martin Dibelius, *From Tradition to Gospel* (New York: Scribners, 1934)

W. L. Knox, *Sources* — Wilfred L. Knox, *The Sources of the Synoptic Gospels* (2 vols.; Cambridge: Cambridge University, 1953-1957)

H.-W. Kuhn, *Ältere Sammlungen* — Heinz-Wolfgang Kuhn, *Ältere Sammlungen im Markusevangelium* (SUNT 8; Göttingen: Vandenhoeck & Ruprecht, 1971)

14

W. Kümmel, *Introduction* — Werner G. Kümmel, *Introduction to the New Testament* (rev. ed.; Nashville: Abingdon, 1975)

Mishnah (H. Danby) — *The Mishnah* (trans. Herbert Danby; Oxford: Oxford University, 1933)

NT Apocrypha (Hennecke-Schneemelcher/Wilson) — *New Testament Apocrypha* (2 vols.; ed. Edgar Hennecke & rev. Wilhelm Schneemelcher; trans. Robert McL. Wilson; Philadelphia: Westminster, 1963-1965)

V. Taylor, *Formation* — Vincent Taylor, *The Formation of the Gospel Tradition* (2nd ed.; London: Macmillan, 1935)

II. Frequently Cited Commentaries

B. H. Branscomb, *Mark* — B. Harvie Branscomb, *The Gospel of Mark* (New York: Harper, 1939)

J. Creed, *Luke* — John M. Creed, *The Gospel According to St. Luke* (London: Macmillan, 1957)

E. Ellis, *Luke* — E. Earle Ellis, *The Gospel of Luke* (CB; rev. ed.; London: Oliphants, 1974)

E. Gould, *Mark* — Ezra P. Gould, *A Critical and Exegetical Commentary on the Gospel According to St. Mark* (ICC; New York: Scribners, 1896)

W. Grundmann, *Markus* — Walter Grundmann, *Das Evangelium nach Markus* (THKNT; 3rd ed.; Berlin: Evangelische Verlagsanstalt, 1965)

S. Johnson, *Mark* — Sherman E. Johnson, *A Commentary on the Gospel According to St. Mark* (HNTC; New York: Harper, 1960)

E. Klostermann, *Markus* — Erich Klostermann, *Das Markus-Evangelium* (HNT; 3rd ed.; Tübingen: Mohr, 1936)

W. Lane, *Mark* — William L. Lane, *The Gospel According to Mark* (NICNT; Grand Rapids: Eerdmans, 1974)

E. Lohmeyer, *Markus*   Ernst Lohmeyer, *Das Evangelium des Markus* (MeyerK; 17th ed.; Göttingen: Vandenhoeck & Ruprecht, 1967)

D. Nineham, *Mark*   David E. Nineham, *The Gospel of St. Mark* (Baltimore: Penguin, 1963)

A. Plummer, *Luke*   Alfred Plummer, *A Critical and Exegetical Commentary on the Gospel According to St. Luke* (ICC; 5th ed.; Edinburgh: Clark, 1922)

A. Rawlinson, *Mark*   A. E. J. Rawlinson, *St. Mark* (London: Methuen, 1947)

E. Schweizer, *Mark*   Eduard Schweizer, *The Good News According to Mark* (Richmond: John Knox, 1970)

E. Schweizer, *Matthew*   Eduard Schweizer, *The Good News According to Matthew* (Richmond: John Knox, 1975)

H. Swete, *Mark*   Henry B. Swete, *The Gospel According to St. Mark* (London: Macmillan, 1909)

V. Taylor, *Mark*   Vincent Taylor, *The Gospel According to St. Mark* (London: Macmillan, 1952)

III. Journals, Reference Works, and Serials

AB	Anchor Bible	BAG	W. Bauer, W. F. Arndt, and F. W. Gingrich, *Greek-English Lexicon of the NT*
ALGHJ	Arbeiten zur Literatur und Geschichte des hellenistischen Judentums		
ANF	The Ante-Nicene Fathers	BDF	F. Blass, A. Debrunner, and R. W. Funk, *A Greek Grammar of the NT*
APOT	R. H. Charles (ed.), *Apocrypha and Pseudepigrapha of the Old Testament*		
		BEvT	Beiträge zur evangelischen Theologie
ASNU	Acta seminarii neotestamentici upsaliensis	BJRL	*Bulletin of the John Rylands University Library of Manchester*

BZNW	Beihefte zur ZNW	JQR	*Jewish Quarterly Review*
CBQ	*Catholic Biblical Quarterly*	*JSS*	*Journal of Semitic Studies*
CBQMS	Catholic Biblical Quarterly — Monograph Series	*JTS*	*Journal of Theological Studies*
ConNT	*Coniectanea neotestamentica*	KD	*Kerygma und Dogma*
EvT	*Evangelische Theologie*	LCC	Library of Christian Classics
ExpTim	*Expository Times*	LCL	Loeb Classical Library
FRLANT	Forschungen zur Religion und Literatur des Alten und Neuen Testaments	MeyerK	H. A. W. Meyer, Kritischexegetischer Kommentar über das Neue Testament
HNT	Handbuch zum Neuen Testament	*NEB*	*New English Bible*
HNTC	Harper's NT Commentaries	NICNT	New International Commentary on the New Testament
HTR	*Harvard Theological Review*	*NovT*	*Novum Testamentum*
HTS	Harvard Theological Studies	NovTSup	Novum Testamentum, Supplements
HUCA	*Hebrew Union College Annual*	*NRT*	*La nouvelle revue théologique*
ICC	International Critical Commentary	NTD	Das Neue Testament Deutsch
IDB	G. A. Buttrick (ed.), *Interpreter's Dictionary of the Bible*	*NTS*	*New Testament Studies*
IDBSup	Supplementary volume to *IDB*	*PCB*	M. Black and H. H. Rowley (eds.), *Peake's Commentary on the Bible*
Int	*Interpretation*		
JBC	R. E. Brown et al. (eds.), *The Jerome Biblical Commentary*	*RevScRel*	*Revue des sciences religieuses*
JBL	*Journal of Biblical Literature*	RSV	Revised Standard Version
JBR	*Journal of Bible and Religion*	SBLDS	SBL Dissertation Series
JE	*Jewish Encyclopedia*	SBLMS	SBL Monograph Series
JJS	*Journal of Jewish Studies*	SBLSS	SBL Semeia Supplements

SE	*Studia Evangelica*	THKNT	Theologischer Hand-kommentar zum Neuen Testament
SHR	Studies in the History of Religion	TLZ	*Theologische Litera-turzeitung*
SJLA	Studies in Judaism in Late Antiquity	TRu	*Theologische Rund-schau*
SNTSMS	Society for New Testament Studies Monograph Series	TS	*Theological Studies*
SPB	Studia postbiblica	VC	*Vigiliae christianae*
Str-B	[H. Strack and] P. Billerbeck, *Kommentar zum Neuen Testament*	WMANT	Wissenschaftliche Monographien zum Alten und Neuen Testament
SUNT	Studien zur Umwelt des Neuen Testaments	ZAW	*Zeitschrift für die alttestamentliche Wissenschaft*
TDNT	G. Kittel and G. Friedrich (eds.), *Theological Dictionary of the New Testament*	ZEE	*Zeitschrift für evangelische Ethik*
		ZNW	*Zeitschrift für die neutestamentliche Wissenschaft*

Introduction

Although the conflict stories occupy a large portion of the synoptic gospels, they have received surprisingly little attention. There is only one significant volume devoted exclusively to them, and that appeared in German over fifty years ago, the work of Martin Albertz, *Die synoptischen Streitgespräche: ein Beitrag zur Formgeschichte des Urchristentums* (Berlin: Trowitzsch, 1921). Aside from this work by Albertz, the only other important treatments of the conflict stories are those given in the more general form critical studies of R. Bultmann, M. Dibelius, and V. Taylor.[1]

This study is informed by the works of these pioneers in form criticism, but it goes beyond them in its attention to other relevant exegetical, form critical, and redaction critical studies which have appeared since their works were published.[2] Furthermore, this book attempts to reassess former assumptions and prior form critical conclusions, and to describe the form and function of the conflict stories in new ways. The thesis that emerges is that while analogies to rabbinic and Hellenistic forms of debate and pronouncements are useful, comparative studies should not obscure the peculiar genre and various *Sitze im Leben* of the conflict stories themselves. (*Sitze im Leben* is a technical term meaning "settings in life," but more appropriately the term signifies those aspects of early Christian practice—worship, preaching, catechetical instruction, or apologetics—within which units of tradition were formed and put to use. *Sitz im Leben* is the singular.) What one observes through comparative study, more detailed than heretofore, is that the conflict stories have features peculiar to themselves, because of the circumstances and purposes surrounding their composition, and that they have been composed at various periods in the history of tradition for functions which differ at each period.

This book is divided into three main sections. Part One consists of two chapters. In Chapter I there is a delineation of the materials

19

which are considered conflict stories in the present work. (Compare Appendix A for other proposals which have been made along different lines, using different terminology and methods, by Albertz, Bultmann, Dibelius, and Taylor.) This is followed by a review and critique of the work in this field. Attention is drawn especially to analogies from rabbinic and Hellenistic literatures, which have been used to illustrate the synoptic form and to make judgments concerning the *Sitze im Leben* in which, it has been concluded, these synoptic units were formed and put to use. The point is made that there are not only similarities between the synoptic units and these analogies, but differences as well. The result is that we are then freed from certain prevailing preconceptions about form and *Sitz im Leben* and we can go on to reconsider the form and function of the conflict stories in their own right.

In Chapter II a reconsideration of form is made. There are places in the synoptic tradition at which we can observe the actual formation of conflict stories from materials not originally having that form. These instances are reviewed in order that we can observe more carefully the actual emphases and structure worked out in the history of tradition. This is followed by a description of the conflict story form (as well as a statement indicating why the term "conflict story" is used in this work) including not only a delineation of its basic structure, but also a discussion of how the individual parts function within the broader structure.

Part Two consists of studies in the formation of the various conflict stories individually. The stories have been classified broadly into two sub-categories: unitary conflict stories (Chapter III) and non-unitary conflict stories (Chapter IV). Unitary conflict stories are those in which the closing saying of Jesus could have circulated only as a unit together with the rest of the conflict story (the opponent's question and, usually, the immediate setting). Non-unitary conflict stories, on the other hand, are those in which the closing saying of Jesus could have circulated independently of the rest of the story; the latter (made up of a narrated scene and the opponent's question) is a secondary, artificial construction.[3] The decision to divide the conflict stories into these two sub-categories within the conflict story form has been arrived at as the best of three methods of classification.

One could, as a second possibility, classify the conflict stories according to the framework of the gospel narrative and place them under the categories "Galilean Conflict Stories" and "Jerusalem Conflict Stories." This is the classification used by Albertz for most of the conflict stories.[4] But this alternative has been rejected, since the Galilean and Jerusalem settings alone have nothing to do with similarities and differences among the stories from a formal point of view. Furthermore, these settings in Mark's Gospel have more to do with the editing of the stories than with their actual formation.

A third possibility is to classify the conflict stories according to thematic considerations, e.g., (1) stories that end with a saying having to do with Jewish law; (2) stories that contain a saying on doctrine; and (3) stories that have a saying concerning the role or authority of Jesus. But this method of classification of the stories has been rejected too, since one should not use the end-point of the stories' full development in the gospels in making judgments about prior purposes for which, and settings in which, they were formulated. The classification by unitary and non-unitary, however, allows one to study the individual stories with flexibility. By classifying them in terms of these two types of formation process one can observe more readily the dynamics at work in the primitive church by which the conflict stories, as brief narratives with dialogue, were composed.

Part Three is devoted to the collecting and use of the conflict stories in the primitive church. In Chapter V it is argued that the five conflict stories in Mark 2:1—3:6 existed as a collection prior to the writing of Mark's Gospel. An attempt is made to designate the approximate time, place, and church situation in which the collecting of these stories would have taken place. Then in Chapter VI the whole of the previous discussion is drawn upon to deal with the question of the function of the conflict stories at various stages in the synoptic tradition. Their function in the period prior to the evangelists is probed first, and then their function in each of the three gospels is observed. Our concern is to discover ways in which the evangelists made use of the conflict stories within the over-all composition of their works. Here we make some connection with redaction criticism.

A Conclusion is provided which brings together some of the more important results of the study. And an Afterword follows on "Christian and Jew in Light of the Conflict Stories" in which the problem of interpreting certain conflict stories in the church is addressed briefly, and which is a part of the volume no reader should neglect.

A methodological point should be made at the outset. Time and again an attempt is made to discover the form and substance of traditions prior to their being written in their present form in the gospels. The degree to which that attempt is possible is debatable. Yet nearly everyone engaged in synoptic studies (especially in redaction criticism) is involved in it in one way or another. It should be said that in the following study whenever an earlier form of a given conflict story is presented, we are dealing with approximate results. No one would deny that certain editorial phrases by Mark can be removed from a given pericope. But what remains is not to be thought of as a text free from Marcan influence; we are still dependent on Mark's version (and language) even in our claim to have recovered what is pre-Marcan. Nevertheless, it is necessary to try to identify the approximate material with which Mark worked, and the author assumes that one can get at least a step closer to the pre-Marcan tradition by removing that which is most obviously Marcan.

NOTES

1. R. Bultmann, *Synoptic Tradition*, 11-27, 39-54, 61-69; M. Dibelius, *Tradition*, 37-69; V. Taylor, *Formation*, 63-87.

2. The first edition of three of these studies was prepared at approximately the same time: 1919 is the date of publication of the work of Dibelius; 1921 is the date of publication of the works of Bultmann and Albertz, although Albertz, *Streitgespräche*, v, indicates that his work was completed in 1919. Taylor's first edition appeared in 1933.

3. These two categories (unitary and non-unitary) have been suggested from an observation made by R. Bultmann, *Synoptic Tradition*, 46-47. After his critical work on the individual conflict stories, he observes: "This individual analysis of the Synoptic controversy dialogues has further shown that we must always raise the question whether we are dealing with a unitary composition, or whether the scene is a secondary construction for a saying originally in independent circulation. If the saying is comprehensible only in terms of its contextual situation, then it clearly has been conceived together with it. But that is commonly not the case either in the controversy or scholastic dialogues. Instances such as Mark 2:15-17; 7:1-23; 10:2-12, where the artificiality of composition is clear as day; or such as Mark 2:1-12; Luke 7:41-43, where the insertion into an alien narrative is quite plain; or such as Matthew 12:11f. and Luke 14:5, which are proverbs given different places in the tradition—all these show that the arguments were in many places already there before the narrative themselves." For a similar judgment concerning rabbinic debates, see Jacob Neusner, *The Rabbinic Traditions about the Pharisees before 70* (3 vols.; Leiden: Brill, 1971) 3. 17.

4. M. Albertz, *Streitgespräche*, 5-36.

Part One
Form Criticism

I. The Conflict Stories in
Modern Study

The synoptic gospels contain several episodes prior to the passion narrative (Mark 14-15 and parallels) in which there is a verbal exchange between Jesus and his contemporaries on some crucial issue, and in which Jesus and the other party are adversaries. The crucial issue normally arises because of some action of Jesus or his disciples which is unacceptable to the other party, or because Jesus or someone else asks a question which provokes conflict. Mark 2:15-17 is such a story:

> 15 And as he sat at table in his house, many tax collectors and sinners were sitting with Jesus and his disciples; for there were many who followed him. 16 And the scribes of the Pharisees, when they saw that he was eating with sinners and tax collectors, said to his disciples, "Why does he eat with tax collectors and sinners?" 17 And when Jesus heard it, he said to them, "Those who are well have no need of a physician, but those who are sick; I came not to call the righteous, but sinners."

The story opens with a narrated scene in which Jesus and his disciples are sitting with "many tax collectors and sinners." Furthermore, Jesus is eating with them (2:16), sharing in table fellowship, which was an affront to Pharisaic sensibilities. The activity, in short, provokes conflict, and the "scribes of the Pharisees" take up the challenge with the question, "Why does he eat with tax collectors and sinners?" (2:16). Jesus replies with a statement (2:17) which justifies his conduct. He does not seek a legal precedent to defend himself; he merely states his position, and that closes the discussion.

There are several passages in the synoptic gospels which share the same form, which is called a "conflict story" in this study. (Why this term is used is discussed in Chapter II, Part B.) They are found in all three of the synoptic gospels. From a source-critical standpoint,

however, they originate in only three (Mark, Q, and L) of the four
(M is excluded) major synoptic sources and streams of tradition, as
follows:

1. Eleven Conflict Stories in Mark (with parallels in Matthew and
   Luke)
   2:1-12, The Healing of the Paralytic (Matt. 9:1-8//Luke 5:17-
   26)
   2:15-17, Eating with Tax Collectors and Sinners (Matt. 9:10-13
   //Luke 5:29b-32)
   2:18-22, The Question about Fasting (Matt. 9:14-15//Luke
   5:33-35)
   2:23-28, Plucking Grain on the Sabbath (Matt. 12:1-8//Luke
   6:1-5)
   3:1-5, Healing on the Sabbath (Matt. 12:9-13//Luke 6:6-10)
   3:22-30, The Beelzebul Controversy (Matt. 12:22-32//Luke
   11:14-23)
   7:1-8, The Tradition of the Elders (Matt. 15:1-9)
   10:2-9, On Divorce (Matt. 19:3-9)
   11:27-33, The Question about Authority (Matt. 21:23-27//
   Luke 20:1-8)
   12:13-17, Paying Taxes to Caesar (Matt. 22:15-22//Luke
   20:20-26)
   12:18-27, On the Resurrection (Matt. 22:23-33//Luke 20:27-40)

2. A Conflict Story in Q
   Matt. 12:22-32//Luke 11:14-23, The Beelzebul Controversy
   (cf. Mark 3:22-30)

3. Two Conflict Stories in the Special Lucan Material
   13:10-17, Healing the Crippled Woman on the Sabbath
   14:1-6, Healing the Man with Dropsy on the Sabbath

4. Three Conflict Stories in Matthew Based in Part on Marcan and
   Q Materials
   12:38-42, The Refusal of a Sign (in part from Mark 8:11-12 and
   Q, Luke 11:29-32)
   22:34-40, The Double Commandment of Love (in part from
   Mark 12:38-42 and Q, Luke 10:25-28)
   22:41-46, The Question about David's Son (in part from Mark
   12:35-37)

5. A Conflict Story in Luke Based in Part on Marcan Material
   7:36-50, The Sinful Woman at Simon's House (in part from
   Mark 14:3-9)

Whether this list can be considered complete—or whether other passages should be added—can be debated. A major problem in this area of study is the amount of material which can be classified under this form. Appendix A provides lists of synoptic materials which other scholars have included in this area of study, and it will be seen that while considerable agreement exists among these four, there is also disagreement. Our own list shares a basic commonality with these lists, but there are differences here too. Of the eighteen pericopes above, seven appear in all four of the other lists; five more appear in three of them. There are no pericopes accepted by three or four other scholars which do not appear in our own. The eighteen pericopes have been selected on the basis of their sharing the conflict story form as it is described in Chapter II, Part B.

Closely related to the problem of what pericopes should be considered to share a common form is the problem of terminology. The term "conflict story" itself does not have universal usage in English. The next section of this chapter is devoted to the twin questions of terminology and descriptions of form in major studies.

A. Terminology and Descriptions in Major Studies

In the earlier, pioneering form critical works several terms have been used to designate the material which we are here calling conflict stories. In German scholarship the term *Streitgespräche* (controversy dialogues) was used by Martin Albertz and Rudolf Bultmann.[1] Martin Dibelius, however, used the term *Paradigmen* (paradigms).[2] And the British scholar Vincent Taylor used the term pronouncement stories.[3] Sometimes the term controversy stories has been used as a general designation in English as well.

Each of the authors mentioned has described the conflict story form in his own way. The differences are due in large part to the differing assumptions of the various writers concerning the *function* of the stories in their pre-literary stages of formation and transmission. In fact it is clear that their various formal descriptions, as well as the terminology which they have used, have been determined in each case by the functions a given form critic assumes that the stories served. It is our purpose in this section to review the descriptions and terminology of these writers.

1. *Martin Albertz*

According to Albertz, the normal structure of the controversy dialogues consists of two, sometimes three parts.[4] There is, first of all, introductory material (which he calls *Exposition*) which prepares the way for a question and introduces the questioner(s). To go back to our earlier example, Mark 2:15-17, the introductory material is found in 2:15, 16a. These verses describe the situation (Jesus sits at table with tax collectors and sinners; the scribes see him eating with them). The second part in the formal pattern is the dialogue *(Gespräch)*, which consists of one or more brief speeches by Jesus and his opponents, as in Mark 2:16b, 17:

> Scribes: "Why does he eat with tax collectors and sinners?"
> Jesus: "Those who are well have no need of a physician, but those who are sick; I came not to call the righteous, but sinners."

These two parts *(Exposition* and *Gespräch)* are found in all controversy dialogues, and the major interest falls on the dominical saying (i.e., the Lord's saying), which often brings the story to a close. Occasionally, however, there is a third part as well, namely closing remarks *(Schlussbemerkungen)*. Closing remarks do not appear in our example, but can be found elsewhere at the end of certain stories (for example, Mark 2:12; 3:6; 12:17b, 34b, and 37b).

Albertz wrote his work prior to the appearance of the form critical works of Dibelius and Bultmann.[5] He does not deal with the question of what factors existed in the primitive church to give the controversy dialogues their form. Therefore Bultmann could criticize his work as not a truly form critical one.[6] Albertz assumed that, while some abridgement and expansion took place during the oral period of transmission, the controversy dialogues generally give us reports of disputes between Jesus and his opponents from Jesus' own life situation. He concludes that the stories give us glimpses of the activities of Jesus, and that their form is modelled on speech forms in the Old Testament prophets. Certain prophets, he says, engaged in verbal struggles with their own people and their leaders (royalty, false prophets, and priesthood).[7] Likewise, he says, Jesus took up a prophetic stance; he stood, "called by God, in struggle against the false leaders of the people, as they did." [8] The stories are therefore considered by Albertz—from a formal point of view—based on Old Testament models, the controversies of the prophets, but are nevertheless considered virtual transcripts of controversies carried on by Jesus as a prophetic figure.

2. Rudolf Bultmann

Although Bultmann's work (first edition, 1921) appeared after that of Dibelius (first edition, 1919), it stands somewhere between Albertz and Dibelius in outlook. He uses the same term (controversy dialogues) as Albertz, and he finds analogies for this form in Palestinian Judaism.

Bultmann considers the controversy dialogues as one sub-category within the larger category of *apophthegms*.[9] He deals with the controversy dialogues, however, as a distinct form, and therefore his treatment of apophthegms in general need not detain us here.

The controversy dialogues consist of three parts: [10] first, there is an action or a description of an attitude of Jesus or his disciples; second, this is seized upon by an opponent and used in an attack by accusation or question; and, third, Jesus replies to the attack. The latter follows a set form. Special preference is given for a counter-question or a metaphor (or both together), or it may consist of a Scripture quotation.

The most important part of the controversy dialogues is the reply of Jesus. It was because of the dominical sayings that the controversy dialogues were composed, shaped, and preserved. It can be said that there was an "increasing tendency of the Church to clothe its dominical sayings, its views and its fundamental beliefs in the form of the controversy dialogue." [11] In order to do so, the situation (i.e., the activity of Jesus or his disciples, and the attack by opponents) has frequently been composed out of the dominical saying.[12] These artificial situations Bultmann calls "imaginary" or "ideal" scenes.[13] The conflict stories do not necessarily give reports of particular historical events, but illustrate by means of incidents various principles which the church ascribed to Jesus.

Bultmann affirms that Jesus undoubtedly entered into debates with opponents during his historical ministry.[14] But as a form critic he asks what church setting or life situation is presupposed in the shaping of these stories into the form of controversy dialogues. His conclusion is that the carrying on of disputes as portrayed in the stories is "typically rabbinic." Therefore their *Sitz im Leben* is in the discussions which the church had with its opponents outside the church (Palestinian Jews) and among its own members on questions of law.[15]

3. *Martin Dibelius*

As already indicated, Dibelius uses the term paradigm, not controversy dialogue,[16] as a form critical category.[17] He argues that dialogue form *(Gesprächsform)* is not decisive for the category; interest falls not on the dialogue, but rather on the word or activity of Jesus.[18]

What we have, he says, are paradigms, and paradigms are illustrative narratives which were used in the preaching of early Christian missionaries to illustrate and support their message. In form they are (1) rounded off at beginning and end, independent of their context within the framework of the rest of a given gospel; (2) brief and simple, lacking portraiture of the persons on the scene; (3) religious or edificatory in style; (4) didactic, having an emphasis on the final word of Jesus; and (5) ending with a thought useful for preaching purposes, whether it be a general phrase, an exemplary act of Jesus, or an exclamation of onlookers.[19]

While Bultmann claims that the controversy dialogues were formed already in the Aramaic-speaking Palestinian church,[20] Dibelius thinks otherwise. The paradigms, for him, were formed in the Greek-speaking (Hellenistic) Jewish church as it launched its mission into the Hellenistic world.[21] He turns to popular Hellenistic literature and finds that the closest analogy to the paradigms is the Hellenistic chria form. The chriae consist of short pointed sayings of popular teachers couched within brief descriptions of their situations. He says that the chria form can be illustrated in the works of Diogenes Laertius, Xenophon, Lucian, Philostratus, and the fifth century work entitled *Philogelos*.[22]

The *Sitz im Leben* of the paradigms is missionary preaching. Preaching requires, says Dibelius, short anecdotes which speak "of the divine power of Jesus, of his words, his acts, his person" and which "do not wander off into description" and other secondary matters.[23] For Dibelius, "preaching" was "the original seat of all tradition about Jesus." [24]

4. *Vincent Taylor*

Taylor accepted the terminology of neither Bultmann nor Dibelius. Nor did he accept their skepticism concerning the origins of the materials. He affirms in his own form critical study that the personal testimony of eyewitnesses in the formative process of gospel traditions must be taken much more seriously.[25]

Taylor uses the term "pronouncement stories," and for him this leaves open the question of origins. (Bultmann and Dibelius find origins of materials in primitive church disputation and preaching, respectively, but in each case this means that the church produced some traditions.) While Taylor admits that traditions about Jesus were applied to the needs of the primitive church, he refrains from saying that the church, in short, *invented* any of these traditions. Rather, he says, the practical needs of daily life, the necessity of understanding and explaining the faith, and the necessity of defending it "would *kindle recollections* and prompt the relating of His words and deeds" [26] in the primitive churches.

Taylor, then, does not look for analogies in Jewish and Hellenistic literature of the period,[27] which might shed light on the *Sitz im Leben* of the pronouncement stories. He gives attention instead to the form given in the gospels themselves. The pronouncement stories, in his view, consist of brief narratives introduced by a question or description of events, ending with a "pronouncement" of Jesus. Each of the pronouncements has a bearing on some aspect of life, belief, or conduct in the primitive church.[28] "Everything leads up to the final word of Jesus, which for the early Christians must have had the force of a Pronouncement." [29]

B. Assessment of Major Studies

A comparison of the studies by Albertz, Bultmann, Dibelius, and Taylor demonstrates that there is no agreed-upon approach, description, or terminology concerning the conflict stories, but a polyphony of critical views. Nor has there been an independent study in which their views have been assessed, followed by a new approach. This section consists of an assessment; the next chapter provides a reconsideration.

Albertz's claim that the origin of the controversy dialogue form lies in the Old Testament will not do. As Erich Fascher pointed out shortly after the appearance of Albertz's study, there is no real dialogue in the passages from the prophets to which Albertz refers.[30] These passages contain antitheses formulated by the prophets themselves as words of their opponents. Certainly the prophets were involved in religious disputations, but we do not have dialogue forms in the prophetic books comparable to those in the synoptic gospels.

Bultmann does better than Albertz when he turns to rabbinic literature.[31] There one finds disputes which have similarities to the controversy dialogues. One may take, for example, the following dialogue in the Babylonian Talmud tractate *Sanhedrin* 91a, in which a certain "sectarian," who does not believe in the resurrection of the dead, challenges Rabbi Gebiha ben Pesisa: [32]

> A sectarian said to Gebiha b. Pesisa, "Woe to you, ye wicked, who maintain that the dead will revive; if even the living die, shall the dead live?"
>
> He replied, "Woe to you, ye wicked, who maintain that the dead will not revive: if what was not [now] lives, surely what has lived will live again!" [33]

Many such dialogues can be found in rabbinic literature,[34] and their similarity to the controversy dialogues cannot go unnoticed. (Appendix B provides examples.) Through extensive reading of rabbinic disputes one notices the following characteristics common to many of them:

1. The views of the parties entering into debate are set forth in direct discourse.[35]

2. Generally they close with a decisive statement of a rabbi which ends the discussion.

3. Generally they have a certain concreteness about them; the parties of a dispute are often named specifically, or at least what they represent is made clear, and there is often some narration giving the circumstances or occasion for the dispute.

4. Sometimes counter-questions by the one being questioned are presented to the opponent.

5. Sometimes Scripture is appealed to by the parties in debate.

Such characteristics can be found in the conflict stories—not in all of them (nor in all of the rabbinic disputes)—but in a degree sufficient enough to show that the conflict stories belong to a setting similar to that of the rabbinic debates, and therefore Bultmann speaks of the controversy dialogues as "typically rabbinic." [36]

Nevertheless, allowing for the similarities, there are features about the conflict stories which set them apart from the rabbinic debates, as follows:

1. The synoptic conflict stories are brief, while the rabbinic disputes can be, and often are, quite long in comparison; the latter can involve several interchanges.

2. In the synoptic conflict stories there are only two parties to a dispute (Jesus and an opponent—either an individual or a delegation), but in the rabbinic disputes there are frequently several parties to a dispute, each entering into the dialogue.

3. In the synoptic conflict stories the closing statements are generally merely *asserted,* and their authority is based on the fact that Jesus has made them,[37] but in the rabbinic disputes the closing statements are usually arrived at by the rabbi's having followed established procedures of rabbinic disputation, by which his authority is derived.

4. In the synoptic conflict stories the opening questions or statements to Jesus by his opponents are critical; the opponent objects to Jesus' conduct on some legal pretext, and his words are in essence ad hominem attacks upon Jesus. But in the rabbinic disputes such a feature is missing. A person asks a rabbi a question or challenges him with a statement, but he does not object to the rabbi's conduct.[38]

These contrasts show that the conflict stories have peculiarities which must be taken into account. As the next chapter will indicate, they are a unique form of expression—unique in part due to the significance of Jesus himself in Christian thinking—created by primitive Christian storytellers in a unique environment.

The form of the chria, to which Dibelius looks for analogies to the paradigms, also has similarities—and differences—when set beside the gospel materials. The chriae of Hellenistic literature, he says, typically open with an initial question, personal remark, or description of circumstances, followed by a saying of a popular teacher. A chria, he says, is "a short pointed saying of general significance, originating in a definite person and arising out of a definite situation." [39] Examples of chriae follow from a work of Diogenes Laertius concerning Aristotle: [40]

> Being asked how much the educated differ from the uneducated, "As much," he said, "as the living from the dead." He used to declare education to be an ornament in prosperity and a refuge in adversity. Teachers who educated children deserved, he said, more honour than parents who merely gave them birth; for bare life is furnished by the one, the other ensures a good life. To one who boasted that he belonged to a great city his reply was, "This is not the point to consider, but who it is that is worthy of a great country."

Other examples of chriae are listed by Dibelius,[41] but one of the weaknesses of his work is that he does not quote many of them. He asserts similarities between the paradigms and the chriae without sufficiently demonstrating them. (Appendix C contains the actual texts cited by Dibelius.)

A study of both the chriae themselves and the statements of ancient writers about the chriae shows that the similarities between them and the conflict stories are minimal. Dibelius himself must have been aware of this, since he points out that the sayings in the chriae are "often given in connection with a longer narrative, or interwoven with a biographical description" [42]—features not found in the conflict stories. Furthermore, "In place of a terse sentence we may find a longer one, or even a dialogue. The description of the situation may require several sentences." [43]

The Greek term chria can be translated roughly as "use" or "service," and it appears that the chriae were considered "useful sayings" of popular teachers put to use in the moral and rhetorical education of children. Seneca (ca. 5 B.C.–A.D. 65) compares the chriae to proverbs which are given to children to memorize.[44] Hermogenes of Tarsus (born ca. A.D. 150) provides a definition: "A *chria* is a record of a certain word or deed, or both together, having a brief explanation . . . designed for its usefulness." [45] And Quintilian (ca. A.D. 35–100) gives a more detailed description:

> Of *chriae* there are various forms: some are akin to aphorisms and commence with a simple statement "he said" or "he used to say"; others give the answer to a question and begin "on being asked" or "in answer to this he replied," while a third and not dissimilar type begins, "when someone has said or done something." Some hold that

a *chria* may take some action as its text; take for example the statement "Crates on seeing an ill-educated boy, beat his pedagogus," or a
very similar example which they do not venture actually to propose
as a theme for a *chria,* but content themselves with saying that it is of
the nature of such a theme, namely, "Milo, having accustomed himself
to carrying a calf every day, ended by carrying it when grown into a
bull." All these instances are couched in the same grammatical form
and deeds no less than sayings may be presented for treatment.[46]

From what has been said about the chriae by the ancients themselves, and from a reading of various chriae,[47] it is apparent that the
chriae differ from the synoptic conflict stories in three major ways: [48]

1. The conflict stories portray specific situations and issues in which
   and concerning which Jesus is challenged by his opponents, but
   the chriae have about them the character of " 'once upon a time,'
   when the speaker was asked 'such-and-such,' he replied 'such-
   and-so.' "

2. Central to the conflict stories is the dialogue between Jesus and his
   opponent, of which the saying of Jesus is most important, but
   chriae need not contain sayings material at all; some are brief anecdotes (short narratives) of human interest. "Deeds no less than
   sayings can be presented," Quintilian says.

3. The specific settings in the conflict stories are portrayed by narrated
   scenes, and the dialogue is given in direct discourse. Furthermore,
   neither the narrated scenes nor the dialogues are submerged into
   one another. The chriae, however, may lack narrated scenes or dialogues, and either the sayings material or the occasion on which it
   was given may be subordinated by use of subordinate clauses or
   indirect discourse. It might be said that the chriae differ in these
   respects only because of the way in which they were edited. As
   Seneca has written about them. "They do not drip forth occasionally; they flow continuously. They are unbroken and closely connected." [49] Nevertheless, the differences are due to factors other
   than editing alone. The chriae belong to a broader category of
   anecdotal biography, and as such any given chria may lack either
   of two features found in all conflict stories, viz., narrated scenes
   and sayings in direct discourse.

The significance of this critical response to the views of Bultmann
and Dibelius must now be made clear. Both Bultmann and Dibelius
make judgments on the synoptic materials on the basis of analogies
to rabbinic and Hellenistic literature, respectively. Bultmann thinks of

the controversy dialogues as "typically rabbinic" and concludes therefore that their *Sitz im Leben* is debates concerning points of law which the church carried on with Jewish opponents and within its own membership. Dibelius, on the other hand, thinks of the paradigms as similar to the chriae; both are written to "preserve expressions and events in order to maintain the mind and the manner of the hero as the normative standard." [50] And, as the chriae were used in the moral education of children in Hellenistic culture, so the paradigms were used in preaching to illustrate doctrinal and moral principles. In short, both Bultmann and Dibelius draw conclusions about the form and function of the conflict stories from the study of materials outside the gospels which are roughly analogous. But when it is observed that these analogies break down, one must conclude that what they say about form and function must be taken with caution. And a fresh attempt must be made.

NOTES

1. M. Albertz, *Streitgespräche* (passim); R. Bultmann, *Die Geschichte der synoptischen Tradition* (1st ed., 1921; 3rd ed., Göttingen: Vandenhoeck & Ruprecht, 1957) 9-26. Cf. R. Bultmann, *Synoptic Tradition*, 12-27.
2. M. Dibelius, *Die Formgeschichte des Evangeliums* (1st ed., 1919; 3rd ed., Tübingen: Mohr, 1959) 34-66. Cf. M. Dibelius, *Tradition*, 37-69.
3. V. Taylor, *Formation*, 63-87.
4. M. Albertz, *Streitgespräche*, 86-87.
5. Although his work was published in 1921, he indicates (ibid., p. v) that his work was completed in 1919.
6. R. Bultmann, *Synoptic Tradition*, 40 (n. 2). Cf. also Erhardt Güttgemanns, *Offene Fragen zur Formgeschichte des Evangeliums* (BEvT 54; Munich: Kaiser, 1970) 167, who criticizes Albertz for "historicizing" the concept of *Sitz im Leben* by directing his attention to questions concerning the historical Jesus at the expense of attending to the sociological factors in the formation process.
7. M. Albertz, *Streitgespräche*, 157-158. He gives dozens of examples, including Amos 8:4-8; Hos. 6:1-4; Isa. 28:7-13; Mic. 2:1-11; Jer. 28:1-17; 44. Most of his examples are from Isaiah, Jeremiah, and Ezekiel.
8. Ibid., 163.
9. R. Bultmann, *Synoptic Tradition*, 11-69. Other forms falling under the general category of apophthegms include the scholastic dialogues and biographical apophthegms.
10. Ibid., 39-41.
11. Ibid., 51.
12. Ibid., 61.
13. Ibid., 39-40.
14. Ibid., 40.
15. Ibid., 41.
16. M. Dibelius ("Zur Formgeschichte der Evangelien," *TRu* N. S. 1 [1929] 195) writes, "Because I hold at least questionable the origin of these scenes from debates of the church, it appears to me therefore that the term controversy

dialogues does not follow, which Bultmann as well as Albertz use." (Translation mine.)

17. M. Dibelius, Tradition, 37-69.
18. M. Dibelius, *Die Formgeschichte des Evangeliums*, 65. Cf. p. 68 of English translation.
19. M. Dibelius, *Tradition*, 44-58.
20. R. Bultmann, *Synoptic Tradition*, 48. Cf. also his essay, "The Study of the Synoptic Gospels," *Form Criticism* (1st ed., 1934; 2nd ed., New York: Harper, 1962) 41.
21. M. Dibelius, *Tradition*, 28-36.
22. Ibid., 153-157.
23. M. Dibelius, "The Structure and Literary Character of the Gospels," *HTR* 20 (1927) 162.
24. M. Dibelius, *Tradition*, 14.
25. V. Taylor, *Formation*, 41-43.
26. Ibid., 37 (italics mine).
27. He does, however, cite an example of Jewish disputation from the Talmud; ibid., 29.
28. Ibid., 30; cf. p. 71.
29. Ibid., 65.
30. Erich Fascher, *Die formgeschichtliche Methode* (Giessen: Töpelmann, 1924) 168.
31. M. Albertz (*Streitgespräche*, 162-163) refers to rabbinic disputations too, but he contrasts them with the controversy dialogues; while the former contain "learned discussions," the latter portray "opposition against Jesus."
32. Gebiha is thought to be a legendary figure (so I. Levi, *JE*, 1. 342). Quotation from *Babylonian Talmud* (I. Epstein).
33. Meaning: if it is the case that human life in the present had no pre-existence, which surely is the case, it is possible to conceive that human life will exist in the world to come, since it has a pre-existence (the present life). This form of argument is the familiar rabbinic technique known as argument from major to minor *(kal wa-homer)*, which is described in various studies. See Herman L. Strack, *Introduction to the Talmud and Midrash* (Philadelphia: Jewish Publication Society of America, 1931) 285; or Jacob Z. Lauterbach, "Talmud Hermeneutics," *JE*, 12. 32.
34. R. Bultmann (*Synoptic Tradition*, 42-44) and M. Dibelius (*Tradition*, 134-141) list and illustrate several. Others can be found listed by Kaufman Kohler, "Disputations," and Isaac Broyde, "Polemics and Polemical Literature," *JE*, 4. 614-618 and 10. 102-109, respectively. More can be found in *The Exempla of the Rabbis* (ed. and trans. Moses Gaster; New York: Ktav, 1968) 54, 56, 63, 65, and 72.
35. Cf. J. Neusner, *Rabbinic Traditions*, 3. 5-6.
36. R. Bultmann, *Synoptic Tradition*, 41.
37. J. Neusner (*Rabbinic Traditions*, 3. 78) writes, "Jesus gets both the first and the last lemma; the opposition is allowed only a single argument, then is overwhelmed. No effort is made to balance the arguments of the two parties."
38. In this respect the rabbinic disputations are closer in form to the scholastic dialogues *(Schulgespräche)* of Bultmann's work than to the controversy dialogues. J. Neusner (ibid., 3. 80) writes, "I do not find among Bultmann's ten rabbinic examples a single debate. He has been misled by combining debates with scholastic dialogues, which are in both form and type entirely separate."
39. M. Dibelius, *Tradition*, 152.

40. Diogenes Laertius, *Lives of Eminent Philosophers* (trans. R. D. Hicks; LCL; London: Heinemann, 1925) 1. 463.

41. M. Dibelius, *Tradition*, 151-172.

42. Ibid., 154.

43. Ibid., 155.

44. Seneca, *Ad Lucilium Epistulae Morales*, 33.5-7.

45. *Progymnastica* c. 3; Greek text given in Rudolf Hirzel, *Der Dialog: ein literar-historischer Versuch* (2 vols.; Leipzig: Hirzel, 1885) 1. 145.

46. Quintilian, *Institutio Oratoria*, 1.9.3-6 (trans. H. E. Butler; LCL; Cambridge: Harvard University, 1920) 1. 157-159.

47. Cf. Appendix C. Appendix C contains those units which M. Dibelius (*Tradition*, 151-172) classifies as chriae, and our comparison is limited to these illustrations, as well as the statements of Hermogenes of Tarsus, Quintilian, and Seneca concerning the chriae. Several essays have appeared recently concerning materials in extra-biblical texts which have been categorized by the essayists as pronouncement stories, which to the essayists is a category broader than that of chriae. The work of these scholars does not, however, affect our own evaluation of Dibelius' proposals for the Hellenistic chria as an analogy for the conflict stories. These essays appear in the Society of Biblical Literature 1977 and 1978 *Seminar Papers*, ed. Paul J. Achtemeier, Number 11 (1977) 257-284, and Number 14 (1978) 2. 1-46. Both volumes are published at Missoula by Scholars Press.

48. For a study of the chria form in ancient Jewish sources, in which the author demonstrates both similarities to Hellenistic models and their adaptation within Hebrew culture, see Henry A. Fischel, "Studies in Cynicism and the Ancient Near East: The Transformation of a *Chria*," *Religions in Antiquity: Essays in Memory of Erwin R. Goodenough* (SHR 14; ed. Jacob Neusner; Leiden: Brill, 1968) 372-411. The points indicated above concerning the conflict stories, however, have no correspondence to the points which Fischel makes.

49. Seneca, *Ad Lucilium Epistulae Morales*, 33.6 (trans. Richard M. Gummere; LCL; Cambridge: Harvard University, 1961) 1. 237.

50. M. Dibelius, *Tradition*, 156.

II. The Form of the Conflict Stories Reconsidered

The conflict stories in the synoptic gospels have no formal dependence on other literary or popular forms of the period. They are as new in form as they are in content. They are presented in a form composed by early Christian storytellers specifically for the needs of the newly developing Christian movement.

To make such a claim, and to develop a study of the conflict stories on the basis of the claim, is to depart from the views of Bultmann and Dibelius. It is to violate the notion that there are "laws of style" [1] or "laws which operate as formative factors" [2] common to the gospel traditions and to other popular literary traditions (Jewish and Hellenistic) in the environment of the early church.

But more recent criticism opens the way to making such a claim with justification. Amos Wilder has written that, while rhetorical patterns of the early Christian environment certainly conditioned the speech forms of the early Christians, they did not determine them. The "cultural crisis," he says, "demanded new styles." [3] "The Christian movement was creative in various ways, including the phenomena of human discourse. This impulse brought forth not only a new vocabulary and oral patterns but also new literary forms and styles." [4] These forms were deeply determined by the faith, life-orientation, and social setting that produced them, and not so much by general world views and rhetorical models of the time.

Erich Auerbach, likewise, has written concerning the distinctive forms and styles of early Christian narrative and dialogue. He says that the dialogue we find in the synoptic tradition has no similarity in all the literature of antiquity. Most significant about the gospel dialogues, he says, is their use of direct discourse, "a symptom which at first glance may seem insignificant." But, he says, "I do not believe that there is a single passage in an antique historian where direct discourse is employed in this fashion in a brief, direct dialogue." When dialogues do exist, "they appear in anecdotal biography, and there the function they serve is almost always to lead up to famous pregnant retorts, whose importance lies not in their realistically concrete content but in their rhetorical and ethical impact." One does not find in ancient literature "face-to-face dialogues" given the "salience and immediacy" characteristic of the dialogues presented in the gospels." [5]

It is our purpose in this chapter to describe the conflict story form. This is to be accomplished in two steps. First, we shall demonstrate that, for whatever reasons, there were early Christian transmitters of tradition, including the evangelists themselves, who quite deliberately formed materials into conflict stories. We shall examine certain texts in which we can observe formal features emerge over against other closely related texts that serve as a control. Second, we shall go on to describe the conflict story form on the basis of these observations and by examining other texts which share formal features with the texts that have been formed into conflict stories.

A. Evidence of Conflict Story Formation in the Synoptic Tradition

The New Testament arose during a period of history in which various dialogue forms were common and highly developed.[6] Socratic dialogue and refutation, Stoic diatribe, dramatic dialogue, rabbinic disputation, Gnostic dialogue, as well as dialogue forms in the Old Testament are well known to have existed in the period. By the time the gospel traditions were being transmitted, certain canons of dialogue existed in educated circles. Dialogue forms were used, for instance, in rhetorical competition. Aristotle's *On Rhetoric* was used as a manual to train orators involved in pleading cases at court in rhetorical methods. In one place [7] Aristotle tells how to go about refutation and interrogation of one's opponent. In rabbinic circles, too, the ability to carry on oral disputation was highly prized, and the masters of the technique were emulated by their successors in the schools. In an anonymous tradition of the Mishnah tractate *'Abot* there is the saying: "Any controversy that is for God's sake shall in the end be of lasting worth, but any that is not for God's sake shall not in the end be of lasting worth. Which controversy was for God's sake? Such was the controversy of Hillel and Shammai." [8]

In the writing of literature also—in distinction from rhetorical competition—the dialogue form is held up as a model for would-be dramatists (specifically, writers of tragedies). Aristotle holds Aeschylus in high regard who, he says, "first raised the number of actors from one to two. He also curtailed the chorus and gave the dialogue the leading part." [9] Every tragedy has six parts: plot, character, diction, thought, spectacle, and song.[10] Under thought "come all the effects to be produced by the language. Some of these are proof and refutation, the arousing of feelings like pity, fear, anger, and so on." [11]

When we turn to the New Testament we find various dialogue forms. Our attention here is limited to that dialogue form in the synoptic gospels in which Jesus is confronted by various adversaries on issues arising out of teaching or conduct. Four examples are discussed below in which we observe the formation of a dialogue form, characterized by direct confrontation between Jesus and his adversaries, out of units of tradition. The first is found in Mark, and the parallel in the Gospel of Thomas is used (as a control) to show that an alternative form could be used to present the teaching of Jesus. Nevertheless, Mark, or more likely some traditionist before him, has formed the unit as a dialogue between Jesus and his adversaries. The other three examples show that Matthew formed dialogues between Jesus and his adversaries out of material which is not presented that way in his sources (which are our controls). These four examples give evidence that there was indeed a process of formation of gospel materials into a form of dialogue portraying conflict. What happened in that process of formation is itself of great importance for our attempt at describing the characteristics of that form. Only by observing the process can we describe the characteristics accurately and avoid postulating a form from outside the material itself (i.e., from Hellenistic and/or Jewish analogies, or from a hypothetical "original form" arising from our understanding of the function which the dialogues served in primitive Christian communities).

1. Paying Taxes to Caesar

This pericope, which appears in Mark 12:13-17 and its synoptic parallels (Matt. 22:15-22; Luke 20:20-26) has a parallel also in the Gospel of Thomas, logion 100. It reads in Thomas as follows:

> They showed Jesus a gold (coin) and said to him: Caesar's men ask taxes from us. He said to them: Give the things of Caesar to Caesar, give the things of God to God and give to Me what is Mine.[12]

This pericope differs formally from others in the Gospel of Thomas.

Most of the pericopes in this gospel are revelatory sayings beginning with the words "Jesus said," "He said," or "Jesus said to his
disciples." Others begin with a question usually from the disciples
who ask for a teaching on a particular subject; the stylized introduction is, "His disciples said to him," or "the disciples said to Jesus." [13]
What is peculiar to the pericope above is that it (1) begins with an
action (i.e., they show Jesus a coin)[14] and (2) opens with a problem
from outside the circle of Jesus' followers (i.e., Caesar's men have
demanded taxes). We do not simply have disciples asking the Revealer
for knowledge. "They"—whoever they are, but presumably Jesus' followers—come with a practical problem, a problem which has a direct
bearing on life in the Roman world. The problem has arisen out of
contact with "Caesar's men," and in the view of the questioners there
is an issue to be resolved.

What we have in the Gospel of Thomas, however, is not a fully
stylized story portraying conflict in comparison to that found in Mark.
While there is a conflict situation described, which has arisen from
contact with those outside the circle of Jesus and his followers, this is
not expressed in story form as it is in the synoptic account. We have a
conflict-situation report, not a conflict story. In the Gospel of Thomas
it is the followers of Jesus who come on the scene, show the coin, and
report the conflict issue. In Mark's Gospel, in contrast, there is open
confrontation in story form and in direct dialogue: opponents, who are
identified as a group, arrive on the scene; they ask a question to entrap
Jesus; the question is followed by an interchange of dialogue and the
showing of the coin at Jesus' request; and Jesus gives a final reply
which amazes and silences his opponents.

A comparison shows, then, that we have the same incident related
in two different forms. The critical issue which arises is that of the
relationship between these two accounts in their respective forms.
Are the two pericopes from parallel and independent traditions, lying
behind the respective gospels, or did the collector of the traditions in
the Gospel of Thomas reformulate the synoptic account? The issue is
a highly complex one.

There are scholars who claim that the Gospel of Thomas contains
an independent and very old gospel tradition.[15] By "independent" is
meant that the sayings in this gospel were not taken from the canonical gospels or their sources, nor was this gospel tradition a source of
the canonical gospels. It has also been held, on the other hand, that
the writer of Thomas made use of the canonical gospels. Either he

made use of the traditions which underlie them, or, at the most, he relied on written documents.[16] If either of the latter viewpoints is accepted (that he made use of our gospels either as oral traditions or as written documents), one would have to conclude that the conflict story framework of the pericope found in Mark 12:13-17 has been dismantled in the post-synoptic tradition, and the result of dismantling is the briefer pericope in Thomas, logion 100, which simply reports the problem posed by Caesar's men and gives the remark of Jesus.

There is, however, another solution to the problem which has gained wide acceptance. The materials in the Gospel of Thomas are varied and fall into four general groups: [17] (1) logia which agree verbally with the words of Jesus in the canonical gospels; (2) logia which have variants from canonical parallels; (3) logia which are not found in any form in the canonical gospels, but are found in the apocryphal gospels, church fathers, and Manichean writings; and (4) logia heretofore unknown. No uniform judgment can be made summarily on all of these types of material as to their tradition backgrounds. While those in the first category might be judged as taken over directly from canonical sources, it does not follow that those in the second category were. Oscar Cullmann's position is that these have origins in a Jewish-Christian tradition parallel to and independent of the synoptics.[18] This view has been accepted, with modifications, by others.[19] Robert McL. Wilson modifies it with a cautious qualification. He suggests that these variants have their origin in parallel, independent traditions, but that some of them were influenced later by the form and wording of the canonical gospels prior to the final Gnostic redaction of the material as a whole.[20]

Even if we do not press for the view that there are two completely independent traditions before us,[21] it is difficult to believe that the synoptics have been used as a written source for the Gospel of Thomas, logion 100. If one claims that they were, one must deal not only with the question of form but also with the question as to why the Gnostics would have omitted the reference to the Teacher as being "true" and as one who truly "teaches the way of God" (Mark 12:14). The term "way" is frequently found in Gnostic literature.[22] The words in Mark 12:14 would lend themselves readily to the Gnostic pericope, since the words attributed to Jesus in the Thomas logion, "give to Me what is Mine," are in fact a teaching which teaches "the way of God": tribute belongs to Caesar; the things of this world to the God of this world (i.e., the Demiurge); but persons in their true and essential nature belong to Jesus.[23] In light of this significant difference between the two accounts, it is better to assume that at the most the Gnostic traditionists (or writers) had access to the synoptic tradition in a primitive form which did not include the words of Mark 12:14, or—and this is more likely—they had access to an independent tradition which they fashioned for their own purposes.

It is apparent that the pericopes in the Gospel of Thomas and in Mark have been formulated with different ends in view; therefore they are presented in different forms in the two gospels. In the Gospel of Thomas the material is formulated without traces of direct conflict between Jesus and opponents. But the "pronouncement" of Jesus is still provided for the readers. It would appear that in this circle of readers the interest was simply that of having a teaching on the question of paying taxes to Caesar.

But we must ask the question: Why does the Marcan pericope differ in form? Why is there the portrayal of a conflict between Jesus and his opponents? If the primitive church wished to preserve merely a "pronouncement" of Jesus on the tax issue, the setting and dialogue of conflict would not have been necessary, as the Thomas form illustrates so well. It might be argued that the synoptic traditionists presented the material in this particular dialogue form because they remembered that "that's the way it happened," i.e., that the traditionists have given us a virtual transcript of an actual conflict between Jesus and his adversaries on the issue. But studies in the history of the synoptic tradition militate against such a point of view. One must allow for the likelihood that in this pericope, as in others, the final product has been influenced both in form and wording by the work of the traditionists within the early Christian communities to serve some purpose, even if the pericope should contain a reminiscence of an actual event in the ministry of Jesus. The synoptic traditionists have presented the material, then, not merely to give a "pronouncement" on the issue at stake. They have presented the material in a form which itself has significance: a form in which spirited dialogue takes place between Jesus and opponents. We shall attempt to determine later (Chapter III, Part B) the specific motive for the formation of the material into this form. Here we simply register the phenomenon, viz., that while other forms of presentation are viable for preserving a pronouncement (of which the Thomas pericope is one illustration), the synoptic traditionists have presented the material in the form of a story which contains dialogue within conflict.

2. *The Question about David's Son*

This pericope is found in Mark 12:35-37a and its parallels (Matt. 22:41-46; Luke 20:41-44). In Mark and Luke the tradition is not presented in the form of a conflict story. In the Marcan account Jesus is teaching in the temple and asks how the scribes can say that the Messiah is the Son of David since David, inspired by the Holy Spirit, calls the Messiah Lord (in Psalm 110). There is no opening question asked of Jesus by opponents, nor by Jesus to opponents. The question asked by Jesus is a rhetorical one (12:35), and there is no closing pronouncement but, rather, an additional question which illustrates how impossible it is to speak of the Messiah as the Son of David.

The Marcan pericope is didactic, and it lacks a confrontation between Jesus and opponents. Bultmann classifies it as a "legal saying." [24] It apparently originated in early Christian exegetical work. Barnabas Lindars has suggested that the pericope is a formulation related to a more primitive exegetical tradition which has been preserved in its more pristine form in Acts 2.[25] Here the Lord, who is seated at the right hand of God, is considered superior to the Son of David, who sits on an earthly throne: "For David did not ascend into the heavens; but he himself says, 'The Lord said to my Lord, Sit at my right hand . . .'" (Acts 2:34). If we may accept the judgment of Lindars, we have a community product which speaks of a lordship that was greater than anything that David could claim for himself. To the transmitters of the tradition, Jesus fulfills the qualification of lordship, and they place the saying on his lips as a teaching for the church concerning him.

In Matthew's Gospel, however, the incident is in the form of a story which portrays conflict between Jesus and the Pharisees (22:41-46). While in Mark the question is raised by Jesus concerning the teachings of the scribes—and we are not told that the scribes were even present; rather, if 12:37b belongs to this pericope, Jesus was addressing a great crowd—in Matthew the question is put by Jesus directly to the Pharisees: "What do you think of the Christ? Whose son is he?" The Pharisees answer: "The Son of David." Jesus then raises the question, as in Mark, as to how the Messiah can be the Son of David in light of Psalm 110. This does not mean that in this passage the Messiah's Davidic Sonship is denied, of course, but what is being said is that, while the Messiah is the Son of David, even more is he the Son of God.[26] The pericope closes, "And no one was able to answer him a word, nor from that day did any one dare to ask him any more questions" (22:46).

Here it is important to emphasize again the difference in form in the parallel accounts. In the one case, Mark, we do not have a narration of conflict, but rather a saying which relates a rhetorical question. In Matthew we have a fully stylized story portraying conflict: opponents, who are identified as a group, are present; they are asked a question by Jesus which is designed to provoke conflict; they answer; and they are refuted by Jesus in an appeal to Scripture and a closing question.

3. *The Refusal of a Sign*

This pericope appears in Mark 8:11-12; in Matt. 12:38-42 and 16:1-4; and in Luke 11:29-32. It is necessary to review the complex relationships between the various texts before going on to establish the point of this section, viz., that Matthew has created a story portraying conflict (12:38-42) out of materials originally not in that form.

Luke's parallels to Mark 8:11-12 appear in two different places. At 11:16, set within the Beelzebul Controversy (from Q: see Chapter IV below), certain persons are said to seek from Jesus a sign from heaven, thereby testing him. This verse corresponds roughly with Mark 8:11. But there is no refusal of a sign by Jesus here. At 11:29, however, at the beginning of another pericope (11:29-32), there is a statement by Jesus concerning the "present generation's" seeking a sign, followed by the statement that none shall be given, "except the sign of Jonah." This verse roughly parallels Mark 8:12.

In Matthew's Gospel there is a demand for a sign in two places. First, it is given at the beginning of the Refusal of a Sign pericope (12:38-42) at 12:38. Second, it is given at the beginning of a similar pericope (16:1-4) at 16:1. In both instances a verse follows which is roughly parallel to Mark 8:12. These are at Matt. 12:39 and 16:4.

It is clear from a comparison of the texts that neither Matthew nor Luke has made use of the Marcan (8:12) version of the dominical saying. It must be concluded that both have taken the saying from Q (Luke 11:29; Matt. 12:39; 16:4), since their dominical sayings have agreements over against Mark's version.[27]

The question of the relationships of the various texts must now be faced. There is no indication, first of all, that Luke has made use of Mark 8:11-12 as a basis for his pericope (11:29-32).[28] Here Luke is dependent on Q, as the close similarities of 11:29b-32 and Matt.

12:39-42 over against Mark show. Second, at Matt. 16:1-4 it must be concluded that Matthew has made use of Mark 8:11-12, but that he has conflated it with Q material and his own special material. Matthew's first verse (16:1) is based on Mark 8:11; furthermore, the fact that Matthew has located the pericope in exactly the same context as Mark 8:11-12 (after the Feeding of the Four Thousand) shows his dependence on Mark. Matt. 16:2-3 consists of Matthew's own special tradition. And his closing statement (16:4), as indicated above, is taken from Q.

But our main interest in this discussion concerns Matt. 12:38-42. The pericope opens with a statement by certain "scribes and Pharisees" addressed to Jesus: "Teacher, we wish to see a sign from you" (12:38). This statement, given in direct discourse, is not found in Mark 8:11, nor would it have appeared in the Q material. Luke's parallel (11:29-32) begins with the words, "When the crowds were increasing, Jesus began to say. . . ." (11:29). Various reasons can be given to support the view that the Lucan introduction (lacking a challenge to Jesus) would have existed in Q,[29] and that Matthew has replaced this, bringing the scribes and Pharisees on stage, and having them address Jesus in direct discourse. It is also clear that Matthew has fashioned this opening verse on the basis of Mark 8:11, at which Mark writes that "the Pharisees" sought a sign from Jesus, testing him. Matthew picks up this verse and rewrites it, adding the scribes to the scene, and composing a question to Jesus in direct discourse. The rest of the pericope is constructed from Q materials (Matt. 12:39-42//Luke 11:29b-32).

The upshot of this discussion is that Matthew has composed a conflict story at 12:38-42. He preserves the Q tradition on the Refusal of a Sign, but he attaches to its beginning a request in direct discourse—a challenge—which did not appear in the Q material. Taking a suggestion from Mark 8:11, he has "some of the scribes and Pharisees" say to Jesus: "Teacher, we wish to see a sign from you." The response of Jesus is the traditional Q material (12:39-42). The passage, as Matthew has reformulated it, falls easily within the category of a conflict story.[30]

4. *The Double Commandment of Love*

This pericope appears in Mark 12:28-34; Matt. 22:34-40; and Luke 10:25-28. The question of the relationship between these three texts is complex, and there is little agreement on its answer. The one point on which there is considerable consensus is that Luke did not make use of Mark at all, but was dependent either on Q or his own special traditions (L).[31] The claim that he made use of Q, however, is the more convincing.[32]

The major problem of interrelationships is that of the relationship of Matthew's pericope to the others. Here there is virtually no consensus. Some typical solutions are the following:

(1) Matthew used Mark's text but revised it;[33]

(2) Matthew (and Luke) used Mark's text, but it was an older form of the text than that available to us;[34]

(3) Matthew conflated parallel traditions in Mark and Q;[35]

(4) Matthew used (but also revised) an already existing conflation of Mark and Q;[36]

(5) Matthew used the Q text alone, but adapted it;[37] and

(6) all three evangelists used independent traditions.[38]

As we have shown elsewhere in more detail than can be offered here,[39] it can be concluded that Matthew's story (22:34-40) is based ultimately on his own special traditions (special M) which have been influenced at the time of writing his gospel by the accounts in Mark (12:28-34) and Q (as given in Luke 10:25-28). The original Matthean story contained the double commandment of love as it is still given in Matt. 22:37, 39, followed by the comment in 22:40. The double commandment in Matthew's tradition listed only three faculties (heart, soul, and mind) by which one is to love God, and it contained the preposition *en* reflecting the Hebrew *b^e*.[40] These features of Matthew stand over against Mark (12:30) and Luke (10:27, from Q) who have four faculties listed (heart, soul, strength, and mind) and over against Mark and the LXX (Deut. 6:5) which uses the preposition *ex*. (Luke, using Q, has *ex* initially, but then uses *en*.) Furthermore, the closing statement in Matt. 22:40 ("On these two commandments depend all the law and the prophets") is peculiar to Matthew. This statement must also have been a part of Matthew's earlier tradition. Originally it would have had nothing to do with the question raised in Mark's Gospel (12:28) concerning which commandment is first of all, but would have been a programmatic statement concerning interpretation of the Torah and the prophets: "The whole law and the prophets can be exegetically deduced from the command to love God and the neighbor, they 'hang' exegetically on these." [41]

When Matthew wrote his gospel, however, he was influenced by both the Marcan and Q versions of the double commandment. That he was influenced by Mark is clear from the fact that he placed his pericope in the same sequence as Mark has it. Second, he attached the question of Mark 12:28 at the head of his pericope, but he used the term "great," instead of "first," and he added the words of 22:38, 39a ("first" appears in 22:38). The use of "great," instead of "first," is an improvement upon the question. The term "great" (a positive in Greek, but expressing a Semitic superlative [42]) expresses quality, i.e., the "greatest." By using this term Matthew attempted a connection between the Marcan question and his own original tradition. Now the double commandment of love—from which exegesis of the "law and the prophets" is to proceed (22:40)—becomes the "greatest" commandment within the law itself. Despite the Marcan influence, however, Matthew retained the wording of his double commandment in its Semitic form (retaining the preposition *en* throughout and using only three faculties by which one is to love God).

The influence of the Q version can be seen in that Matthew took over from it three elements: (1) that the questioner was a "lawyer"; (2) that the questioner was "testing" Jesus; and (3) perhaps the address "Teacher."

Finally, Matthew added his own introduction in 22:34: "But when the Pharisees heard that he had silenced the Sadducees, they came together." This forms a transition between the previous story on the Question of the Resurrection (22:23-33), in which the Sadducees were Jesus' opponents, and the dialogue at hand, and it identifies the questioners as Pharisees (as over against Mark's scribes and the solitary lawyer of Q).

The conclusion to be drawn is that Matthew has created a story in which Jesus is in conflict with the Pharisees. To his own special tradition, containing the double commandment of love and its application (22:37, 39-40), he has added the question given in Mark 12:28 (revised) and the Q tradition of testing (Luke 10:25); moreover, he has identified the questioners as Pharisees. Now it is from among the Pharisees that one of their members, a lawyer, questions Jesus, "testing him." In Mark's Gospel the story does not portray conflict. From a form critical standpoint his pericope is classified as a scholastic dialogue: [43] the questioner is a scribe who asks the question as to which commandment is first of all purely out of religious and intellectual interest, and the dialogue is amiable, not controversial, in tone.[44] But Matthew has formed a different type of story, a story showing conflict between Jesus and the Pharisees. If we search for a reason why Matthew composed the story in this form, not least was the fact that he was aware of the division between current Pharisaic (i.e., rabbinic) exegesis—which to Matthew misses the true meaning of Scripture (cf. especially 23:23-24, but also 23:13 and 15:3)—and the exegetical program which he prescribed for his own church.

5. *Conclusions*

There are two major conclusions to be drawn from observing these four instances of conflict story formation. First, it is clear that in the first-century church there was an active tendency on the part of certain traditionists to present material in the form of spirited dialogues between Jesus and his opponents on certain issues.[45] It appears that there was actually a primitive church consciousness of presenting materials in what we have designated the conflict story form. One can support this claim not only by the studies above, but also by the fact that conflict stories were collected together (there are five collected together in Mark 2:1-3:6) in the pre-Marcan stage of their transmission. (See Chapter V for a discussion of Mark 2:1-3:6 as a pre-Marcan collection.) Just as parables and miracle stories were collected together, so conflict stories were too; there must have been a recognition that these pericopes share a common form. As indicated by our four studies above, traditionists did not compose "pronouncement stories" to provide a pronouncement of Jesus on an issue, nor did they compose "paradigms" with a saying useful for preaching. For the pronouncements and sayings useful for preaching were already in the units of tradition prior to the formation or reformation of these units as conflict stories. Rather, the traditionists composed "conflict stories" by introducing opponents and their questions who enter into dialogue with Jesus as adversaries.

In form critical work on the conflict stories there has been a correct but somewhat exaggerated emphasis on the closing dominical word at the expense of the action or drama of the conflict story as a whole. Comments by Bultmann, Dibelius, and Taylor illustrate the point:

> Upon a survey of all this material, it becomes possible to talk of a productive power of the controversy dialogue, of the increasing tendency of the Church to clothe its dominical sayings, its views and its fundamental beliefs in the form of the controversy dialogue.[46]

> The action of the narrative has no independent value for the preacher. . . . The attractive working out of the details for their own sake . . . all these things Paradigms must lack, and, in fact, they do so.[47]

> Everything leads up to the final word of Jesus, which for the early Christians must have had the force of a Pronouncement.[48]

> Provided a narrative ends in a pronouncement of Jesus, expressed or implied, it does not matter materially whether it is introduced by a question or a description of events.[49]

Nothing in our studies above would lead one to deny the rightful emphasis that has been placed upon the dominical sayings. There are indications, however, that the drama of exchange between Jesus and his adversaries is an element which has not been given sufficient attention, as Robert Tannehill has also indicated.[50] If the traditionists were concerned about retaining the dominical sayings only, alternative (or less-developed) forms would have served this purpose. Certain questions (for instance, that in Mark 12:14) *could* have been asked by the disciples (cf. Thomas, logion 100) or by interested bystanders (cf. Mark 12:28), rather than by opponents, as in the many pericopes known as scholastic dialogues. Or questions need not necessarily be asked at all. A dominical saying *could* be clothed in a conflict situation with the request expressed in the form of a report of what Jesus' opponents had in mind (as in Mark 12:35; 8:11). Furthermore, while there are instances (Matt. 22:41-46; 12:38-42; 22:34-40) in which tradition is reformulated into fully developed conflict stories, there are no instances in which the latter are transformed into any other form.[51] The dramatic interchange between Jesus and his adversaries is of interest to the synoptic traditionists. In contrast to the statement of Dibelius above, the action of the narrative does indeed have value for the traditionists and the primitive churches—not independently (as he says), but intrinsically.

A second conclusion is to be derived from our study to this point. The view of Dibelius that the more closely a pericope conforms to the regular pattern of a form, the more primitive that pericope is [52] cannot be sustained. We see, on the contrary, that conflict stories are formulated in Matthew out of Marcan materials which were originally in non-conflict story form. In these instances it is clear that pericopes conforming to the regular pattern are relatively late in origin. This does not mean, on the other hand, that conformity to the conflict story form is an indication of a pericope's being late, either. Subsequently (in Chapters III and IV) it will be shown that there are conflict stories in the synoptic tradition which are indeed primitive in origin. The degree of conformity to the regular pattern of a conflict story form, therefore, is no indication of a pericope's age.

B. The Form of the Conflict Stories

The form of the conflict stories has been described in different ways. Albertz found three parts to the formal structure of the controversy dialogues consisting of (1) exposition (as he called it; more properly this might be called an introductory narrative)·, (2) dialogue, and (3) closing remarks.[53] Bultmann described the form along different lines. Each story has a "starting point" in "some action or attitude which is seized on by the opponent and used in an attack by accusation or by question." This is followed by a "reply" which contains a counter-question, metaphor, or quotation from Scripture.[54] Pressing Bultmann's language, it appears that for him the form has a three-part structure too, although it differs from that described by Albertz, consisting of (1) an opening scene, (2) question or attack, and (3) Jesus' reply. Dibelius and Taylor gave less attention to the formal aspects of the stories, but described their characteristics (see Chapter I, Part A, 3 and 4).

The fact that the "closing remarks" do not appear in all the controversy dialogues (as Albertz himself acknowledged)—e.g., in the stories of Mark 2:15-17, 18-20, 23-28, plus others—militates against this element as being essential to the form, and it can therefore be passed over. Yet it cannot be denied that Albertz was aware of something important. By calling attention to the frequently used "closing remarks," he sensed that narrative serves more than simply an introductory function. What we have is dialogue set within a narrative structure. We have not simply controversy dialogues but *narratives containing dialogue,* and the narrative itself is of such importance that the dialogues cannot exist independently. It is to the credit of Dibelius too that he observed the importance of the narrative and therefore placed the paradigms among narratives, while Bultmann included them under the sayings material of the gospels. It is here that their methods of classification diverge fundamentally.

It is because of the importance of the narrative that the term "conflict stories" has been adopted in this book. There are some who might

prefer to use "controversy stories." Both usages appear in the literature written in English. The terms "conflict" and "controversy" are
almost synonymous, but there is a slight difference. Controversy
(etymologically, a turning against) is dispute or contention over some
matter, and it usually has a duration over a length of time. Conflict
(etymologically, a striking together) is discord, collision, or incom-
patibility of one stance over against another, and it usually has more
of a "punctiliar" (less than "linear") character. The materials with
which we are dealing do not portray extended discussion or debate
as we actually experience them. As R. Tannehill has written, "while
actual conversations usually go on at some length with inconclusive
results, many of these stories contain only a single exchange and end
with a striking word of Jesus." [55] They portray a clash or conflict of
positions, and controversy in the usual sense is lacking. Therefore
while "controversy stories" may be acceptable—and will be continued
in usage by some—my preference is "conflict stories." The form of
these stories is that of (1) introductory narrative, (2) opponent's question or attack, and (3) dominical saying. How each of these actually
appears and functions within the conflict stories deserves attention.

1. *Introductory Narrative*

There is always narrative at the beginning of the conflict stories, and
it is sometimes found also within them and at their end. The introductory narratives serve not only as transitional links, but also describe
a setting in such a way that the reader is prepared for an inevitable
conflict. Sometimes the narrative is extremely brief, and neither Jesus
nor his disciples gives occasion for an attack or question; we are told
only that scribes and Pharisees (Matt. 12:38), chief priests, scribes,
and elders (Mark 11:27) or "people" (who have nevertheless observed
the conduct of the Pharisees, Mark 2:18) approach Jesus. Yet even in
these instances a polarity is thereby staged, however briefly, by reference to opponents through use of code words. More often the introductory narrative portrays Jesus (Mark 2:1-6, 15-16; Matt. 12:22-23;
Luke 7:36-38; 13:10-14a) or his disciples (Mark 2:23-24; 7:1-4)
involved in an activity in the presence of scribes, Pharisees, or
synagogue officials, and the narrative thereby serves to heighten the
tension explicitly.

In other cases the adversaries of Jesus are portrayed as watching
to see whether he will perform an act they consider inappropriate

(Mark 3:1-2; Luke 14:1-2). In still other cases the adversaries have gathered together to "entrap" Jesus (Mark 12:13-14) or "test" him (Mark 10:2; Matt. 22:34-35), or they have gathered to provide an occasion for a question by Jesus (Matt. 22:41). On one occasion it is the Sadducees who gather and whose denial of the resurrection is stated, so a conflict of ideas is staged (Mark 12:18).

Narrative within the conflict stories and at their end is not so frequent, and it does not have the importance of narrative at the beginning of a pericope in terms of its heightening the tension between Jesus and his opponents. An exception to this would be Mark 3:6, but this is a pre-Marcan or Marcan composition which serves as an ending to the whole section Mark 2:1-3:5,[56] rather than an ending to 3:1-5 alone. Other narratives appearing late in a pericope consist of words of praise by the bystanders at the end of a conflict story (Mark 2:12) or brief references to the opponents' fear (Matt. 22:46) or inability to answer questions—either internally (Mark 11:31-32), or at the end of a pericope (Luke 14:6).

This review of narrative material in the conflict stories leads to the conclusion that narration is used to describe a situation which prepares for an inevitable conflict. Scribes, Pharisees, chief priests, elders, Herodians, a ruler of the synagogue, Sadducees, a lawyer, and "they" (Mark 3:2b, presumably synagogue leaders or officers) are on the scene as potential opponents. These opponents question Jesus' conduct, or that of his disciples, seek to entrap him or test him, or gather against him. All these important details are provided by the narratives. Therefore the narratives are supportive frameworks for the dialogues. One may grant that the narrative material is not as important as the dialogue material; this becomes obvious in some pericopes (e.g., Mark 2:12, 18; 3:22; 11:31-32; Matt. 12:38; 22:46; Luke 14:6). Nevertheless, in other pericopes there would be no conflict story without it (e.g., Mark 2:6, 8; 3:1-2, 5; Luke 7:36-38; 13:10-14), and in the remaining cases it serves to heighten the tension between Jesus and his opponents. As R. Tannehill has indicated, we have in these stories a type of "tensive language, one in which the tension assumes narrative form, with the speaking and acting persons as the poles." [57]

2. *The Opponent's Question or Attack*

Most of the conflict stories open with a question or accusation directed toward Jesus. In two instances the situation is reversed so that the question is asked by Jesus of his opponents, viz., Matthew 22:41-46 and Luke 14:1-6, and once, Mark 3:1-5, there is only a narrative introduction.[58] Given the fact that, except for Mark 3:1-5, all of the conflict stories begin with a question or accusation (usually directed toward Jesus or his disciples, but twice from him), we sense how important the question or accusation is for the form of the conflict story. (Concerning 3:1-5, Bultmann says that the "lurking silence of the opponent (3:2)" can have the significance of a statement.[59])

There are some conflict stories in which the question or accusation is integral to the story; that is, that the dominical saying depends on the question or accusation, and it could not have existed in independent circulation. Bultmann calls these stories "unitary" compositions.[60] For instance, the dominical saying in Mark 12:13-17 (Question of Taxes to Caesar) can hardly have circulated independently of the question of the payment of taxes, and, furthermore, it depends on the dialogue concerning the image and description on the coin. In Chapter III we shall deal with further examples.

There are others, however, in which the question of the opponent is contrived; it is a composition by a traditionist. In Chapter IV we shall discuss these "non-unitary" conflict stories in a comprehensive way. Here it is sufficient to point out a few examples. We have seen above that in Matt. 12:38-42 we have a conflict story which draws upon material in Q. We proposed that in that source there was no initial request for a sign, but rather a report of the crowds being present, as we find in Luke's parallel. In Matthew, however, certain scribes and Pharisees ask Jesus for a sign in direct discourse (12:38). The question was composed for the sake of producing a fully-developed conflict story. Questions have also been composed at the beginning of other stories analyzed above (Matt. 22:34-40; 22:41-46). As another example—one which has not yet been analyzed—the question in Mark 7:5 appears to have been composed for the sake of the dominical saying in 7:6-8.[61]

To give more examples one would have to go into much greater detail than can be done here. The point to be made is that the conflict stories customarily begin with a question or accusation. It is apparent that the question or accusation has importance for the story. This is seen in instances in which they are composed secondarily, even if they are lacking in the sources. We saw above (Chapter II, Part A, 3), for instance, that Matthew placed the reference to a demand (given in Mark 8:11) into a direct discourse question of the Pharisees. By

doing so he created a conflict story. Bultmann lists certain dominical —
sayings which *could* have been framed within a conflict story setting
(Mark 4:21; Matt. 5:13; 7:3-4, 9-10, 16; Luke 6:39),[62] but which
remained independent; neither settings nor conflict questions were
composed for them. What is of interest is that when traditionists did
compose conflict stories, they consistently, except for Mark 3:1-5,
composed a question or accusation as an important element.

The conflict stories portray Jesus in debate with one other party
only, never two or three. By "party" is meant here an individual
opponent or group of opponents. It does not mean that the group is
made up of one party in the sense of sect (e.g., Pharisees), but that
Jesus is in debate with one opponent or group of opponents only,
even if that group is made up of several officers (e.g., Mark 11:27)
or two or more subgroups (e.g., Mark 7:1; 12:13). Never is Jesus portrayed in debate on an issue in an extended dialogue with first one
party and then another.[63] The interchange is solely between two
parties: Jesus on one side, his opponents (individually or collectively)
on the other.

The opponents are identified in general terms alone (Pharisees, —
scribes, Sadducees, elders, or whatever), and no further details are
given. As Albertz says, their names and origins "remain in the dark,"
and we are given no details as to their outer or inner characteristics.[64]
We are not told of former relationships to Jesus, which might explain
animosity, or whether the same opponents appear in more than one
scene. They are simply described in the most general terms, usually
by sect or office, and that is sufficient to set up the necessary polarity —
for the conflict dialogue. Bultmann says that originally the opponents
were for the most part unspecified persons, but that there was a
tendency to characterize them as Pharisees and scribes in the later —
development of the tradition.[65] We have seen instances of this in
Matt. 22:34-40 (as over against Mark 12:28-34) and in Matt. 22:41-46
(as over against Mark 12:35-37). Nevertheless, while the polarity for
conflict is thereby made more clear, the opponents as persons "remain
in the dark."

3. *The Dominical Saying*

The dominical saying, which brings the dialogue to a close, dom-
inates the conflict story. It is held by form critics that all the materials
of the conflict stories serve to stress it.[66]

The fact that the dominical saying comes at the close of the dialogue in conflict stories is an indication of its importance. It does not always come at the end of the entire pericope, as in those which have closing remarks or brief narration following (Mark 2:1-12; 3:1-6; 3:22-30; Matt. 22:41-46; Luke 13:10-17; 14:1-6), but it does come at the end of the dialogue itself in every case, and it actually closes the discussion. A review of these sayings shows that they address three major concerns.

(1) In some cases the dominical saying is a teaching concerning the conduct of Jesus or his disciples in *relationship to Jewish law*. These teachings are pointed, memorable, and usually quite brief; never are they lengthy discourses. Five of them are set in parallelism, either synonymous or antithetic (and either complete or incomplete forms): [67]

(a) On the question of associating with tax collectors and sinners (Mark 2:15-17), "Those who are well have no need for a physician, but those who are sick" (2:17a).[68]

(b) On the question of plucking ears of grain on the sabbath (Mark 2:23-28), "The sabbath was made for man, not man for the sabbath" (2:27).[69]

(c) On the question of healing on the sabbath (Mark 3:1-5), "Is it lawful on the sabbath to do good or to harm, to save life or to kill?" (3:4).

(d) On the question of eating with unwashed hands (Mark 7:1-8), a quotation from Isa. 29:13 (LXX) is given, a verse containing two couplets with lines in parallelism. This is followed by an additional saying (7:8) which is also in parallelism: "You leave the commandment of God, and hold fast the tradition of men."

(e) On the question of divorce (Mark 10:2-9), "What therefore God has joined together, let not man put asunder" (10:9).

There are two conflict stories concerning conduct in relationship to Jewish law in which the dominical saying is a Scripture quotation which closes the controversy:

(a) On the question of eating with unwashed hands (Mark 7:1-8), a quotation from Isa. 29:13 (LXX) is given. As indicated above, there is an additional saying which, in conjunction with the quotation, closes the controversy.

(b) On the question of which is the greatest commandment (Matt. 22:34-40), the quotations from Deut. 6:5 and Lev. 19:18 are given.

There are other conflict stories concerning conduct in which the dominical saying is less stylized, but it is given in a direct and fairly brief manner:

(a) On the question of fasting, Mark 2:19, followed by the parables of the unshrunk patch on the garment and of new wine in old wineskins.

(b) On the question of healing on the sabbath, Luke 13:15-16; 14:3, 5.

(c) On the question of associating with sinners, Luke 7:41-47.

(2) In other cases the dominical saying is a teaching on some matter in *relationship to Jewish doctrine.* The dominical saying provides Jesus' answer vis-à-vis that of certain contemporaries:

(a) On the question of whether there is a resurrection of the dead (as over against the Sadducees), Mark 12:26-27.

(b) On the question as to whether the Messiah is the Son of David (as over against the Pharisees), Matt. 22:43-45.

(3) In still other cases the conflict stories portray a direct attack upon Jesus as a person, calling his ministry into question. In these cases the dominical saying is a *defense of Jesus' ministry:*

(a) On the charge that he casts out demons by Beelzebul, Mark 3:23-29 (cf. Matt. 12:25-32//Luke 11:17-23).

(b) On the question of authority, Mark 11:33.

(c) On the question of a sign, Matt. 12:39-42.

In all of the above, the dominical saying deals with a vital issue within the context of a Jewish and/or primitive Christian context: [70] an issue of law, doctrine, or Jesus' ministry. The emphasis which form critics have placed on the dominical saying within the conflict story form is well founded. In none of the pericopes is the dominical saying completely submerged into the framework; it always stands out prominently. The facts (1) that it is frequently stylized and (2) that it is the decisive conclusion of each story indicate its dominance in the conflict stories.

C. Addendum

Besides these characteristics common to all the conflict stories, three other features should be mentioned which are common to a few of the stories. First, some of them have within them a counter-question of Jesus following upon the initial question or accusation by the opponents. This is found in the following pericopes: Mark 10:2-9; 11:27-33; 12:13-17; and Luke 7:36-50. Second, some of the dominical sayings are in part made up of Scripture quotations. These sayings are found in the following pericopes: Mark 7:1-8; 10:2-9; 12:18-27; Matt. 22:34-40; and 22:41-46. Finally, as already indicated, several dominical sayings are cast in the form of parallelism. In addition to the five mentioned already, which have to do with Jewish law (Mark 2:17, 27; 3:4; 7:8; and 10:9), there is antithetic parallelism at Mark 12:17 (concerning taxes) and synonymous parallelism at Mark 2:19 (concerning fasting).

NOTES

1. R. Bultmann, *Form Criticism*, 30.
2. M. Dibelius, *Tradition*, 7-8.
3. Amos N. Wilder, *The Language of the Gospel: Early Christian Rhetoric* (New York: Harper, 1964) 12.
4. Ibid., 15.
5. Erich Auerbach, *Mimesis: The Representation of Reality in Western Literature* (Princeton: Princeton University, 1953) 40.
6. The most comprehensive study of these forms of dialogue is that of R. Hirzel, *Der Dialog*, which has a chapter on "Der Dialog in der altchristlichen Literature" (2. 366-380), but it lacks entirely a study of dialogue forms in the gospels.
7. Aristotle, *On Rhetoric* 3.17.13–3.18.4.
8. *m. 'Abot* 5:17. From the translation of H. Danby, *Mishnah*, 457-458. R. Travers Herford (*The Ethics of the Talmud: Sayings of the Fathers* [New York: Schocken, 1962] 138-139) says concerning this saying: "If the object of the controversy be to establish truth and not to flout authority, then the truth will in the end be established and the authority will be vindicated. . . . Both the contending parties may be equally sincere in their desire to serve the truth, while differing in their opinion of what the truth is. . . . The main result will be that the truth will be established and God thereby served. . . . The two famous teachers, or rather the two 'houses' of their disciples, were sharply opposed; but both were sincere in desiring to establish the truth, as it was finally said, 'the words of both are the words of the living God' (jBer. 3b)." Cf. the similar comment by J. Israelstam in *Babylonian Talmud* (I. Epstein), *'Abot* 71.
9. Aristotle, *The Poetics* 4.16 (trans. W. Hamilton Fyfe; LCL; London: Heinemann, 1927) 19.
10. Ibid., 6.9 (p. 25).

11. Ibid., 19.3-4 (p. 73).
12. *The Gospel According to Thomas* (trans. A. Guillamont, H.-Ch. Puech, G. Quispel, W. Till and Yassah 'Abd Al Masih New York: Harper, 1959) 51.
13. Outside of these, the following are exceptions: "Mary said to Jesus" (21); "A man said to him" (72); "A woman in the crowd said to him" (79); "Simon Peter said to them" (114); and "They said to him" (91, 100).
14. Logia 22 and 60 are closely related in form. They do not begin with an action per se, but they, along with 100, are the only ones which have narrated introductions giving a setting for the saying to follow.
15. G. Quispel, "The Gospel of Thomas and the New Testament," *VC* 11 (1957) 189-207; idem, "Some Remarks on the Gospel of Thomas," *NTS* 5 (1959) 276-290; Claus-Hunno Hunzinger, "Aussersynoptisches Traditionsgut im Thomas-Evangelium," *TLZ* 85 (1960) 843-846; Hans Werner Bartsch, "Das Thomas-Evangelium und die synoptischen Evangelien," *NTS* 6 (1960) 249-261; Hugh Montefiore, "A Comparison of the Parables of the Gospel According to Thomas and of the Synoptic Gospels," *NTS* 7 (1961) 224, 237; and Helmut Koester, *GNOMAI DIAPHOROI*. The Origin and Nature of Diversification in the History of Christianity," *HTR* 58 (1965) 293-296.
16. Robert M. Grant and David Noel Freedman, *The Secret Sayings of Jesus* (Garden City: Doubleday, 1960) 107-108; Ernst Haenchen, *Die Botschaft des Thomasevangeliums* (Berlin: Töpelmann, 1961).
17. For this classification, see Oscar Cullmann, "Das Thomasevangelium und die Frage nach dem Alter der in ihm enthaltenen Tradition," *TLZ* 85 (1960) 331-334. This article appears in English translation as "The Gospel of Thomas and the Problem of the Age of the Tradition Contained Therein," *Int* 16 (1962) 418-438, and the classification is given on pp. 433-438.
18. Ibid. (German), 332-333.
19. Robert McL. Wilson, *Studies in the Gospel of Thomas* (London: Mowbray, 1960) 4, 145-148; Bertil Gärtner, *The Theology of the Gospel of Thomas* (London: Collins, 1961) 53-55; Henri-Charles Puech, *NT Apocrypha* (Hennecke-Schmeemelcher/Wilson) 2. 293-294; and Wolfgang Schrage, *Das Verhältnis des Thomas-Evangeliums zur synoptischen Tradition und zu den koptischen Evangelienübersetzungen* (Berlin: Töpelmann, 1964) 2-11.
20. R. Wilson, *Studies in the Gospel of Thomas*, 147-148.
21. Some scholars have suggested that one should assume the independence of the two traditions as a "working hypothesis" in exegetical work. See Norman Perrin, *Rediscovering the Teaching of Jesus* (New York: Harper, 1967) 36-37; cf. Joachim Jeremias, *The Parables of Jesus* (rev. ed.; New York: Scribners, 1963) 24. This is probably sound procedure in many cases, but not universally.
22. In the Hermetic writings there are several references to *gnosis* as the way, *Corp. Herm.*, 4.11; 6.5–6; 10.15; 11.21. These references are given by Wilhelm Michaelis, *TDNT* 5. 46-48. The Mandaean texts abound with examples of the use of the term "way"; see Ernst Käsemann, *Das wandernde Gottesvolk* (2nd ed.; Göttingen: Vandenhoeck & Ruprecht, 1967) 54-56.
23. R. Wilson, *Studies in the Gospel of Thomas*, 60; R. Grant and D. Freedman, *The Secret Sayings of Jesus*, 109.
24. R. Bultmann, *Synoptic Tradition*, 66, 136-137.
25. Barnabas Lindars, *New Testament Apologetic* (London: SCM, 1961) 46-47.
26. Cf. Jack D. Kingsbury, *Matthew: Structure, Christology, Kingdom* (Philadelphia: Fortress, 1976) 101-102, and idem, "The Title 'Son of David' in Matthew's Gospel," *JBL* 95 (1976) 595-596. Kingsbury (*Matthew*, 101-102) also cites the following: W. Wrede, "Jesus als Davidssohn," *Vorträge und Studien* Tübingen: Mohr, 1907) 174; J. M. Cribbs, "Purpose and Pattern in Matthew's

Use of the Title 'Son of David,' " *NTS* 10 (1963-1964) 461-464; Alfred Suhl, "Der Davidssohn im Matthäus-Evangelium," *ZNW* 59 (1968) 61; and David M. Hay, *Glory at the Right Hand* (SBLMS 18; Nashville: Abingdon, 1973) 116-117.

27. Luke 11:29//Matt. 12:39; 16:4 contain *ponēra* (modifying *genea*), which is lacking in Mark 8:12. Second, they have the words (in common) *kai sēmeion ou dothēsetai autē ei mē to sēmeion Iōna* over against Mark's *ei dothēsetai tē genea tautē sēmeion*. Various scholars claim that the Q version is more primitive than that given by Mark. These include Werner Kümmel, *Promise and Fulfilment* (Naperville: Allenson, 1957) 68; H. E. Tödt, *The Son of Man in the Synoptic Tradition* (London: SCM, 1965) 211; and N. Perrin, *Rediscovering the Teaching of Jesus*, 193. A contrary view is expressed by F. W. Beare, *Earliest Records*, 103.

28. At Luke 11:16, however, within the Beelzebul Controversy, Mark 8:11 is used.

29. The reasons are as follows. First, in Luke the pericope follows two Q passages, the Beelzebul Controversy (11:14-15, 17-23) and the Return of the Evil Spirit (11:24-26), and one special L passage, On True Blessedness (11:27-28). In none of these passages are Pharisees present. But in Matthew, who also draws upon Q materials from the Beelzebul Controversy (with some rearrangement, however), there is an insertion of a short anti-Pharisaic polemic (consisting of special M Tradition) on Good and Bad (12:33-37) immediately prior to 12:38-42. (The phrase "brood of vipers" at 12:34 within the discourse on Good and Bad applies to the Pharisees, as elsewhere in Matthew's Gospel; cf. 3:7; 23:33.)

Second, while in Q (and at Luke 11:29) the "evil generation" applies to the generation (in general) upon whom the Son of man's parousia will come as an affliction (cf. H. Tödt, *Son of Man*, 267), in Matthew the "evil generation" has been made to refer to the Pharisees. Cf. 12:39 with the adjective "evil" applied to the Pharisees in the discourse on Good and Bad (12:34, 35). It must be concluded that the presence of the Pharisees in Matt. 12:38 is due to Matthew's purposeful editing. For a detailed treatment of Matt. 12, in which it is concluded that the section is intended to portray conflict between Jesus and the Pharisees, and that Matthew is responsible for the presence of the Pharisees in 12:38, see O. Lamar Cope, *Matthew: A Scribe Trained for the Kingdom of Heaven* (CBQMS 5; Washington: Catholic Biblical Association, 1976) 32-52, esp. pp. 40-44, 49-52.

30. Of course it should be asked whether Mark 8:11-12 should be considered a conflict story. M. Albertz considers it (and all its parallels) to be a controversy dialogue (*Streitgespräche*, 52-54), and V. Taylor considers it to be a pronouncement story (*Formation*, 78-79). R. Bultmann and M. Dibelius, on the other hand, do not admit the pericope (or any of its parallels) to their respective categories. Within Mark 8:11-12 there are features of a conflict story, but it is also correct, surely, to make a distinction between this pericope and the fully developed stories as we find them, for instance, in Mark 2. It lacks a question by opponents (or Jesus) and merely reports a conflict situation, followed by the dominical saying. In this respect, of course, it is not much unlike Mark 3:1-5, but in respect to its lack of a narrated scene, it is not like it either.

31. B. H. Streeter, *The Four Gospels: A Study of Origins* (London: Macmillan, 1930) 210; T. W. Manson, *The Sayings of Jesus* (London: SCM, 1949) 259-260; V. Taylor, *Mark*, 484; and F. W. Beare, *Earliest Records*, 158-159. Of these, Taylor and Beare think Luke to be dependent on Q; Streeter allows for dependence on Q or L; and Manson assigns the material to L.

32. There are terms common to Matthew and Luke, against Mark, as follows: lawyer (Matt. 22:35//Luke 10:25); testing him (Matt. 22:35//Luke 10:25); and teacher (Matt. 22:36//Luke 10:25).

33. Krister Stendahl, *The School of St. Matthew and Its Use of the Old Testament* (Lund: C. W. K. Gleerup, 1954; American ed., Philadelphia: Fortress, 1968) 75.

34. Günther Bornkamm, "Das Doppelgebot der Liebe," *Neutestamentliche Studien für Rudolf Bultmann* (ed. Walther Eltester; BZNW 21; Berlin: Töpelmann, 1954) 92.

35. Sherman E. Johnson, "The Biblical Quotations in Matthew," *HTR* 36 (1943) 147-148; V. Taylor, *Mark*, 484; F. W. Beare, *Earliest Records*, 159. Georg Strecker, *Der Weg der Gerechtigkeit: Untersuchung zur Theologie des Matthäus* (Göttingen: Vandenhoeck & Ruprecht, 1962) 135-137, could perhaps be included here; he says that Matthew's text is based on Mark but "contaminated" by Q.

36. Kenneth J. Thomas, "Liturgical Citations in the Synoptics," *NTS* 22 (1975-1976) 209-214. The complexity of the theory proposed by Thomas is so great that it appears improbable. It requires (1) that a revision of the LXX text was made by and circulated among early Christians as a common tradition; (2) that Mark and Q are dependent on this common tradition; (3) that a conflation was made of Mark and Q prior to Matthew's writing of his gospel; and (4) that Matthew revised this conflation.

37. K. Berger, *Die Gesetzesauslegung Jesu*, 1. 203.

38. Ernst Lohmeyer, *Das Evangelium des Matthäus* (MeyerK 3rd ed.; Göttingen: Vandenhoeck & Ruprecht, 1962) 327, 330.

39. Arland J. Hultgren, "The Double Commandment of Love in Mt. 22:34-40: Its Sources and Composition," *CBQ* (1974) 373-378.

40. No known version of the OT lists four faculties. The MT has "with all your heart, and with all your soul, and with all your might" (Deut. 6:5). The preposition used is b^e. The LXX has the same three faculties, but it uses *ex* as the preposition. The fact that Matthew has "mind" as the third faculty, over against "strength" in the Hebrew and LXX, remains a puzzle. K. Stendahl *(The School of St. Matthew*, 75-76) may be correct in saying that Matthew is dependent at this point on Mark 12:30 (where the third faculty is "mind"). But this does not militate against the claim that Matthew drew initially on his own material; it means only that Matthew has substituted (consciously or otherwise) Mark's term for his own when he composed his gospel. Concerning the claim above that Matthew's material reflected a distinctive Hebraic tradition, it is clear that Matthew did occasionally make use of the Hebrew OT (although the LXX is his usual working version). This is the conclusion of O. L. Cope *(Matthew*, 124), who cites other scholars (K. Stendahl, G. D. Kilpatrick, and R. Gundry) as well. Cope bases his claim on other passages in Matthew (15:1-20; 19:16-22) without reference to 22:34-40.

41. Gerhard Barth, "Matthew's Understanding of the Law," *Tradition and Interpretation in Matthew* by Günther Bornkamm, G. Barth, and H. J. Held (Philadelphia: Westminster, 1963) 77. Cf. also Victor P. Furnish, *The Love Command in the New Testament* (Nashville: Abingdon, 1972) 33-34; Jack T. Sanders, *Ethics in the New Testament* (Philadelphia: Fortress, 1975) 42; Robert J. Banks, *Jesus and the Law in the Synoptic Tradition* (SNTSMS 28; Cambridge: Cambridge University, 1975) 169; and Birger Gerhardsson, "The Hermeneutic Program in Matthew 22:37-40," *Jews, Greeks, and Christians*

(W. D. Davies Festschrift; SJLA 21; ed. R. Hamerton-Kelly and R. Scroggs; Leiden: Brill, 1976) 129-150.

42. BDF, 127, "The positive can also be used in the sense of a comparative (superlative), as sometimes in classical, but more so after the Semitic pattern which does not provide for degree at all." Cf. also the vast lexical evidence given by K. Berger, *Die Gesetzesauslegung Jesu,* 1. 203-205.

43. Cf. G. Bornkamm, "Das Doppelgebot," 85, 92; R. Bultmann, *Synoptic Tradition,* 51; and V. Furnish, *The Love Command,* 26. K. Berger *(Die Gesetzesauslegung Jesu,* 1. 581) designates the Marcan version a teaching dialogue *(Lehrgespräch).*

44. The Lucan pericope is not in the form of a conflict story either. In spite of the phrase "testing him" (10:25), which appeared in Q, the interchange is amiable, ending with Jesus' acceptance of the lawyer's answer to the counter-question. It too is a scholastic dialogue.

45. It is of interest to notice a similarity to this phenomenon of reformulation of tradition into dialogue form in early Gnostic literature. H.-Ch. Puech *(NT Apocrypha* [Hennecke-Schneemelcher/Wilson] 1. 248) has made a comparison of the Gnostic gospel *Sophia Jesu Christi* with the Gnostic *Epistle of Eugnostos.* These two documents contain essentially the same material, but in different forms. Puech says that "the Sophia is only a simple re-casting of the letter: its author has taken over the content of the letter. . . . By slight alterations, by placing the content of the epistle in a fictitious frame, by a setting as artificial as the questions posed by the characters introduced, *he has transformed a treatise* written for a correspondent of the author or for his pupils *into a dialogue* of the risen Savior with his disciples." (Emphasis mine.)

46. R. Bultmann, *Synoptic Tradition,* 51; cf. pp. 41, 47.

47. M. Dibelius, *Tradition,* 48.

48. V. Taylor, *Formation,* 65.

49. Ibid., 71.

50. Robert C. Tannehill, *The Sword of His Mouth* (SBLSS 1; Philadelphia: Fortress, and Missoula: Scholars, 1975) 201.

51. We allow logion 100 in the Gospel of Thomas over against Mark 12:13-17 as a possible but unlikely exception (i.e., possible only if the former used the latter as a source). This, however, does not in either case affect the validity of our statement in regard to the synoptic tradition.

52. This is applied by Dibelius to the paradigms in particular; *Tradition,* 61.

53. M. Albertz, *Streitgespräche,* 86-87.

54. R. Bultmann, *Synoptic Tradition,* 39-41.

55. R. Tannehill, *The Sword of His Mouth,* 153.

56. See Chapter V, in which it is maintained that Mark 3:6 is a pre-Marcan composition which concludes the collection of Mark 2:1–3:5 as a whole.

57. R. Tannehill, *The Sword of His Mouth,* 154.

58. It might be argued that Mark 3:1-5 should not be considered a conflict story, since it does not contain a question (as it does in Matt. 12:10). Like Mark 8:11-12, one could say, this pericope is not fully developed into a conflict story until Matthew's reworking it. This will have to be taken up again, but two points can be made here: (1) the pericope does (much more than 8:11-12) portray dramatic interchange between Jesus and his opponents who seek to accuse him; and (2) it appears along with four other stories (Mark 2) in an apparent collection of conflict stories ending with 3:6.

59. R. Bultmann, *Synoptic Tradition,* 390-391.

60. Ibid., 47.

61. See Chapter IV, Part E.
62. R. Bultmann, *Synoptic Tradition,* 47.
63. Contrast the lengthy dialogue in the *Clementine Recognitions* 1.55-58, which is a public controversy at Jerusalem after Jesus' death. The disciples debate with several parties in succession: the high priest, a Sadducee, a Samaritan, a scribe, a Pharisee, a disciple of John the Baptist, and "all the people."
64. M. Albertz, *Streitgespräche,* 87-88.
65. R. Bultmann, *Synoptic Tradition,* 52-53, 67.
66. M. Albertz, *Streitgespräche,* 95; R. Bultmann, *Synoptic Tradition,* 41, 51; M. Dibelius, *Tradition,* 56, 65, 67; V. Taylor, *Formation,* 63, 65, 71.
67. For discussion of this form, see C. F. Burney, *The Poetry of Our Lord* (Oxford: Clarendon, 1925) 63-99; Matthew Black, *An Aramaic Approach to the Gospels and Acts* (3rd ed.; Oxford: Clarendon, 1967) 143-149. Of those passages cited above, the third (Mark 3:4) is in synonymous parallelism (cf. Burney, 64); the others are antithetic.
68. Whether 2:17b is to be considered an original part of this saying, or whether it is a freely floating saying which has been attached here, is discussed in Chapter III, Part B.
69. Mark 2:28b is discussed in terms of the same question posed regarding 2:17b (preceding note) in Chapter IV, Part D.
70. Analysis of each pericope is given in Chapters III and IV. There the question of context (Jewish or primitive Christian) is explored.

Part Two
Studies in
the Formation of the
Synoptic Conflict Stories

III. The Formation of the Unitary Conflict Stories

It has been stated in the Introduction that some conflict stories can be considered unitary, while others are non-unitary.[1] A unitary conflict story is one in which the dominical saying is comprehensible only in terms of its contextual situation. That is to say, the opponent's question, and often the setting, is indispensable to the closing saying, and the latter would not have been preserved and circulated independently of it. Conversely, a non-unitary conflict story is one in which the opponent's question and the narrated scene prove to have been composed to create a conflict story out of an originally independent saying.

It is our purpose in this chapter to analyze those conflict stories which are of the unitary type. Our particular interest is the *Sitz im Leben* of the formulation of each. We shall ask whether there is a *Sitz im Leben* common to them. Form critical work on the conflict stories has drawn some conclusions on their *Sitz im Leben*, but there has been no agreement between critics as to what that is. Is it discussions of a rabbinic type which the church had with its opponents (Bultmann)? Is it preaching (Dibelius)? Is it the need for pronouncements on conduct (Taylor)? Or is it something else?

By definition, the dominical saying and the opponent's question come from the same stage of tradition in the unitary conflict stories.[2] Therefore it is the unitary conflict stories only which could possibly come from the earliest stage of tradition intact and preserve the memory of a *conflict* between Jesus and an adversary.[3] Obviously this will not be so in every case; a unitary conflict story can be a community creation. But the history of some unitary conflict stories can be traced back to the very beginnings of the gospel tradition about Jesus. We should ask the question, in these cases, as to whether these stories preserve authentic memories, and if so why these memories have been presented in conflict story form. What attitudes and purposes were operative in the transmission of these units of tradition in the form of conflict stories?

A. The Question about Authority

(Mark 11:27-33//Matthew 21:23-27//Luke 20:1-8)

The three synoptic parallels have extensive verbal agreements, and it can be assumed that both Matthew and Luke used Mark. The major problem concerning the synoptic interrelationships is that of the order of presentation of this pericope in Luke over against Mark-Matthew. In parallel columns the order is as follows:

Mark-Matthew	Luke
Cleansing the Temple (Mark 11:15-17//Matt. 21:12-13)	Cleansing the Temple (19:45-46)
Chief Priests and Scribes Conspire (Mark 11:18-19; not in Matthew)	Chief Priests and Scribes Conspire (19:47-48)
Healing in the Temple (Matt. 21:14-17; not in Mark)	
Remarks on Withered Fig Tree and Prayer (Mark 11:20-26//Matt. 21:18-22)	
Question about Authority (Mark 11:27-33//Matt. 21:23-27)	Question about Authority (20:1-8)

The passage Mark 11:18-19//Luke 19:47-48 (chief priests and scribes conspire against Jesus) is a "concluding formula" which forms a unit with the Cleansing of the Temple. While in Mark there is a pericope (Mark 11:20-26) which separates the Temple Cleansing with concluding formula (11:15-19) from the Question about Authority (11:27-33), such is not the case in Luke. In Luke the Question about Authority is thereby related to Jesus' action in the Temple Cleansing. This is also the case in the Fourth Gospel (John 2:18-22). But it is not so related in Mark and Matthew. Rather, in Mark and Matthew the pericope on authority begins without an apparent reference to any particular action which Jesus has done.

The problem of the relationship of this pericope to the Temple Cleansing cannot be dealt with fully until the pericope has been analyzed in further detail. Then we shall have to deal with the question whether the connection to the Temple Cleansing has been made by Luke and the Fourth Evangelist, or whether the connection has been severed by Mark (whom Matthew follows). Our immediate interest, however, is to trace the history of the formation of this pericope in the synoptic tradition.

1. *The Formation of the Pericope*

We begin our analysis with the double quotation of Jesus' opponents in Mark 11:28:

> By what authority are you doing these things?
> Who gave you this authority to do these things?

These two questions have the same object in view; each questions the authority by which Jesus has done some action. Initially it appears that the second question is redundant.

Whether both of these questions belong to the most primitive form of the pericope may be questioned. The phraseology of the first question appears in two other verses of the pericope (11:29, 33). The second does not appear again. With Mark, therefore, the dominating question is the first, and the second has no further importance to the pericope.

There are reasons, however, for maintaining that the second question is more original and that the first question, even though it appears three times (11:28, 29, 33), is an interpretive revision and restatement of the original. The reasons are as follows:

First, the counter-question of Jesus in 11:30 [4] actually addresses the second question directly, not the first.[5] Implicit in 11:30 is an affirmation that either God or men gave authority. It makes connection with the question of *who* gave authority, rather than *by what* authority Jesus acted.

Second, if the Question about Authority had to do originally with the Temple Cleansing (a point we shall maintain subsequently,) it is likely that the temple authorities would ask "*Who* gave you authority to do this?" The implication is that those who sold in the temple had been permitted by the authorities themselves to conduct their business. Therefore the authorities ask him *who* gave him permission to expel them. This type of question is also found in the extra-canonical fragment *Oxyrhynchus Papyrus* 840, in which there is a similar confrontation between a temple authority (the chief priest Levi) and Jesus: "*Who* gave you permission to tread this place of purification?" [6]

Third, the second question is in good Semitic form. Matthew Black has drawn attention to the *hina*-clause in the second question and has asserted that it represents the consecutive *d*ᵉ in Aramaic.[7] It is one of the most frequent gospel Aramaisms. (Ordinarily one expects the conjunction *hōste* to introduce a consecutive clause in Greek.) Furthermore, the main clause of the second question contains a phrase which reflects a Semitic form of expression. The phrase *didonai exousian* occurs many times in the LXX and Josephus.[8]

Fourth, in a Palestinian Jewish milieu authority is generally personal, and the question "*Who* gave you authority," not "By *what* authority,"[9] expresses the personal nature of the transfer of authority. In the Jewish sources authority is given by certain persons to others; the former thereby authorize the latter to teach (cf. Sir. 45:17) or to perform a certain action (cf. 1 Macc. 1:13; 10:35; 11:58; Sir. 30:11; 1 Esdr. 8:22; Acts 9:14; 26:10, 12; John 19:10).[10] The phrase "by what authority" does not refer to authority given to Jesus by someone else, but refers to the nature of his own authority. We shall show later that it refers to his authority as the Son of man on earth, and that it is therefore an interpretive Christian composition.

On the basis of the foregoing, and on the basis of additional remarks below, the following is suggested as the earliest recoverable form of the pericope:

> [27b] And as he was walking in the temple, the chief priests and the scribes and the elders came to him, [28] and they said to him . . . "Who gave you . . . authority to do these things?" [29] And Jesus said to them, "I shall ask you a question. . . . [30] Was the baptism of John from heaven or from men?"

This is a complete unit, and it contains all the essential features of a conflict story as described in Chapter II.[11] The secondary elements are (1) Mark 11:27a, which is a Marcan connecting link;[12] (2) the first question about authority (11:28a) and its inclusion within a conditional statement in 11:29; and (3) the material in 11:30b-33.[13]

2. The Question of Authority and the Temple Cleansing

The question was raised earlier concerning the relationship of the Question about Authority and the Temple Cleansing. Since the two are related in Luke and John, but not in Mark (whom Matthew follows), did Luke and John make this connection, or was it in the tradition from the beginning, but severed by Mark?

There have been several suggestions as to what the term "these things" which Jesus does refers in the Gospel of Mark. Some have suggested that the phrase does, in fact, refer to the temple cleansing.[14] Others have suggested that it refers to a baptizing ministry of Jesus.[15] Still others have suggested that it refers to Jesus' ministry of words and deeds as a whole.[16]

Upon examination of the possible alternatives, the following is the solution which is the most probable in light of evidence. While Mark conceives no connection between the Question about Authority pericope (11:27-33) and the Temple Cleansing pericope (11:15-17) in his own gospel, this connection did in fact exist at an earlier stage of the synoptic tradition. The first part of our assertion rests on the following observations:

First, as D. Nineham has suggested, Mark has enhanced the story of the Temple Cleansing by breaking up the primitive sequence consisting of Triumphal Entry (11:1-10), Temple Cleansing (11:15-17), and Question about Authority (11:27b-33) and by inserting the two parts of the Cursing of the Fig Tree (11:12-14, 20-27a). The Temple Cleansing is enhanced in that, according to Mark, "the Messiah comes to [the temple] and when he finds that the outward foliage of ceremony hides no fruit of righteousness, his only possible reaction is one of judgment and cleansing."[17]

Second, either Mark or a predecessor has added the first question about authority. This question is placed in the second person; it is a question about the person of Jesus, i.e., a question about his authority as Son of man on earth. For Mark, as for his predecessors, the question is a challenge to Jesus' earthly ministry as a whole (for, as Mark knows, he teaches and acts with *exousia*, 1:22, 27; 2:10), not a challenge to any one act which he has done.

At the earliest stage of the tradition, however, it can be maintained that the *tauta* in the Question about Authority referred to the Temple Cleansing. This claim rests on the following points:

First, as Nineham suggests, it is likely that the natural sequence of events would be that of Triumphal Entry, Temple Cleansing, and Question of Authority. The Cursing of the Fig Tree is a miracle story which is undoubtedly a formulation of the early church.[18] It cannot be assigned to the same stratum of tradition to which one assigns the other pericopes in the sequence.[19]

Second, there is the witness to this connection between the Question of Authority and Temple Cleansing in the Fourth Gospel. There, in immediate response to the Cleansing, the opponents ask (2:18), "What sign have you to show us for doing this?" If the author of the Fourth Gospel worked independently, this is an independent tradition which is conscious of the connection. If he worked with knowledge of the synoptic tradition (but not of the written gospels themselves), the connection may have existed in that tradition at an early stage.[20]

Third, the Question of Authority, both in John *(hoti tauta poieis)* and in Mark *(hina tauta poiēs)*, has to do with some *action* of Jesus. It is difficult to believe that the pericope could have been used independently in the primitive church without some rather clear reference as to what the *tauta poiein* refers. It must have been used in connection with the decisive occasion, still remembered, by which the confrontation was provoked. That was most likely the Temple Cleansing.[21]

3. *The Function of the Pericope in the Primitive Church*

Assuming that the earliest form of the pericope was as we have given it above, and that the question of the opponents originally referred to the Temple Cleansing, we can attempt an answer to the question, What is its *Sitz im Leben?* What is the historical context (debate, preaching, or otherwise) in which it was used, formulated, and indeed composed as a conflict story?

In all probability we have here a pericope which relates a scene out of the historical life of Jesus of Nazareth. This can be maintained in a preliminary way on the grounds of multiple attestation, since we have not only the synoptic account but also the account in the Fourth Gospel and a similar account in the *Oxyrhynchus Papyrus* fragment 840. But, more significantly, the historicity of material in this pericope can be maintained by means of the so-called "criterion of dissimilarity,"[22] i.e. the saying of Jesus is dissimilar to characteristic emphases both of ancient Judaism and of the early church. The question of the opponents to Jesus in the temple would have been a question about authority in its most elementary sense: "Who authorized you (or gave the permission or the right) to do this?" The meaning of the Hebrew and Aramaic equivalents of *exousia* is simply "right" or "permission."[23] That is the case for such terms as *rasut* and *r⁰suta'* in rabbinic literature.[24]

The burning issue in the minds of those who confronted Jesus was the authority (right or permission) by which he cleansed the temple.[25]

Jesus' reply, on the other hand, involves something characteristic about his own message. When he asked whether the baptism of John was from heaven (God) or from men, he raised the issue of authority to a different level. D. Daube has written:

> [Moses] had received the Law—and his authority—"from Sinai," a circumlocution meaning "from God (at Sinai)." When Jesus claimed, in scarcely veiled language, that his authority, like John's baptism, was "from heaven," another circumlocution meaning "from God (in heaven)," he was applying to himself a doctrine which all Jews admitted at least in the case of Moses.[26]

Jesus' act of temple cleansing, by which he sought to drive the vendors out of God's house at the coming of the new age, was an eschatological sign.[27] In the counter-question the implication is that the authority by which he acts is an authority "from heaven." While the opponents ask a simple question of who—what jurisdiction—it was that gave him the right to do what he did, the question is met with an implied affirmation that the *exousia* is from above: it is the eschatological *exousia* of God that is coming into being in these actions which appear disruptive, illegitimate, and unauthorized. Just as one must decide whether the baptism of John was the eschatological baptism of repentance, or a misguided human activity which came to nought, so one must decide concerning the temple cleansing. This counter-question silences the opponents, for they are not prepared to make a public decision about John's baptism. Because they are not so prepared, they are left with a dilemma.

The tradition of this conflict was preserved and interpreted by the primitive church for its own purposes. At the earliest stage this purpose could hardly have been, as Dibelius affirms for the paradigms, that of preserving a statement of Jesus useful for preaching. Nor could it have been, as Bultmann claims for the apophthegms, for the purpose of resolving debates on issues of conduct. Rather, it is apparent that in the formulation and preservation of this conflict story the interest was from the beginning centered upon Jesus as an agent of God's eschatological authority. That is to say, the interest was Christological.

The Question about Authority tradition, used in conjunction with the Temple Cleansing, was an account which proclaimed to the primitive community the eschatological victory of Jesus over the powers of the old age. During the pre-Marcan period, and certainly for Mark, this purpose was made even more clear by interpretive additions to the pericope. The first question of authority in Mark 11:28 was added, and this made the pericope more understandable to those who heard it. For with this addition we no longer have a question as to who gave the right or permission to cleanse the temple, but we have a question concerning Jesus himself: "By what authority do *you* do this?" The early hearers would have understood that it is by the authority of the Son of man in his earthly role that Jesus acted. The idea of Jesus as Son of man on earth was an early conception, used already in the Palestinian church,[28] and it is the one idea in which Jesus was conceived as acting with authority in the tradition of both Q and Mark. H. E. Tödt has shown that in Q passages the sayings about Jesus as Son of man on earth designate Jesus' *exousia* over against opponents who attack him, and that sayings in Mark (2:10, 28) about Jesus as Son of man are in accord with this.[29] "In both cases," he says, "Jesus appears as the one having full authority at whom his opponents take offense." [30] Possibly already in the pre-Marcan transmission, but certainly for Mark in any case, the use of this pericope served to proclaim Jesus' authority as Son of man on earth.

In a sense, then, Dibelius is correct in claiming a *Sitz im Leben* of preaching for this and, perhaps, other conflict stories. But, contrary to Dibelius, this conflict story would not have served the purpose of preaching in the sense that he would have it. It does not end with a statement of Jesus which is of obvious use in illustrating the "mind and manner" of Jesus as the "normative standard." Rather, the pericope would more likely have been used to proclaim and teach the unique status of Jesus. It preserved the memory of how the earthly Jesus had once acted in the temple with authority "from heaven" and silenced his opponents, when they called his activity into question, by means of a counter-question concerning John.

But, furthermore, it was used to make explicit that the activity of Jesus in the temple was in fact an act of the Son of man working with authority from above. Those who have discerned the events of God's salvation, beginning with the baptism of John, know Jesus as the Son of man who had been active on earth and who shall appear again at the end of time. The old temple, its authorities, and the former activities in the temple continued to be a part of the familiar world. But in faith the Christian community believed that the Son of man is the one endowed with authority from heaven, which relativizes temple authority known in daily life. The Son of man will return to judge and save those who belong to the community of faith in him, not the community about the temple. Such a view carries with it, of course, a harsh judgment against contemporary Judaism. It implies that tensions between Jew and (Jewish) Christian had been heightened to such a degree that authority was conceived by Jewish Christians to have been taken away by God from the religious leadership of Judaism in Jerusalem and granted to Jesus, the Son of man.

B. Paying Taxes to Caesar
(Mark 12:13-17//Matthew 22:15-22//Luke 20:20-26)

In our discussion of this pericope earlier (Chapter II, Part A, 1), we observed that the Marcan form differs from that in the Gospel of Thomas, logion 100. The incident is presented in the form of a conflict story in Mark, whereas in Thomas there is merely a pronouncement of Jesus on the issue of paying taxes to Caesar in response to a question by his disciples.

It should be observed that the conflict story in Mark is a unitary one.[31] It is hardly possible that the closing saying (Mark 12:17) would have circulated independently of the rest of the story, for it is directly dependent on the production of the coin and the dialogue concerning the coin.[32] The question is asked: "Whose likeness and inscription is this?" The reply: "Caesar's." And the saying follows: "Render to Caesar the things that are Caesar's, and to God the things that are God's." The latter saying presupposes the production of the coin and the acknowledgment of the opponents that Caesar's inscription is on it. Therefore the conflict story would have originated as a unit. Moreover, it would have originated in the Palestinian church. For the denarius was used in Judea to pay the head tax, and the denarius bore Caesar's inscription.[33] It is possible, as some major critics have contended,[34] that the pericope preserves the memory of an incident in the ministry of Jesus on the issue of paying taxes. But having allowed for this, the pericope in Mark is nevertheless a primitive church composition, containing narration as well as dialogue, which has been formulated and transmitted to serve some purpose.

1. *The Formation of the Pericope*

The pericope is unitary, and there is little in Mark which would not have been in the pericope from its original formation. However, it appears that 12:13 is a Marcan addition as well as 12:17b. The former verse ("And they sent him to some of the Pharisees and some of the Herodians to entrap him in his talk") serves to identify the opponents of Jesus, who are not named in the opening verse of the conflict story proper (12:14), and it seeks to establish that the opponents were sent by officers of the Sanhedrin. It begins, "and they sent . . . . ," but who "they" are is not specified. One must check back to 11:27 to find a reference to the officers of the Sanhedrin.[35] The half-verse at the end of the pericope (12:17b, "and they were amazed at him") is most likely a Marcan comment too, since similar endings are seen elsewhere as Marcan endings to traditional materials (cf. 1:27, 45; 5:20; 12:34b, 37b).

Having removed the Marcan additions, the conflict story which Mark would have received reads as follows:

> [14] And they came and said to him, "Teacher, we know that you are true, and care for no man; for you do not regard the position of men but truly teach the way of God. Is it lawful to pay taxes to Caesar, or not? [15] Should we pay them, or should we not?"
>
> But knowing their hypocrisy, he said to them, "Why put me to the test? Bring me a coin, and let me look at it." [16] And they brought one.
>
> And he said to them, "Whose likeness and inscription is this?"
>
> They said to him, "Caesar's."
>
> [17] Jesus said to them, "Render to Caesar the things that are Caesar's, and to God the things that are God's."

The conflict story (Mark 12:14-17a) fits the conditions of Jesus' ministry and must have been based on memory of an incident in the life of Jesus. Certain persons—unspecified in the pre-Marcan conflict story (and they needn't have been opponents in the actual interchange [36])—asked Jesus concerning the payment of taxes to Caesar. Jesus gave a reply in parallelism and in which the second half has the major weight: [37]

> Render to Caesar the things that are Caesar's,
> and to God the things that are God's.

There has been a great deal of discussion of the political consequences of this saying. S. G. F. Brandon wrote concerning the dominical saying (12:17) that it was "a saying of which any Zealot would have approved," and that it was intended to assert that "payment of tribute to Caesar was an act of disloyalty to Yahweh," [38] for the land of Israel and all its resources belong to him. Robert Eisler wrote that even the statement "render to Caesar" was loaded with political meaning; he says it "really means: 'Throw Caesar's, i.e., Satan's, money down his throat, so that you may then be free to devote yourself wholly to the service of God.' " [39]

But such views are extreme. Martin Hengel writes that no real Zealot would handle the silver denarius bearing Caesar's image.[40] The issue of whether one should pay taxes to Caesar had been decided a long time before the ministry of Jesus,[41] and his saying (12:17) merely acknowledges that those who use Caesar's money are obliged to pay tribute when he demands it.[42] Nevertheless, the paying of taxes to Caesar is a temporary obligation. The important thing in view of the nearness of the kingdom is that people render to God what belongs to him, namely, themselves.[43]

2. *The Function of the Pericope in the Primitive Church*

On the basis of the foregoing, our purpose is to inquire into the setting in which this conflict story was composed in its most primitive stage. The essential question we pose is this: Why would the primitive church preserve a tradition about paying taxes to Caesar if it conceived itself to be the eschatological community of the last days? Furthermore, why did it preserve this tradition in the form of a conflict story?

At the earliest stage of the tradition this pericope would not have been used to govern church conduct in relation to the state as an end in itself. This is how the passage was used later, as the references to it in Justin, Irenaeus, and Tertullian make clear,[44] and perhaps in Mark as well. It became a timeless general proposition (i.e., not understood in terms of eschatological expectation) on the relationship of the Christian to the state. But it does not follow that the pericope had normative significance for the Christian's relationship to the state at the most primitive stage.

At the time of the story's initial composition there would not yet have existed a fixed boundary between "two kingdoms," a civil sphere ruled by Caesar, and a religious one ruled by God.[45] The tradition would not yet have been "de-eschatologized" to the point that a two-kingdom way of thinking—with two spheres coexisting for an indefinite duration—was intended. Rather, the dominical saying (12:17), central to the story, called the hearer to a worldly abandon and eschatological expectation so characteristic of the teaching of Jesus as a whole. And the primitive church would have composed the story with similar ends in view.

Living after the resurrection of Jesus and believing that the eschatological events were taking place, the Palestinian Christian community would have been confronted by opponents [46] who called its worldly abandon and eschatological expectation into question. The opponents would want to know what the church has to say about the world "as is" or "ought to be," and how its position differs or conforms to their own. The conflict story was composed as a response, for the conflict story form *as form* is still a vehicle for citing the position of Jesus, and therefore the community, over against that of his opponents. Using a traditional saying of Jesus, the church affirmed that the questions asked by opponents are secondary.

The universal problem of people is that, although they belong to God, they do not render themselves to him in self-and-worldly abandon, faith, and expectation. Political obligations, though important, are to be seen for what they are—temporary and penultimate. Undoubtedly the Palestinian Christians took the attitude of Jesus on paying taxes to Caesar, and at that point the conflict story has political consequences and provides for the community and posterity an authoritative position. But the thrust of their concern was that in light of the one kingdom to come—not two kingdoms which are—present urgency requires one's rendering of one's self to God. Caesar's reign is temporal, but God's is eternal. The individual Christian is left with responsibility before God. No guideline is given by which one might negotiate between the claims of God and Caesar for all time and in all circumstances. Nothing is endorsed—neither political conservatism, revolutionary activity, nor apathy. One is to render the self to God and stand responsible for decisions and activities *coram deo*.

C. The Question about Fasting
(Mark 2:18-20//Matthew 9:14-15//Luke 5:33-35)

Our sources indicate that fasting on certain days is a very old custom. It was practiced in Judaism prior to the time of Jesus.[47] In the familiar parable of the Pharisee and the Tax Collector (Luke 18:9-14) the Pharisee prays, "I fast twice a week" (Luke 18:12).

Certain Pharisees customarily fasted on Mondays and Thursdays

as a special act of piety.[48] Sometime already in the first century A.D.
certain Christians took up the practice of fasting too.[49] Rather than
keeping the Pharisaic fast days, however, they fasted on Wednesdays
and Fridays—Wednesdays because that was the day on which the
betrayal of Jesus was arranged, and Fridays because that was the
day of the crucifixion.[50]

The conflict story on fasting[51] must be seen as having been composed in a setting in which fasting was a live issue. The story appears
to have been composed out of a saying of Jesus on the issue of fasting, given in response to a question about it, and certain secondary
additions.

The story opens with a question concerning the disciples. They
don't fast. Why? The response of Jesus is given in a question and a
statement:

> Can the wedding guests fast while the bridegroom is with them? As
> long as they have the bridegroom with them, they cannot fast (Mark
> 2:19).

Much of the story surrounding (and even within) this saying must
be considered material composed in a primitive Christian setting.
What is generally agreed on as authentic (an actual statement of
Jesus) is the question (19a) i.e., the first half of the verse quoted
above. Even that, however, cannot be accepted as unretouched in its
present form. The term "bridegroom" poses a critical problem, since
elsewhere in the New Testament it stands allegorically for Jesus whose
"bride" is the church (2 Cor. 11:12; Matt. 25:1-3; cf. Eph. 5:23-33; Rev.
19:7-9; 21:9), a way of thinking which developed after the lifetime
of Jesus. The term surely has allegorical meaning in Mark 2:19a too.

Joachim Jeremias has suggested that the present wording of the
verse is a circumlocution for an original question which would have
been, "Can the wedding guests fast during the wedding?"[52] And, according to him, there is no reason to question its authenticity when
reconstructed in some such form.[53]

The saying asserts that there is no need for fasting. The present
moment, for Jesus, is a time of rejoicing, since the kingdom of God
is at hand. Jesus was not an ascetic, nor is there a basis for claiming
that he enjoined any type of ascetic practices, including fasting, upon
his disciples. There is a saying from Q (Matt. 11:19//Luke 7:34) in
which it is said of Jesus, "the Son of man came eating and drinking,
and they say, 'Behold, a glutton and a drunkard, a friend of tax col-

lectors and sinners.' " While there is undoubtedly hyperbole in that, the verse does, nevertheless, dash cold water on the idea that Jesus was an ascetic. It must summarize the general tone and style of his ministry.[54]

The words which follow in Mark 2:20 (together with 2:19b) must be considered a secondary formulation,[55] for they enjoin fasting: "As long as they have the bridegroom with them, they cannot fast. The days will come, when the bridegroom is taken away from them, and then they will fast on that day." These words presuppose Christian reflection on the death of Jesus after the fact. That the bridegroom (Christ) will be "taken away" refers to his death. And that his disciples will fast "on that day" refers to Christian fasting on Friday in commemoration of his death.[56]

The rest of the pericope (Mark 2:18) was composed at two different stages. The initial statement in Mark 2:18a ("And John's disciples and the Pharisees were fasting") can be considered an editorial link written by Mark himself. But the rest of the verse (2:18b) is more complicated. Various writers claim that it would have originally contrasted only the conduct of Jesus' disciples with those of John the Baptist: "Why do John's disciples . . . fast, but your disciples do not fast?" The words "and the disciples of the Pharisees," in their view, would have been added later.[57]

Reasons can be offered in support of such a view. In the first place, the words "and the disciples of the Pharisees" present a problem. There is no evidence elsewhere that the Pharisees had "disciples." The phrase appears to be an anachronism. And, second, there is a tradition in Q (Matt. 11:18//Luke 7:33) that John the Baptist did in fact fast, and we may infer that his disciples would have done the same.[58] Mark 2:18 would therefore report things accurately if the disputed phrase were left out.

But we must deal with the question: Why was the conflict story on fasting composed? Can one account for its composition as a conflict story without reference to the Pharisees? It is not likely that it would have been composed to portray a polarity between the church and a sect of John.[59] Furthermore, why would Mark himself write "and the Pharisees" into his introduction (2:18a), unless there had been reference to the Pharisees in his source (2:18b)?

Another approach can be made. It can be held that the central core of the story is based on memory. On a particular occasion Jesus was asked why his disciples do not fast, in contrast to John's,[60] but without reference to the Pharisees, to which Jesus gave a reply. That reply—given in Mark 2:19a (but probably in the form given above)—was remembered, since it was a radical statement for its time. Both 2:18b (without reference to the Pharisees) and 2:19a, then, are based on a remembered question and a remembered answer from the ministry of Jesus, and the conflict story can therefore be classified as a "unitary" one.

But these are not sufficient for the creation of a conflict story. The story would have been developed at a time and place in which fasting had become an issue in the primitive Palestinian church. That which was remembered—Jesus' characteristic freedom from fasting for himself and his disciples—was considered applicable no longer after his death. The Palestinian Christians could not think of the present as a time of festivity characteristic of a wedding celebration. They had shifted their thinking so that the messianic wedding feast was considered eschatological, a future hope (which comes to expression in Matt. 22:2-14; 25:1-3). The practice of fasting on Friday came to be observed by them in commemoration of Jesus' death.

Fasting on Friday, however, is a departure from practices best known in the culture, that is, the fasting of certain Pharisees on Mondays and Thursdays. The question was raised therefore by the church's critics, certain Pharisees, Why do you not keep the traditional fast days? And the conflict story was composed in response to this question. Memory had it that Jesus had once dealt with the question of fasting. But that question was revised so that it would meet the needs of the present: "Why do John's disciples *and the disciples of the Pharisees* [61] fast, but your disciples do not fast?" (2:18b; the italicized words were added). And the response to the question was composed on the basis of the traditional response of Jesus (Mark 2:19a): From the beginning, since the ministry of Jesus, his disciples have not kept the traditional fast days. Since the coming of the Bridegroom, and in keeping with his own attitude, there is no need to keep those days. The Bridegroom, however—and here the church relates the traditional saying to present circumstances—has been "taken away." Therefore the church has set aside a day of fasting in commemoration of "that day" on which he was taken away.

The fact that the material is presented in the form of a conflict story indicates that the primitive church in Palestine was interested in distinguishing the basis for Christian fasting from that of Judaism in light of the tradition that Jesus and his disciples did not fast during his ministry. Christian fasting is based on the absence of the Bridegroom, not Jewish tradition. It can be seen also that Mark the evangelist understood the conflict story essentially along the same lines. It is he who added the two little similes in 2:21-22 [62] (on the new patch on old clothes and new wine in old skins). By so doing he highlights the claim in the conflict story, namely that Christian fasting has no basis in Jewish tradition, but is for a new time and for a new and different purpose. [63]

D. The Healing on the Sabbath
(Mark 3:1-5//Matthew 12:9-13//Luke 6:6-10)

The Healing on the Sabbath pericope in Mark 3:1-5 and parallels is one of four synoptic conflict stories concerning Jesus' or his disciples' activities on the sabbath. [64] One of these appears immediately before the present pericope in all three gospels, viz., the Plucking of Grain on the Sabbath (Mark 2:23-28//Matthew 12:1-8// Luke 6:1-5). The other two are in Luke's Gospel only (13:10-17; 14:1-6), and both have to do with healings on the sabbath. [65]

The conflict story in Mark 3:1-5 can be considered a complete unit in itself. The concluding narrative in 3:6 can be considered an addition to the pericope, made by the collector of the conflict stories of 2:1–3:5 as a conclusion to the whole series. [66] The conflict story, furthermore, can be considered a unitary type. The dominical saying in 3:4 could not have circulated independently in the primitive church without some reference to an action. The saying is an interrogative reply to the charge implied in 3:2. [67] It would have depended on a setting of this type to have survived in transmission.

1. *The Formation of the Pericope*

In order to describe the earliest recoverable form of the pericope, the Marcan additions must be identified. The opening descriptive words in Mark 3:1a ("again he entered the synagogue") are Mark's own—a redactional link. [68] The phrase "and they were silent" in 3:4 appears to be a Marcan addition. [69] And the words at 3:5a, "having looked around at them, grieving at their hardness of heart," are quite certainly Marcan too. [70] With these various additions omitted, the pericope in its pre-Marcan form approximates the following:

[1] And a man was [in the synagogue] who had a withered hand.

[2] And they watched [Jesus] to see whether he would heal him on the sabbath, in order that they might accuse him. [3] And he said to the man who had the withered hand, "Come here." [4] And he said to them, "Is it lawful on the sabbath to do good or to harm, to save life or to kill?" [5b] [He] said to the man, "Stretch out your hand." He stretched it out, and his hand was restored.

2. The Function of the Pericope in the Primitive Church

This pericope relates a miracle, but the miracle is not at the center of attention. "The spotlight falls on the conflict between Jesus and his opponents, and the cause of controversy is not the healing as such, but the fact that it is done on the sabbath." [71] The pericope has to do with conduct on the sabbath, and one expects that the community in which it originated was one in which the observance of sabbath law along Pharisaic lines was a live issue. The pericope would not, however, have originated in a community which had ceased observing the sabbath. The content of 3:4 has been preserved (whether authentic to Jesus or not) [72] in a community which continues to observe the sabbath, albeit in its own way.

The conflict story portrays Jesus as departing from Pharisaic law in his act of healing. Pharisaic law allowed for the suspension of sabbath law to preserve life, [73] but that is not at stake here. The man's life is clearly not in danger. If there is a historical basis for the incident in the life of Jesus, it appears that he was conscious that saving life does in fact override sabbath law. Thus far his attitude would have been consistent with Pharisaic attitudes concerning the sabbath.

But "to save life" on the sabbath is not the issue. The issue is whether healing (and healing a not very serious malady—or at least a malady which could wait another day) on the sabbath is permitted. But, contrary to what we might expect, the question of healing on the sabbath is not raised by Jesus before his opponents (3:4). His question is of deeper significance. Using the familiar technique of inference from minor to major (*kal wa-homer* [74]), Jesus raises the question: If it is the case that "to save life" (a particular, or minor, principle) is permitted, does not the law in its fundamental thrust affirm that "doing good" on the sabbath (a major principle) is the will of God? The Pharisaic concession to permit the saving of life on the sabbath is, in the thinking expressed here, merely an expression of the fundamental principle that "doing good" is permitted. Moreover, the sabbath is understood here as an anticipation of life in the new age to come, which has drawn near, and therefore a shift of emphasis is made from the typological to the eschatological.[75]

This conflict story, which may very well have as its basis a reminiscence out of the life of Jesus,[76] must have been composed at a time in which the primitive church was attempting to arrive at a position regarding sabbath practices over against that of Pharisaic Judaism. It would have been composed in a community which continued to observe the sabbath, but which raised the question of the extent to which Pharisaic law was applicable. The question was raised whether the church can with justification do "good works" on the sabbath, although what those "good works" would have been—acts of healing or other benevolent activities in general—can no longer be determined. In any case, the expression "to do good" contains the controlling conception of the entire pericope; it is that which stands apart from, and is thought to be the presupposition of, the accepted practice ("to save life"). And it became the principle for sabbath conduct in the church within which the story was composed.[77]

While it might be concluded from the foregoing that the conflict story originated in a "typically rabbinic" debate, as Bultmann describes the background of the various conflict stories,[78] such a conclusion is neither necessary nor necessarily accurate. To be sure, a "typically rabbinic" method is employed (viz., "from minor to major"). Nevertheless, at the level of the story's composition and actual usage it is clear that the church justified *its own* conduct through appeal to Jesus' conduct of "doing good" on the sabbath (i.e., his sabbath healings, which have a multiple attestation in the traditions about Jesus [79]). And it is evident that it is not merely Jesus as teacher, equipped with interpretive skills, to whom appeal is made. His acts of "doing good" on the sabbath are the acts of the Messiah,[80] whose authority is self-evident for the Christian community. The principle that "doing good" on the sabbath is God's will is agreed to not merely because the argument "from minor to major" is persuasive, but even more so because it is the Messiah who puts forth the argument and paradigmatically acts on it.

E. The Sinful Woman at a Pharisee's House

(Luke 7:36-50)

The story is found only in Luke's gospel. An examination of it shows, however, that it has several similarities to another story, not found in Luke, the Anointing at Bethany (Mark 14:3-9//Matt. 26:6-13; John 12:1-8).[81]

Although these similarities exist, the story given by Luke is clearly more than another version of the Anointing at Bethany. Furthermore, its own structure and content can be seen more clearly if these similarities to the latter story are removed. Once these are removed, there is a fully coherent conflict story, which either Luke or a predecessor has conflated with the Anointing at Bethany.[82] This story does not tell of an anointing, but of a penitent woman who entered a Pharisee's house, wept at Jesus' feet, and quickly loosened her hair to wipe her tears from his feet. This aroused the Pharisee's indignation, since it was a disgrace for a woman to unbind her hair in the presence of men.[83] In response Jesus speaks to the Pharisee in defense of the woman and her activity. Reconstructed from the text of Luke, this story would appear as follows:

[36]One of the Pharisees asked [Jesus] to eat with him, and he went into the Pharisee's house, and [reclined]. [37] And behold, a woman of the city, who was a sinner, when she learned that he was [reclining] in the Pharisee's house . . . [38] [stood] behind him at his feet, weeping, and she began to wet his feet with her tears, and wiped them with the hair of her head, and kissed his feet. . . .

[39] And when the Pharisee who had invited him saw it, he said to himself, "If this man were a prophet, he would have known who and what sort of woman this is who is touching him, for she is a sinner."

[40] And Jesus answering said to him, "I have something to say to you.

[41] "A certain creditor had two debtors; one owed five hundred denarii, and the other fifty. [42] When they could not pay, he forgave them both. Now which of them will love him more?"

[43] [The Pharisee] answered, "The one, I suppose, to whom he forgave more."

And he said to him, "You have judged rightly."

[44] Then turning to the woman he said to [the Pharisee], "Do you see this woman? I entered your house, you gave me no water for my feet, but she has wet my feet with her tears and wiped them with her hair. [45] You gave me no kiss, but from the time I came in she has not ceased to kiss my feet.

[47] "Therefore I tell you, one whose many sins are forgiven loves much, but to whom little is forgiven, the same loves little." [84]

J. Jeremias, who believes that there is a basis for the story in the ministry of Jesus, has suggested that the woman's action would have been an act of gratitude in response to the preaching of Jesus, perhaps just prior to the banquet, in which Jesus proclaimed God's forgiveness to outcasts.[85] One need not, of course, be quite so specific (that the preaching took place just prior to the banquet), but Jeremias' suggestion is indeed plausible insofar as he says that the action of the woman was a response to Jesus' teaching and attitude concerning outcasts.

The story reconstructed is in the form of a conflict story,[86] although it is longer and more complex than most. Following the introductory narration, there is a charge against Jesus by an opponent identified as a Pharisee, and Jesus gives a response to that charge by a parable, a counter-question, and a final statement. The Pharisee's charge is ad hominem. Jesus has failed the test of proving himself a true prophet (7:39) in the eyes of the Pharisee who had invited him to his house, and who had apparently believed beforehand that Jesus might have been such.[87] The reply of Jesus closes the discussion and justifies his conduct (that of allowing the sinful woman to touch him), as well as the conduct of the woman, by contrasting her action with the Pharisee's and stating that the difference is due to the proportion to which each has been forgiven.[88]

The earlier form of the story, however, was not left untouched. As indicated, elements from the Anointing at Bethany were added: (1) the Pharisee was named Simon,[89] and (2) the anointing activity and statement of Jesus concerning it were introduced.[90] Furthermore, the material in 7:48-50 can be considered secondary.[91] The statement "Your sins are forgiven" (7:48) is superfluous. The action of the woman, the parable of the debtors, and the words of 7:47 ("one whose sins are forgiven loves much") presuppose that the woman *knows* that her sins have been forgiven; that is why she acts the way she does. Nevertheless, 7:48-50 serves to demonstrate that forgiveness of sins is mediated through Jesus to those who have faith.

This conflict story would have originated in a churchly setting in which the forgiveness of sins was affirmed and declared. The church from the beginning—from the original followers of Jesus on—was made up largely from "people of the land" (*'am ha-ares*) [92] who were considered "sinners" in the estimation of the Pharisees.[93] And while it is the case that in Pharaisaism (and Jewish tradition generally) it is affirmed that God is gracious and does indeed freely forgive,[94] the activities of Jesus, as reflected here, as well as the words ascribed to him in 7:48 ("Your sins are forgiven") and in Mark 2:5 and parallels ("My son, your sins are forgiven")—an open declaration that God has indeed forgiven, a declaration which presupposes knowledge of God's disposition in the moment and the authority to declare it—have no similarity in Judaism. Yet this declaration of forgiveness was articulated in the church.

It is no accident that within this story (at 7:37), as elsewhere in the tradition (Mark 2:15-17; and Q, Matt. 11:19//Luke 7:34), Jesus is portrayed as an associate and friend of "sinners." In composing the story of the woman at the Pharisee's house, the traditionist showed that it was a "sinner" (and a woman besides) who responded positively to Jesus. In Jesus' lifetime and after, the Pharisees would deny that he was a prophet (7:39). But those whom the Pharisees considered "sinners"—both formerly and now—accepted him as such. At the time the story was composed, Christians affirmed that those who respond affirmatively to the message of forgiveness are in fact forgiven, while those who trust their own righteousness before God are not able to receive it (Luke 7:44-45). (Compare the parable of the Pharisee and the Tax Collector, in which it is the latter who calls himself a "sinner" and goes home justified; Luke 18:9-14.) The story was composed, in short, to provide for the church a text by which its membership could affirm that God's forgiveness was effective in the present for "sinners" over against the Pharisaic charge that such persons (the church itself) have no grounds for their presumed righteousness before God.[95] And the church rests its claim on the attitude, message, and conduct of Jesus himself.

F. Conclusions

These five unitary conflict stories have common features which can now be recognized. They are all, in the first place, very old in point of origin. They have been formulated at the earliest stage of the gospel tradition about Jesus. It has been suggested that some, if not all, contain information about actual conflicts in the life of Jesus with his adversaries.

Nevertheless, these conflict stories are not to be considered stenographic accounts of such conflicts for their own sake. They have been formulated and preserved by early Christian traditionists for purposes which we can scarcely determine. Our study has shown, however, that previous assumptions concerning the *Sitz im Leben* of the conflict stories cannot rest unchallenged. There are some conflict stories of a unitary nature which clearly could not have been formulated to preserve a statement of Jesus useful for preaching. This is evident above all in the earlier traditions behind Mark 11:27-33; 2:18-19; and Luke 7:36-50. There are others which clearly could not have been formulated in rabbinic-styled debates within the church on points of law—either among church leaders, or between church leaders and those outside. This is evident above all in the earlier tradition behind Mark 11:27-33.

What is common to them, rather, is that they offer for the primitive church a justification for its beliefs and practices in response to Jewish criticism.[96] In each case the primitive church has drawn on traditions about the attitude and conduct of Jesus to affirm that the new life offered between the resurrection of Jesus and the parousia has a legitimacy grounded in the prophetic activity of Jesus. There is no attempt in these stories to argue for the legitimacy of belief or conduct on the basis of contemporary procedures of structuring an argument. Nor do the conflict stories contain new law for Christian conduct over against Jewish law. They center not in law, but in the person of Jesus and his conduct and attitude. As such the conflict stories were at their formative stages a unique genre and quite unlike the stories of rabbinic debates which were transmitted in contemporary Judaism. The primitive community formulated stories which were not patterned on existing models. The primitive community, like Jesus himself, was not interested in justifying its belief or conduct by the *middoth* of rabbinic hermeneutics. It was concerned, like Jesus himself, with meeting criticism by going behind current thinking to the greater controlling principles and motives expressed in the law (cf. Mark 2:18-19; 3:1-5), or simply referring to the words and conduct of its Master (cf. Mark 11:27-33; 12:13-17; Luke 7:36-50).

By means of the unitary conflict stories the church was working out its own patterns of belief and practice, arriving at its own distinctive self-awareness, over against its critics; not by rabbinically styled argument, but by drawing upon reminiscences of Jesus and formulating stories upon them in which the Master is set in bold and victorious relief vis-à-vis his adversaries. Over against the criticism of an independent Jesus-sect within Judaism, the traditionists proclaimed the authority of Jesus over the impressive existing authorities of Judaism (Mark 11:27-33). Over against the political realities of the moment, in which the power of Caesar is so visibly present, the church called

for a commitment to God which transcends present political penultimate urgencies (Mark 12:13-17). And over against criticism on matters
of the legal bases for conduct, it justified its own conduct (Mark
2:18-19; 3:1-5) and status before God (Luke 7:36-50) by appealing to
the actions and attitudes of Jesus.

NOTES

1. The distinction has been made by R. Bultmann, *Synoptic Tradition*, 47. He
   does not, however, speak of "unitary" and "non-unitary" conflict stories. His
   contrast is between stories of "unitary composition" and those of "secondary
   construction."
2. Conversely, the non-unitary stories are made up of elements from differing
   stages of tradition: a saying at hand (from earlier tradition) is embellished
   at a later stage (that in which the conflict story is formulated) with an
   opponent's question and a setting.
3. As a rule, the most which can be claimed for a narrative in a conflict story
   is that it may represent a "typical scene" from the ministry of Jesus, not a
   specific event. Cf. Reginald H. Fuller, *A Critical Introduction to the New
   Testament* (London: Duckworth, 1966) 85; and N. Perrin, *Rediscovering
   the Teaching of Jesus*, 29. But we shall observe below that in some instances
   the conflict story preserves the memory of specific events, e.g., in Mark
   11:27-33 (in relation to the Temple Cleansing) and 12:13-17 (the Question
   of Paying Taxes to Caesar). In these cases we do not merely have "typical
   scenes" from the life of Jesus, but reminiscences of particular (unrepeatable)
   events.
4. At this point the words attributed to Jesus in 11:33 must be left out of
   consideration, since they contain the question in its first form. Verse 30 must
   be considered the dominant dominical saying in terms of the form of a conflict story given in Chapter II.
5. Cf. Günther Dehn, *Der Gottessohn: eine Einführung in das Evangelium des
   Markus* (Hamburg: Furche, 1953) 223.
6. The Greek text reads: *tis epetrespen soi patein touto to hagneutērion*,
   1.12-13. This text is given in Joachim Jeremias, *Unknown Sayings of Jesus*
   (2nd ed., SPCK, 1964) 48-50.
7. Matthew Black, *An Aramaic Approach to the Gospels and Acts* (3rd ed.; Oxford: Clarendon, 1967) 81. Black refers to additional examples in Mark 6:2,
   D; Luke 1:43; John 9:2.
8. For LXX references, see Prov. 17:14; Dan. 5:7, 29; 7:14, 17; Bel 25-26;
   Tob. 7:10; Sir. 17:2; 30:11; 45:17; 1 Macc. 1:13; 10:6, 8; 11:58. For Josephus, see *Ant.* 2.5.7 §90; 20.8.11 §193. The phrase is frequent elsewhere
   in the New Testament: Matt. 9:8; 28:18; Mark 13:34; Luke 4:6; 20:20;
   John 1:12; 5:27; 17:2; Acts 8:19; 2 Cor. 10:8; 13:10; Rev. 6:8; 9:3;
   13:4-7.
9. For the use of *poios* as "what?" (rather than "what kind?"), see Aeschylus,
   Agamemnon 278; Aristophanes, *Aves* 920; 1219; *Paris Papyri* 60.8; *Tebtunis
   Papyri* 1.25.18; *Amherst Papyri* 2.68.7; *Berlin Griechische Urkunden*
   2.7.1047. These references have been collected from James H. Moulton and
   George Milligan, *The Vocabulary of the Greek Testament Illustrated from
   the Papyri and Other Non-Literary Sources* (London: Hodder & Stoughton,
   1930) 524; Edwin Mayser, *Grammatik der griechischen Papyri aus der*

Ptolemäerzeit (2 vols.; Berlin: W. de Gruyter, 1906-1926) 2. 78; and Friedrich Preisigke, *Wörterbuch der griechischen Papyrusurkunden* (3 vols.; Berlin: Selbstverlag der Erben, 1925-1931) 2. 334.

10. For uses of the term "authority" in Jewish literature, illustrating that it is personal (i.e., one's personal right to teach or perform certain actions), see Str-B 1. 859; W. Foerster, *exousia*, TDNT 3. 564-566; and David Daube, *The New Testament and Rabbinic Judaism* (London: Athlone, 1956) 207-210.

11. Cf. R. Bultmann, *Synoptic Tradition*, 20. The proposed unit, however, contains only the minimal amount of material for a dialogue, and it ends abruptly. If it is based on an event from the ministry of Jesus, which is likely, it is possible that the "original dialogue" would have contained more. Yet it does not follow that any of the material in 11:31-33 belonged to the earlier tradition, which has been preserved in 11:27-30.

12. Cf. E. Klostermann, *Markus*, 119. Other instances of the phrase *erchesthai palin* appear in Mark 2:13; 3:20; 7:31; 10:1; 14:39, 40.

13. Cf. the same judgment in E. Lohmeyer, *Markus*, 241; W. Grundmann, *Markus*, 237; R. Bultmann, *Synoptic Tradition*, 19-20; F. W. Beare, *Earliest Records*, 207; D. Nineham, *Mark*, 306-308; E. Schweizer, *Mark*, 236; and Herbert Braun, *Jesus: der Mann aus Nazareth und seine Zeit* (Themen der Theologie 1; 2nd ed.; Stuttgart: Kreuz, 1969) 159-161.

14. Those in this category who say that the connection has existed from the beginning of the tradition include: M. Dibelius, *Die unchristliche Überlieferung von Johannes dem Täufer* (FRLANT 15; Göttingen: Vandenhoeck & Ruprecht, 1911) 21; M. Albertz, *Streitgespräche*, 23; G. Bornkamm, *Jesus*, 159; E. Lohmeyer, *Markus*, 243; Alfred Loisy, *Les evangiles synoptiques* (2 vols.; Haute-Marne: Chez L'Auteur, 1907-1908) 2. 292; T. W. Manson, *Beginnings of the Gospel* (London: Oxford University, 1950) 76; V. Taylor, *Mark*, 469; D. Daube, *The New Testament and Rabbinic Judaism*, 220-221; Ferdinand Hahn, *The Titles of Jesus in Christology* (New York: World, 1969) 155, 206-207; Étienne Trocmé, "L'expulsion des marchands du temple," *NTS* 15 (1968-1969) 10-11; C. H. Dodd, *The Founder of Christianity* (New York: Macmillan, 1970) 49, 147-149; and W. Lane, *Mark*, 413.

Those who say that the connection was made in the transmission of the tradition, but prior to Mark, include: R. Bultmann, *Synoptic Tradition*, 36; D. Nineham, *Mark*, 298, 306; and Gam S. Shae, "The Question on the Authority of Jesus," *NovT* 16 (1974) 1-29.

Those who say that the connection was made by Mark include: C. G. Montefiore, *The Synoptic Gospels* (2 vols.; London: Macmillan, 1927; reprinted, New York: Ktav, 1968) 1. 271-272; G. Dehn, *Der Gottessohn*, 233; and E. Schweizer, *Mark*, 236-237.

Others, who do not suggest at what stage of the transmission the connection to the Temple Cleansing was made, but who belong in this category, are: E. Gould, *Mark*, 217; W. Grundmann, *Markus*, 236; S. Johnson, *Mark*, 193; E. Klostermann, *Markus*, 119; and W. L. Knox, *Sources*, 1. 88, 91.

15. In this category, maintaining that the reference to a baptizing ministry existed at the beginning of the tradition, are R. Bultmann, *Synoptic Tradition*, 20; and D. Nineham, *Mark*, 307.

16. Those who maintain that the reference to the ministry of Jesus as a whole existed at the beginning of the tradition include William Manson, *Jesus the Messiah* (London: Hodder & Stoughton, 1944) 40; Reginald H. Fuller, *The Mission and Achievement of Jesus* (London: SCM, 1954) 61; C. Montefiore, *The Synoptic Gospels*, 1. 271-272; G. Dehn, *Der Gottessohn*, 233. M.

Dibelius (*Tradition,* 45) holds that this connection was made during the transmission of the tradition.

17. D. Nineham, *Mark,* 300.
18. Cf. Bultmann, *Synoptic Tradition,* 54. Several scholars hold that this miracle story was developed out of a parable, such as that in Luke 13:6-9. Cf. V. Taylor, *Mark,* 459 (who says that the suggestion was first made by E. Schwartz, ZNW 5 [1904] 80-84); B. H. Branscomb, *Mark,* 201-202; Reginald H. Fuller, *Interpreting the Miracles* (Naperville: SCM, 1963) 38-39; and F. Hahn, *Titles of Jesus,* 206.
19. Cf. here V. Taylor, *Mark,* 458-459, and his references to other scholars who concur.
20. We assume that the Fourth Evangelist either had no knowledge of the synoptic tradition or at the most had access to the synoptic tradition in its earlier stages before the gospels were written. If, as some claim, he had access to Luke, he must have had some independent tradition connecting the Question about Authority and the Temple Cleansing, because in Luke the Question about Authority is actually asked after Jesus is apprehended for preaching and teaching in the temple, not for cleansing it.
21. So F. Hahn (*Titles of Jesus,* 206-207) says, "In Mk 11:27 . . . the reference is to a concrete occasion. Since moreover the cleansing of the temple and the question about authority are also associated with one another in John 2:13ff., the two may also have originally belonged together in the synoptic tradition."
22. For discussion on this criterion, see N. Perrin, *Rediscovering the Teaching of Jesus,* 39-45.
23. Cf. Str-B 1. 859-862.
24. For references to the literature, see Marcus Jastrow, *A Dictionary of the Targumim, the Talmud Babli and Yerushalmi, and the Midrashic Literature* (2 vols.; New York: Pardes, 1950) 2. 1499.
25. Cf. Victor Eppstein, "The Historicity of the Gospel Account of the Cleansing of the Temple," ZNW 55 (1964) 57. Eppstein says that the question put to Jesus by the temple hierarchy may have been "aimed at finding out whether Jesus was acting by authority of the Sanhedrin or of the Pharisees, since it would have seemed inconceivable that he would act in this way on his own responsibility and initiative."
26. D. Daube, *The New Testament and Rabbinic Judaism,* 219. Cf. also F. W. Beare, *Earliest Records,* 207.
27. Cf. G. Bornkamm, *Jesus,* 159; W. Grundmann, *Markus,* 232; F. Hahn, *Titles of Jesus,* 155-156.
28. Cf. F. Hahn, *Titles of Jesus,* 34-37, and Reginald H. Fuller, *The Foundations of New Testament Christology* (New York: Charles Scribner's Sons, 1965) 120.
29. H. Tödt, *Son of Man,* 114-133.
30. Ibid., 133.
31. Cf. R. Bultmann, *Synoptic Tradition,* and C. H. Dodd, "The Dialogue Form in the Gospels," *BJRL* 37 (1954-1955) 57.
32. This is not the case in the Thomas logion, in which the saying is not related to the production of the coin, but simply to the question asked. The coin is not produced in another late tradition, *Papyrus Egerton* 2, but it is (as *to nomisma*) in Justin Martyr's *Apology* 1.17.2. For Greek texts, see *Synopsis Quattuor Evangeliorum* (ed. Kurt Aland; Stuttgart: Württembergische Bibelanstalt, 1964) 383.
33. It has been held that, since Judea was an imperial (rather than a senatorial)

province, its taxes went not to the treasury of the Senate (the *aerarium*), but into the imperial treasury (the *fiscus*). "Judea therefore, in the strict sense of the word, paid its taxes 'to Caesar,' " writes Emil Schürer, *A History of the Jewish People in the Time of Jesus* (ed. Nahum N. Glatzer; New York: Schocken, 1961) 189. Cf. also G. Bornkamm, *Jesus,* 121. But more recently it has been claimed that "revenues from Judea, though an imperial province, will still have gone to the public treasury *(aerarium)* rather than to the imperial treasury *(fiscus).* None the less, people in Judea spoke of paying taxes 'to Caesar.' " So E. Schürer, *The History of the Jewish People in the Age of Jesus Christ* (1 vol. to date; ed. Geza Vermes and Fergus Miller; Edinburgh: Clark, 1973) 1. 372 (with citation of recent literature). Concerning the denarius itself, the inscription on one side was TI CAESAR DIVI AUG F AUGUSTUS (= Tiberius Caesar Divi Augusti Filius Augustus, translated, "Tiberius Caesar, son of the divine Augustus, Augustus"), and on the reverse was inscribed PONTIF MAXIM (= Pontifex Maximus, "High Priest").

34. M. Albertz, *Streitgespräche,* 29-30; R. Bultmann, *Synoptic Tradition,* 26; V. Taylor, *Mark,* 478; G. Bornkamm, *Jesus,* 121-122; and K. Berger, *Die Gesetzesauslegung Jesu,* 1. 577.

35. Cf. H. Swete, *Mark,* 273; E. Klostermann, *Markus,* 138; V. Taylor, *Mark,* 478; W. Grundmann, *Markus,* 242; D. Nineham, *Mark,* 316; S. G. F. Brandon, *Jesus and the Zealots* (New York: Charles Scribner's Sons, 1967) 250-251 (n. 5); and Theodore J. Weeden, *Mark—Traditions in Conflict* (Philadelphia: Fortress, 1971) 20 (n. 2).

36. It is not clear that "Herodians" existed in the time of Jesus. That they would have been supporters of Herod Antipas, ruler of Galilee from 4 B.C. to A.D. 40 (and therefore contemporaries of Jesus), is not supported by ancient sources, viz., Josephus, *Ant.* 14.15.10 §450; *J. W.* 1.16.6 §319; Epiphanius, "Against the Herodians," *Against Heresies;* and Tertullian, *Against All Heresies* 1. The term applies in Epiphanius to followers of Herod Agrippa I who was king after the time of Jesus' ministry (king in Galilee A.D. 40-44, and in Judea 41-44); see his "Against the Herodians," *Epiphanii Opera* (5 vols.; ed. G. Dindorfius; Leipzig: T. W. Weigel, 1859-1862) 1. 330. See also B. W. Bacon, "Pharisees and Herodians in Mark," *JBL* 39 (1920) 102-111; idem, *The Gospel of Mark* (New Haven: Yale University, 1925) 74-76; and E. Lohmeyer, *Markus,* 67 (n. 2).

The term "Herodians" is used not only at Mark 12:13, but also at Mark 3:6. In the later verse, which is pre-Marcan, the term is anachronistic, as at 12:13, which is Marcan redaction. Apparently the term "Herodians" was the only term for a political party in Palestine which Mark knew (from 3:6). At 12:13 he uses it to demonstrate the political consequences of the question in 12:14. "Herodians" were considered by Mark to be pro-Roman, although the sources mentioned above (Epiphanius and Tertullian) indicate that in fact they supported Herod Agrippa I (A.D. 40/41-44) as a nationalistic leader, and they were consequently anti-Roman.

37. So G. Bornkamm, *Jesus* 122; Rudolf Schnackenburg, *The Moral Teaching of the New Testament* (New York: Herder, 1965) 117-121; W. Grundmann, *Markus,* 244; M. Dibelius, *Jesus* (Philadelphia: Westminster, 1949) 124; E. Schweizer, *Mark,* 244; Martin Hengel, *Was Jesus a Revolutionist?* (Philadelphia: Fortress, 1971) 33-34; Charles H. Giblin, " 'The Things of God' in the Question Concerning Tribute to Caesar (Lk. 20:25; Mk. 12:17; Mt. 22:21)," *CBQ* 33 (1971) 510-527; Hans Conzelmann, *Jesus* (Philadelphia: Fortress, 1973) 67; Werner Kümmel, *Theology of the New Testament* (Nash-

ville: Abingdon, 1973) 73; and R. Tannehill, *The Sound of His Mouth*, 174-177.

38. S. G. F. Brandon, *Jesus and the Zealots*, 347-348; cf. also his *The Trial of Jesus of Nazareth* (New York: Stein & Day, 1968) 67.

39. Robert Eisler, *The Messiah Jesus and John the Baptist* (New York: Dial, 1931) 334.

40. M. Hengel, *Was Jesus a Revolutionist?*, 33. Another who denies that Mark 12:17 is a Zealot statement is C. G. Montefiore, *The Synoptic Gospels*, 1. 279.

41. Cf. Israel Abrahams, *Studies in Pharisaism and the Gospels* (2 vols.; Cambridge: Cambridge University, 1917; reprinted, New York: Ktav, 1967) 1. 62-65.

42. Shailer Matthews (*Jesus on Social Institutions* [ed. Kenneth Cauthen; Philadelphia: Fortress, 1971] 108) writes that Jesus' reply "was a rebuke to insidious quibbling and a refusal to be drawn into politics as an excuse for submission to tyranny or as an incentive to a struggle for independence."

43. Cf. C. Giblin, "The Things of God," 520-525. M. Hengel (*Was Jesus a Revolutionist?*, 33) states, rightly, "Instead of 'and to God, what belongs to God,' it should really be translated adversatively, *but* to God, what belongs to God.'"

44. Justin (*Apology* 1.17) writes, "More even than others we try to pay the taxes and assessments to those whom you appoint, as we have been taught by them. For once in his time some came to him and asked whether it were right to pay taxes to Caesar. [Here Justin relates the gospel account.] So we worship God only, but in other matters we gladly serve you." Translation by E. R. Hardy, *Early Christian Fathers* (LCC 1; ed. Cyril C. Richardson; Philadelphia: Westminster, 1953) 253. See also Irenaeus, *Against Heresies* 3.8.1; and Tertullian, *On Idolatry* 15. The fact that Mark has "Herodians" on the scene (12:13) indicates that even for him the conflict story was loaded with political considerations.

45. Martin Luther made use of the passage to affirm that, while on the one hand, the imperial power does not extend to God's kingdom, "with respect to body, property, and honor [Caesar] has indeed [authority], for such matters are under his authority;" "Temporal Authority: To What Extent It Should Be Obeyed," *Luther's Works* (American ed.; Philadelphia: Fortress, 1962) 45. 111. Mark 12:17 is also found within the "Table of Duties" appended to Luther's *Small Catechism* under "Duties Subjects Owe to Governing Authorities;" see the *Book of Concord* (ed. Theodore G. Tappert; Philadelphia: Fortress, 1959) 355. Cf. also Walther von Loewenich, *Luther als Ausleger der Synoptiker* (Munich: Kaiser, 1954) 233.

46. Opponents, because at 12:15 the questioners are charged with "hypocrisy." The word is not found elsewhere in Mark and must have been embedded within the tradition. The word was probably understood by Mark as a cryptogram for the Pharisees and therefore accounts for his designation of certain opponents in 12:13 as Pharisees.

47. Cf. I. Abrahams, *Studies in Pharisaism and the Gospels*, 1. 121-128.

48. *Didache* 8:2; cf. George Foot Moore, *Judaism in the First Centuries of the Christian Era: The Age of the Tannaim* (3 vols.; Cambridge: Harvard University, 1927) 2. 260. I. Abrahams (*Studies in Pharisaism and the Gospels*, 1. 125) casts doubt on whether this was standard at the time of Jesus; it may have been exceptional and only later became the norm. It is established as the norm in *b. Ta'an.* 12a.

49. Besides Mark 2:20, see Matt. 6:16-18.

50. *Didache* 8.2; *Apostolic Constitutions* 7.23.1.

51. We assume, with most commentators, that Mark 2:18-20 is a complete unit;

and that 2:21-22 were two little similitudes attached to 2:18-20 at a later time, perhaps by Mark himself. See R. Bultmann, "The Study of the Synoptic Gospels," 47-48; M. Dibelius, *Tradition*, 43, 65; V. Taylor, *Mark*, 212; D. Nineham, *Mark*, 103; Joachim Jeremias, *The Parables of Jesus*, 117; F. W. Beare, *Earliest Records*, 79; N. Perrin, *Rediscovering the Teaching of Jesus*, 77-82; E. Schweizer, *Mark*, 67; Howard C. Kee, "The Old Coat and the New Wine," *NovT* 12 (1970) 13-21; and W. Lane, *Mark*, 112-113.

52. J. Jeremias, *The Parables of Jesus*, 52 (n. 14); idem, *Jesus als Weltvollender* (Gütersloh: Bertelsmann, 1930) 22, in which *Exod. Rab.* 15.20 (on Exod. 12:2) is quoted: "In den Tagen des Messias wird die Hochzeit sein" ("In the days of the Messiah, the wedding will take place").

53. J. Jeremias, *The Parables of Jesus*, 52. See also N. Perrin, *Rediscovering the Teaching of Jesus*, 78-80. Others who consider 2:19a authentic or at least expressive of the attitude of Jesus, apart from the question of its original wording, include R. Bultmann, "The Study of the Synoptic Gospels," 45; *Synoptic Tradition*, 105; M. Dibelius, *Tradition*, 65; V. Taylor, *Mark*, 210-211; F. Hahn, *Titles of Jesus*, 133; E. Schweizer, *Mark*, 67; T. A. Burkill, *Mysterious Revelation: An Examination of the Philosophy of St. Mark's Gospel* (Ithaca: Cornell University, 1963) 133; idem, *New Light on the Earliest Gospel: Seven Markan Studies* (Ithaca: Cornell University, 1972) 41, 44; and H.-W. Kuhn, *Ältere Sammlungen*, 62.

54. Cf. G. Bornkamm, *Jesus*, 50, 80-81; N. Perrin, *Rediscovering the Teaching of Jesus*, 119-121; and H. Conzelmann, *Jesus*, 32, 67.

55. Cf. Wilhelm Bousset, *Kyrios Christos* (Nashville: Abingdon, 1970) 78; Julius Wellhausen, *Das Evangelium Marci* (2nd ed.; Berlin: Reimer, 1909) 18-19; M. Albertz, *Streitgespräche*, 9; R. Bultmann, *Synoptic Tradition*, 19; M. Dibelius, *Tradition*, 65-66; E. Klostermann, *Markus*, 27-28; J. Jeremias, *The Parables of Jesus*, 52, 104, 117; T. A. Burkill, *Mysterious Revelation*, 133; N. Perrin, *Rediscovering the Teaching of Jesus*, 79; F. Hahn, *Titles of Jesus*, 133 (n. 4); E. Schweizer, *Mark*, 67; H.-W Kuhn, *Ältere Sammlungen*, 62; K. Berger, *Die Gesetzesauslegung Jesu*, 1. 577; Jürgen Roloff, *Das Kerygma und der irdische Jesus* (Göttingen: Vandenhoeck & Ruprecht, 1970) 223-227; and J. A. Ziesler, "The Removal of the Bridegroom: A Note on Mark II. 18-22 and Parallels," *NTS* 19 (1972) 191. On the other hand, R. Banks (*Jesus and the Law*, 94-96) tries to maintain that the words in Mark 2:19b-20 are authentic; but his attempt is not convincing, since he asserts (against the plain sense of the text) that 2:20 is not a pronouncement concerning actual fasting after the death of Jesus.

56. Cf. M. Dibelius, *Tradition*, 65; T. A. Burkill, *Mysterious Revelation*, 132-133; E. Schweizer, *Mark*, 68; H.-W. Kuhn, *Ältere Sammlungen*, 61-72; and Werner Kelber, *The Kingdom in Mark: A New Place and a New Time* (Philadelphia: Fortress, 1974) 20. Kuhn discusses all the proposals which have been made concerning "that day": a weekly fast on Friday (as proposed here, and which he accepts); an annual fast on Nisan 14 (popularized by Bernhard Lohse, *Das Passafest der Quartadecimaner* [Gütersloh: Bertelsmann, 1953]); an annual fast on the Saturday prior to Easter; and an annual fast on Good Friday.

57. M. Dibelius, *Die urchristliche Überlieferung von Johannes dem Täufer*, 40; V. Taylor, *Mark*, 209-210; W. Grundmann, *Markus*, 65; N. Perrin, *Rediscovering the Teaching of Jesus*, 79; and Walter Wink, *John the Baptist in the Gospel Tradition* (SNTSMS 7; Cambridge: Cambridge University, 1968) 12.

58. Cf. Charles H. H. Scobie, *John the Baptist* (Philadelphia: Fortress, 1964) 131-141.

59. As Burton S. Easton ("A Primitive Tradition in Mark," *Studies in Early Christianity* [ed. Shirley Jackson Case; New York: Century, 1928] 97) has written, "it is by no means clear that followers of the Baptist were conspicuous enough in Palestine after A.D. 30 to attract any particular attention from the Christians."

60. It has been suggested that John's disciples fasted in a commemoration of his imprisonment or death. See A. Loisy, *Les evangiles synoptiques*, 1. 494; C. G. Montefiore, *The Synoptic Gospels*, 1. 58; and A. Rawlinson, *Mark*, 30. But, as indicated above, there is the tradition that John himself fasted (Q, Luke 7:33//Matt. 11:18), and his disciples are most likely to have done so too. The question of fasting need not have originated after the death of John.

61. Perhaps the "anachronistic" wording of 2:18b is due to Mark. His source *could* have read, "Why do the disciples of John and the Pharisees fast . . . ?," and Mark himself could have then revised it slightly for his introduction, "And John's disciples and the Pharisees were fasting" (2:18a). Then, in this view, he rewrote the question of 2:18b as "Why do John's disciples *and the disciples of the Pharisees* fast, but your disciples do not fast?" This places the accent on the conduct of the disciples in all three cases: those of John, those of the Pharisees, and those of Jesus.

62. Cf. R. Bultmann, *Synoptic Tradition*, 19; W. Grundmann, *Markus*, 66; and F. W. Beare, *Earliest Records*, 79.

63. K. Berger (*Die Gesetzesauslegung Jesu*, 1. 583) writes that the logion in Mark 2:21-22 gives expression to the radicality of 2:18-20, but he does not indicate who added these verses. Cf. also J. Ziesler, "The Removal of the Bridegroom," 192.

64. There is also the little episode, not a conflict story, concerning the sabbath in Luke 6:5, Codex D: "On the same day he saw a man performing a work on the Sabbath. Then said he unto him: 'Man! If thou knewest what thou doest, thou art blessed. But if thou knewest not, thou art cursed and a transgressor of the Law.'" This is quoted from the translation given in J. Jeremias, *Unknown Sayings of Jesus*, 61.

65. These two sabbath healing pericopes in Luke may be variants of the sabbath healing pericope which appears in Mark (3:1-5); so M. Dibelius, *Tradition*, 97; R. Bultmann, *Synoptic Tradition*, 12, 62; and F. W. Beare, *Earliest Records*, 173, 175-176. They were, however, transmitted independently in the special Lucan tradition. Although they can be considered conflict stories, they are not discussed at length in our work, because they would have been formulated to serve the same interests of the primitive church as Mark 3:1-5.

66. This point is taken up in the beginning of Chapter V.

67. Cf. R. Bultmann, *Synoptic Tradition*, 12; "The Study of the Synoptic Gospels," 43; and Eduard Lohse, "Jesu Worte über den Sabbat," *Judentum Urchristentum Kirche* (ed. Walther Eltester; Berlin: Töpelmann, 1960) 85.

68. The verb "to enter" *(eiserchesthai)* appears thirty times in Mark's Gospel, frequently in editorial links, such as at 1:21; 2:1; 7:17, 24; 11:11, 15. The adverb "again" *(palin)* appears twenty-five times; examples of its use in editorial links are in 2:1; 4:1; 5:21; 8:1; 10:1; and 11:27.

69. See Mark's use of it in dramatic dialogue situations also at 9:34 and 14:61. The verb *siōpaō* is considered characteristic of Mark by John C. Hawkins, *Horae Synopticae* (2nd ed.; Oxford: Clarendon, 1909; reprinted, Grand Rapids: Baker, 1968) 12-13. The term "connotes a religious silence in the face of the presence of Jesus' power," John R. Donahue, *Are You the Christ? The Trial Narrative in the Gospel of Mark* (SBLDS 10; Missoula: Scholars, 1973) 86. Cf. also K. Berger, *Die Gesetzesauslegung Jesu*, 1. 578.

70. This claim rests on two points: First, the words "having looked around at them" appear frequently in editorial links elsewhere in Mark (3:34; 5:32; 9:8; 10:23; 11:11). Second, the statement that Jesus was "grieved at their hardness of heart" can be considered a composition by Mark, since the theme of "hardness of heart" is Marcan (cf. 6:52; 8:17b-18). On this latter point see Joseph Gnilka, *Die Verstockung Israels—Isa. 6:9-10 in der Theologie der Synoptiker* (Munich: Kösel, 1961) 32. Others who see Mark 3:5a as a composition by Mark include Julius Schniewind, *Das Evangelium nach Markus* (NTD; Göttingen: Vandenhoeck & Ruprecht, 1937) 63; James M. Robinson, *The Problem of History in Mark* (Naperville: Allenson, 1957) 76; Eduard Schweizer, "Ammerkungen zur Theologie des Markus," *Neotestamentica et Patristica* (*O. Cullmann Freundesgabe;* NovTSup 6; ed. W. C. van Unnik; Leiden: Brill, 1962) 41; idem, "Die theologische Leistung des Markus," *EvT* 24 (1964) 344; Edward J. Malley, "The Gospel According to Mark," *JBC* 2. 20; and Werner Kelber, *The Kingdom in Mark*, 21.

71. F. W. Beare, *Earliest Records*, 93.

72. R. Bultmann (*Synoptic Tradition*, 147) considers this verse to reflect the attitude of Jesus, if not his very words. Cf. also R. Banks, *Jesus and the Law*, 125.

73. "Whenever there is doubt whether life is in danger this overrides the Sabbath," *Yoma* 8:6. Quoted from *Mishnah* (H. Danby), 172. For comment, see I. Abrahams, *Studies in Pharisaism and the Gospels*, 1. 132. Additional texts are given in Str-B 1. 623-629.

74. For discussion on this hermeneutical rule (the first of the so-called Seven Middoth of Hillel), see Jacob Z. Lauterbach, "Talmud Hermeneutics," *JE* 12. 32. It is the argument *a minori ad majus* or *a majori ad minus*. Hermann L. Strack (*Introduction to the Talmud and Midrash* [Philadelphia: Jewish Publication Society of America, 1931] 285) cites examples of this rule in the Mishnah tractates *B. Bat.* 9:7; *Sanh.* 6:5; and *'Abot* 1:5. From these three examples it can be seen that the method is used not only in the interpretation of biblical texts, even though it is called a "hermeneutical" rule, but also in rabbinic disputation on other matters which are unrelated to Scripture interpretation.

75. Cf. Harald Riesenfield, "The Sabbath and the Lord's Day in Judaism, the Preaching of Jesus and Early Christianity," *The Gospel Tradition* (Philadelphia: Fortress, 1970) 119.

76. Besides Mark 3:1-5, there are other accounts of healings by Jesus on the sabbath at Luke 13:10-17; 14:1-6; John 5:1-8; and 9.

77. R. Banks (*Jesus and the Law*, 130) asserts that for Jesus, according to Mark 3:1-5, the sabbath "is not only a day upon which it is appropriate to heal, it is the day on which one *must* do so." The same principle would have been current in the church setting in which this pericope (as well as other sabbath healing accounts) was composed.

78. R. Bultmann, *Synoptic Tradition*, 41.

79. See note 76 above. Sabbath healings are attested in the Marcan (from which Matthew draws), special Lucan, and Johannine traditions.

80. Cf. R. H. Fuller, *Interpreting the Miracles*, 52-53, who shows that both "doing good" and "to save life" refer to the saving action of the Messiah. R. Banks (*Jesus and the Law*, 125) agrees that the pericope contains a "christological thrust," and he thinks of 3:4 as authentic. It is puzzling, however, why he allows only that it serves as a call to a decision concerning the person and work of Jesus and, after saying that the verse was not a community creation, intimates that it had nothing to do with conflict between the primitive church and Judaism regarding sabbath practices.

81. Similarities to Mark 14:3-9 include: (1) the host's name is Simon; (2) the event takes place in a house; (3) Jesus reclines at table; (4) an uninvited woman enters; and (5) she brings an "alabaster jar of ointment."

82. The reconstruction offered here is based in part on (but goes beyond) the views of P. Benoit, *L'evangile selon Saint Matthieu* (Paris; Cerf, 1950) 148; A. Legault, "An Application of the Form-Critique Method to the Anointings in Galilee and Bethany," *CBQ* 16 (1954) 131-145; Raymond E. Brown, *The Gospel According to John, I-XII* (AB 29; Garden City: Doubleday, 1966) 449-454; and Barnabas Lindars, *The Gospel of John* (London: Oliphants, 1972) 412-415.

A detailed analysis of the formation of the pericope is given (with different results) by Georg Braumann, "Die Schuldner und die Sünderin Luk. vii. 36-50," *NTS* 10 (1963-1964) 487-493. Braumann concludes that originally the story in 7:36-39, 44-46, and 48-49 stood alone; that the parable in 7:41-43 was inserted (and 7:40 composed); and that 7:47 and 50 were attached. Braumann's analysis has not been followed above. Certainly 7:47 is essential to the story from the moment of its composition. And, if so, the parable and response of the Pharisee (7:41-43) are also essential.

Finally, Robert Holst ("The One Anointing of Jesus: Another Application of the Form-Critical Method," *JBL* 95 [1976] 435-446) tries to show that all of the anointing stories in the gospels (Mark 14:3-9//Matt. 26:6-13; Luke 7:36-50; and John 12:1-8) are based on one incident in Jesus' ministry. Holst tries "to give explanations for changes in the developing tradition and to recover a very primitive story which lies behind all the biblical accounts" (p. 436). For his thesis to stand up, Holst has to assert that Luke used his own tradition (which is clearly the case), and that he made no use of Mark's account whatsoever (pp. 436, 438, 446)—a position which is untenable. Furthermore, Holst ignores the important differences between Luke 7:36-50 and Mark 14:3-9, which are too great to be explained away as due to developments in the transmission of an originally singular story; the differences indicate that more than one tradition stands behind the two accounts.

83. Cf. J. Jeremias, *The Parables of Jesus*, 126, who cites *t. Sota* 5:9 and *y. Git.* 9.50d.

84. The last verse (Luke 7:47) has been altered from the present text of Luke in accordance with a suggestion by M. Black (*An Aramaic Approach to the Gospels and Acts*, 182-183) that a translation error (from Aramaic to Greek) was made. The point of the parable of the two debtors is that one who is forgiven much will love more than one who is forgiven little. In the present (unaltered) reading of Luke 7:47a the point is missed; the woman is forgiven because she loved much. Black writes that 7:47 should be rendered in antithetic parallelism with masculine suffixes: "one whose many sins are forgiven loveth much, but to whom little is forgiven, the same loveth little." C. F. D. Moule (*An Idiom-Book of New Testament Greek* [2nd ed.; Cambridge: Cambridge University, 1959] 147) writes that the *hoti*-clause should be taken as depending on *legō soi:* "I can say with confidence that her sins are forgiven, *because* her love is evidence of it." The *NEB* renders 7:47 as "And so, I tell you, her great love proves that her many sins have been forgiven." Cf. E. Ellis, *Luke*, 122. It should be noted that in connection with 7:47b the suggestions here are required; since "he who is forgiven little loves little" (7:47b), it follows that "he who is forgiven much loves much," and 7:47a should connote such.

85. J. Jeremias, *The Parables of Jesus*, 126-127. Cf. also A. Plummer, *Luke*, 210.

86. Luke 7:36-50 is classified as a controversy dialogue by R. Bultmann, *Synoptic*

Tradition, 20-21, but not by Albertz, and as a pronouncement story (not in its present form, but in the oral period) by V. Taylor, *Formation*, 70-71. M. Dibelius (*Tradition*, 114) classifies it as a legend.

87. Given the fact that for the Pharisees generally prophecy had ceased in Israel (cf. I. Abrahams, *Studies in Pharisaism and the Gospels*, 2. 120-128), it is strange that a Pharisee would entertain such an idea. However, there are indications (Abrahams, 2. 127-128) that prophecy was not thought by some to have ceased, since the Holy Spirit can never cease to operate in the lives of men. See also *b. Ber.* 34b, in which Hanina ben Dosa (first century rabbinical student of Johanan ben Zakkai) is asked by Gamaliel's disciples whether he is a prophet on the basis of his having performed a miracle of healing, to which he replies in the negative. Luke's Pharisee could have made a tentative judgment about Jesus in a positive way, so that he invited him, but concluded that Jesus was a false prophet by his conduct. "A prophet should be able to discern the character of those with whom he consorts," J. Creed, *Luke*, 110-111.

88. The words of Jesus in 7:44-45 (after "Do you see this woman?") are in antithetic parallelism. See M. Black, *An Aramaic Approach to the Gospels and Acts*, 182, where the sayings are written out in parallelism.

89. The name was added at 7:40, 43, and 44.

90. The woman brings an alabaster jar of ointment (7:37) and anoints Jesus' feet (7:38); and Jesus comments on the activity (7:46).

91. Cf. Adolf Jülicher, *Die Gleichnisreden Jesu* (2. vols.; 2nd ed.: Tübingen: Mohr, 1899) 2. 299-300; R. Bultmann, *Synoptic Tradition*, 21; and Joachim Jeremias, *New Testament Theology: The Proclamation of Jesus* (1 vol. to date; New York: Charles Scribner's Sons, 1971) 1. 218 (n. 1). Jülicher and Bultmann claim that basic to Luke 7:36-50 is the parable (7:41-43) and its application (7:47), and they conclude that everything else has been constructed from Mark 14:3-9. The approach taken above, of course, differs from this.

92. For further discussion of this, see Chapter V. Cf. also B. Harvie Branscomb, *Jesus and the Law of Moses* (New York: Richard R. Smith, 1930) 143, 273-274.

93. T. W. Manson (*The Teaching of Jesus* [Cambridge: Cambridge University, 1951] 324-325) discusses the term "sinner." The term "sinners" was variously applied in the Old Testament and Judaism to those who fail to observe the Torah: (1) Gentiles; (2) Sadducees; and (3) the 'am ha-ares, "who cannot or will not observe it in all its details." The latter would be indicated here. Cf. also B. H. Branscomb, *Jesus and the Law of Moses*, 132-138; and K. Rengstorf, *TDNT* 1. 328. It was impossible, in the Pharisaic view, to obey the divine will without knowledge of the law, both written and oral. The first century Hillel is reported as saying, "No 'am ha-ares is pious" (*m. 'Abot* 2:5). And there is the tradition in *m. Dem.* 2:3 that an Associate "may not be the guest of an *Am-haaretz* nor may he receive him as a guest in his own raiment;" quoted from *Mishnah* (H. Danby), 22. For discussion of the 'am ha-ares, see I. Abrahams, *Studies in Pharisaism and the Gospels*, 2. 647-699; Solomon Zeitlin, "The Am-Ha-Ares," *JQR* 23 (1932-1933) 45-61; George F. Moore, "The Am-Ha-Ares and the Haberim," *The Beginnings of Christianity* (5 vols.; ed. F. J. Foakes-Jackson and Kirsopp Lake; London: Macmillan, 1920-1933) 1. 439-445; idem, *Judaism*, 2. 156-161; Marvin H. Pope, "'Am Ha'arez," *IDB* 1. 106-107; and Aharon Oppenheimer, *The 'Am Ha-Aretz: A Study in the Social History of the Jewish People in the Hellenistic-Roman Period* (ALGHJ 8; Leiden: Brill, 1977).

94. Cf. I. Abrahams, *Studies in Pharisaism and the Gospels*, 1. 139-149.

95. This same tendency to affirm the forgiveness of God to "sinners" over against the views of their critics is found in the use of certain parables. J. Jeremias (*The Parables of Jesus*, 124) writes, "The parables which have as their subject the gospel message in its narrower sense are, apparently without exception, addressed, not to the poor, but to opponents. That is their distinctive note, their *Sitz im Leben:* their main object is not the presentation of the gospel, but defense and vindication of the gospel; they are controversial weapons against the critics and foes of the gospel who are indignant that Jesus should declare that God cares about sinners, and whose special attack is directed against Jesus' practice of eating with the despised."

96. Morton Smith ("The Jewish Elements in the Gospels," *HTR* 24 [1956] 96) asserts that "the Gospel passages which show Jesus disputing with the scribes and Pharisees may also represent . . . an adjustment to Judaism. They show a concern to answer Jewish criticisms which Jesus himself may not have had. They try to define the Christian position in relation to that of other Jewish groups and in a way which looks like defense of a party line rather than the work of an original teacher."

IV. The Formation of the Non-Unitary Conflict Stories

Conflict stories classified as non-unitary are those in which the opponent's question and usually some narrative elements are a secondary construction, composed to give a setting for a dominical saying (authentic or not) which originally circulated independently.[1] In Chapter I the composition of conflict stories by Matthew was observed. It was seen that Matthew took pericopes from Mark and, by presenting opponents who ask questions, reformulated those pericopes into the conflict story form (Matt. 12:38-42; 22:34-40; 22:41-46). These Matthean pericopes are all non-unitary by our definition. What is to be observed in this chapter, among other things, is that Matthew was not alone in composing conflict stories out of originally non-conflict story units of tradition. The same process went on in earlier stages of transmission of synoptic materials. It is our purpose to examine the remaining conflict stories, all of which belong to this category, in order to trace the process of their formation into conflict stories. Again, as for the unitary conflict stories, our particular interest is to pursue the question of whether there is a *Sitz im Leben* common to them all.

A. The Beelzebul Controversy
(Mark 3:22-30//Matthew 12:22-32//Luke 11:14-15, 17-23)

The Beelzebul Conroversy is found in all three synoptic gospels. A comparison of the three accounts shows, however, that there are major differences between them, and that Matthew and Luke have not based theirs simply on Mark.

Matthew appears to have based his account on Mark and Q (hence, a conflation), and Luke appears to have based his on Q alone.[2] That Luke was not dependent on Mark at all for his account can be affirmed not only by a comparison of his version with Mark's, but also by the fact that it falls within a long section of his gospel (9:51-18:14) which contains little or no Marcan material.[3]

Our purpose here at the outset will be to reconstruct the Q version of the story, and then to go on to compare it with Mark's version to see whether we can construct an earlier form of the story which would have preceded both Q's and Mark's.

The reconstruction of the Q version can be made by comparing those portions of Matthew and Luke in which there is agreement over against Mark. Furthermore, since Luke's version does not incorporate material from Mark, it follows that his wording is preferable to that of Matthew's in cases where Marcan influence might be detected in the latter.

We shall go on to justify our reconstruction, but essentially the Q version would have read as follows (Luke 11:14-15, 17-18a, 19-23; 12:10):

> [14] And he was casting out a demon that was dumb; and when the demon had gone out, the dumb man spoke, and the people marveled. [15] But some of them said, "He casts out demons by Beelzebul, the prince of demons. . . ."

> [17] But he, knowing their thoughts, said to them, "Every kingdom divided against itself is laid waste, and house falls upon house. [18] And if Satan also is divided against himself, how will his kingdom stand? . . . [19] And if I cast out demons by Beelzebul, by whom do your sons cast them out? Therefore they shall be your judges. [20] But if it is by the finger of God that I cast out demons, then the kingdom of God has come upon you. [21] When a strong man, fully armed, guards his own palace, his goods are in peace; [22] but when one stronger than he assails him and overcomes him, he takes away his armor in which he trusted, and divides his spoil. [23] He who is not with me is against me, and he who does not gather with me scatters. . . . [12:10] And every one who speaks a word against the Son of man will be forgiven; but he who blasphemes against the Holy Spirit will not be forgiven."

Some of the wording above needs justification. First, while Matthew has, "But if it is by the *spirit* of God that I cast out demons" (12:28), Luke has, "But if it is by the *finger* of God that I cast out demons" (11:20). The terminology of Luke is to be preferred. As Norman Perrin has written, "the fact that 'spirit' is a favourite Lukan word makes it difficult to conceive of it having been changed by him into something else, especially in light of Luke 4:18." [4]

Second, Luke 11:16 and 18b have been omitted from our reconstruction. Verse 11:16 ("while others, to test him, sought from him a sign from heaven") does not appear in Matthew's version at this point. It can be considered a Lucan insertion. It is a clause which has been transposed from the pericope concerning the Sign of Jonah in Mark 8:11. And verse 11:18b ("For you say that I cast out demons by Beelzebul"), which is also not found in Matthew, can be considered a Lucan editorial sentence.[5]

Finally, Luke 12:10//Matt. 12:32 ("And every one who speaks a word against the Son of man will be forgiven; but he who blasphemes against the Holy Spirit will not be forgiven") can be considered integral to the Q pericope.[6] While Luke does not have it as the closing statement to the Beelzebul Controversy, but has it appear in a later context, it is given as such in Matthew, and Mark's independent version (3:29) has it, although in different wording (which Matthew does not follow; he uses Q instead).

There are other details about our reconstruction which need not detain us here.[7] The second step of our analysis can now be taken, viz., a comparison of the reconstructed Q version with that of Mark. At once it can be seen that after the Marcan editorial additions are removed, the two versions have an amazing similarity in form. Mark's editorial additions are as follows:

(1) the identification of Jesus' opponents in 3:22a ("the scribes who came down from Jerusalem"), a phrase Mark uses (in slightly different wording) at 7:1 as well;[8]

(2) the words "and he called them to him, and spoke to them in parables" at 3:23;[9]

(3) the words "how can Satan cast out Satan?" in 3:23b;[10]

(4) the little phrase "but he comes to an end" in 3:26;[11] and

(5) the closing words "for they had said, 'He has an unclean spirit'" in 3:30.[12]

Having removed these Marcan additions, and placing the Marcan and Q version (reconstructed) in parallel columns, we get the following: [13]

Q Version (Reconstructed)	Marcan Version (-Additions)
I. And he was casting out a demon that was dumb; and when the demon had gone out, the dumb man spoke, and the people marveled.	

II.	But some of them said, By Beelzebul the prince of demons he casts out demons.	[They] said, He has Beelzebul, and by the prince of demons he casts out demons.
III.A.	But he, knowing their thoughts, said to them, Every kingdom divided against itself is laid waste,	[and he said to them,] If a kingdom is divided against itself, that kingdom cannot stand.
III.B.	and house falls upon house.	And if a house is divided against itself, that house cannot stand.
III.C.	And if Satan also is divided against himself, how will his kingdom stand?	And if Satan rises against himself, he cannot stand.
III.D.	And if I cast out demons by Beelzebul, by whom do your sons cast them out? Therefore they shall be your judges. But if I cast out demons by the finger of God, then the kingdom of God has come upon you.	
III.E.	When the strong man, fully armed, guards his own palace, his goods are in peace; but if one stronger than he assails and overcomes him, he takes away his armor in which he trusted, and divides his goods.	But no one can enter a strong man's house to plunder his goods, unless he first binds the strong man, and then plunders his house.
III.F.	He who is not with me is against me, and he who does not gather with me scatters.	
IV.	And every one who speaks a word against the Son of man will be forgiven;	Truly I say to you, All will be forgiven the sons of men— the sins and the blasphemies, whatever they utter;

but he who blasphemes against the Holy Spirit will not be forgiven.	but whoever blasphemes against the Holy Spirit does not have forgiveness forever, but is guilty of an eternal sin.

Most of what is given above is parallel in content, form, and sequence in Q and Mark, even though specific wording differs. Three items are peculiar to the Q version, however: (1) Part I (the exorcism of Luke 11:14); (2) Part III.D. (the statement of Jesus about his exorcism power, Luke 11:19-20//Matt. 12:27-28); and (3) Part III.F. (the saying that he who is not with Jesus is against him, etc., Luke 11:23//Matt. 12:30). But the similarity between the two versions is otherwise so great that it appears that they are based on a common, primitive version which antedates both. Easton has written that nearly all the Greek words of the Q and Marcan versions are the same, but their order within sentences varies, as does the grammatical construction of the sentences. In short, he says, "it is impossible to prove that the two versions are derived from the same Greek source, although that they are derived from a common source of some kind is obvious." [14] It appears that the Beelzebul Controversy was originally written in Aramaic, that it was translated into Greek by more than one person, and that the writers of Q and Mark have based their versions on separate Greek translations.

Is it possible to recover a more original form of the pericope antecedent to the versions of Q and Mark? Certain suggestions have been made, and these are worthy of attention. Various scholars have suggested that the Q version reproduces the original more faithfully than Mark.[15] The story would most likely have begun with the narrative of the exorcism as Q has it (Luke 11:14; cf. also Matt. 12:22), and it would have ended with a dominical saying more like that of Q (Luke 12:10//Matt. 12:32) than that of Mark (3:29).[16] On the other hand, the sayings found in Parts III.D. and III.F., which are peculiar to Q, can be considered additions to the latter.[17] The net result is that the earlier form of the story would have been as follows (using Q wording where a choice must be made between Mark and Q):

    I. And he was casting out a demon that was dumb; and when the demon had gone out, the dumb man spoke, and the people marveled.

    II. But some of them said, "By Beelzebul the prince of demons he casts out demons."

III. But he, knowing their thoughts, said to them, "Every kingdom divided against itself is laid waste, and house falls upon house. And if Satan also is divided against himself, how will his kingdom stand? When a strong man, fully armed, guards his own palace, his goods are in peace; but if one stronger than he assails and overcomes him, he takes away his armor in which he trusted, and divides his goods.

IV. "And every one who speaks a word against the Son of man will be forgiven; but he who blasphemes against the Holy Spirit will not be forgiven."

This is in the form of a conflict story. It opens with a narrative introduction (I); there is a charge against Jesus by unidentified opponents (II); and it closes—after intervening sayings (III) [18]—with a dominical saying (IV).

Does the story relate to us a scene out of the ministry of Jesus? The question must be answered yes and no. That Jesus was challenged as to the means by which he performed exorcisms may well be historical. What we have in Luke 11:20//Matt. 12:28 ("if it is by the finger of God that I cast out demons, then the kingdom of God has come upon you") has been considered very primitive; Bultmann has written that the saying has "the highest degree of authenticity which we can make for any saying of Jesus." [19] And the statement, as an affirmation by Jesus of the means by which he performs exorcisms, presupposes some type of challenge.

But that the Beelzebul Controversy as such relates a scene from Jesus' ministry must be denied. For the dominical saying just referred to (Luke 11:20//Matt. 12:28), which shows such challenge, has been linked secondarily to its context.[20] The verse preceding it (Luke 11:19 //Matt. 12:27, "And if I cast out demons by Beelzebul, by whom do your sons cast them out? Therefore they shall be your judges.") is a church composition which has been written to introduce the authentic dominical saying (Luke 11:20//Matt. 12:28), and the two have been placed into the Beelzebul Controversy at the time of writing the Q version.

The Beelzebul Controversy would have been formulated at a time and place in which the church dealt with the problem whether forgiveness can be declared to persons who had been originally hostile to Jesus in his earthly ministry, but who now in the postresurrection period acknowledge him as the exalted Son of man. Such a conclusion can be established by focusing attention on the closing dominical saying (Part IV, "And every one who speaks a word against the Son of man will be forgiven; but he who blasphemes against the Holy Spirit will not be forgiven," Luke 12:10//Matt. 12:32). It is a Christian composition—not an authentic statement of Jesus—in which it is said that opposition to Jesus in his earthly life—a thing of the past—can be declared forgiven, but present opposition against the Holy Spirit can and will not.

H. E. Tödt has written concerning the passage that insofar as opponents turned against the Son of man merely in his activities on earth, they can be forgiven. "But there is no forgiveness—in the post-Easter situation—for the one who sets himself in opposition to the manifest activity of the Holy Spirit." [21] Two historical periods are distinguished: the period of Jesus' activity on earth as the Son of man; and the subsequent period of the Spirit's activity. "He who did not follow the earthly Jesus may nevertheless find forgiveness when following the exalted Lord, i.e., if he does not blaspheme against the Spirit." [22]

The Beelzebul Controversy would have been composed, then, in a Palestinian, Aramaic-speaking setting in which the church dealt with the problem of forgiveness and acceptance of persons entering into the Christian community who had rejected Jesus and his message in his historical ministry. Such persons are declared forgiven. What is of particular interest in terms of the history of the conflict story form is that here we have a story which goes back prior to the time of the writing of the Q document, which is usually dated within the years A.D. 50-60, or 50-70 at the most.[23] The conflict story form can therefore be traced back into a Palestinian setting shortly after the ministry of Jesus. In this case we are in touch with the first generation of Christians, some of whom were contemporaries (and possibly disciples) of the historical Jesus.

B. The Healing of the Paralytic
(Mark 2:1-12//Matthew 9:1-8//Luke 5:17-26)

This pericope has been considered by many since the turn of the century to have been composed of two smaller units of tradition.[24] In this view one unit of tradition was a miracle story now preserved in Mark 2:1-5a, 11-12, and the other was a conflict story preserved in Mark 2:5b-10.[25] One reason [26] for holding such a view is that if Mark 2:5b-10 (the conflict story) is removed, the remaining miracle story reads smoothly:

¹ And when he returned to Capernaum after some days, it was reported that he was at home. ² And many were gathered together, so
that there was no longer room for them, not even about the door; and
he was preaching the word to them. ³ And they came, bringing to
him a paralytic carried by four men. ⁴ And when they could not get
near him because of the crowd, they removed the roof above him; and
when they had made an opening, they let down the pallet on which
the paralytic lay.

⁵ And when Jesus saw their faith, he said to the paralytic . . .

¹¹ "I say to you, rise, take up your pallet and go home."

¹² And he rose, and immediately took up the pallet and went out
before them all; so that they were all amazed and glorified God, saying, "We never saw anything like this!"

There are some scholars who have not accepted the view that the
pericope is made up of two former units brought together; they claim
that it existed as a unit from the beginning.[27] The most important
point such persons have made is that, while it may be true that Mark
2:1-5a, 11-12 reads as a complete miracle story, Mark 2:5b-10 does
not appear to have been an original unit. It could not have existed by
itself, since it "has neither beginning nor end." [28]

It is not necessary, however, to consider this latter portion (Mark
2:5b-10) to have been an originally *independent* unit. We can avoid
the notion that Mark 2:1-12 has been put together in scissors-and-paste
fashion from two previous self-contained pericopes. Rather, one can
hold that whoever composed Mark 2:1-12 in its present form had a
miracle story (2:1-5a, 11-12) which he expanded by *composing*
2:5b-10.[29] The expanded pericope reflects the religious issue at stake,
the forgiveness of sins. This means that from a form-critical point of
view the dispute on forgiveness (2:5b-10) was prior in importance to
the healing (2:1-5a, 11-12), but that from a literary-critical point of
view the healing was prior, and that it was put to use in serving the
issue under dispute.

The formation of the pericope as a whole can be accounted for
along the following lines. First, 2:10a ("But that you may know that
the Son of man has authority on earth to forgive sins") can be considered the most important element in the pericope. It can also be
considered, as many have claimed,[30] a Christian composition. It is a
saying about the activities of the Son of man on earth, and all such
sayings have been considered church compositions in recent, important
studies in the development of the synoptic tradition.[31] Taking its cue

from the historical ministry of Jesus who associated—and even had table fellowship—with persons considered sinners by the Pharisees, the primitive Christian community affirmed its right to believe that it had forgiveness before God, and it declared the same openly. As the Son of man in his earthly ministry accepted "sinners," so one can claim that at his coming in the future the same will prevail. "The Son of man has authority on earth to forgive sins," so those who belong to him—still on earth—stand before God as forgiven.

The material in 2:5b-9, which leads up to this most important saying (2:10a), would have been composed in dialogue form to distinguish between the claim of the church (a claim which had its basis in the attitude, conduct, and words of Jesus himself) and that of contemporary Judaism represented by the "scribes" (2:6). To the latter no one can forgive sins except God alone (2:7). But the declaration, "My son, your sins are forgiven" (2:5), means, "My son, God forgives your sins;" the passive verb is a circumlocution for the divine name.[32] And the very act of making such a *declaration*, by which the divine authority is asserted, goes beyond Pharisaic sensibilities. There is nothing wrong —in Pharisaic thinking—with expressing the love of God and proclaiming that God is merciful. But more is at stake here. "God's judgment is not merely 'proclaimed' in the Church; it is exercised." [33] Insofar as the church claimed and declared divine forgiveness, it was open to criticism by its Pharisaic neighbors. The conflict story was composed, then, to provide a justification for ecclesiastical practice. The composer used the methodological argument from major to minor (*kal wa-homer*) [34] and used a previously independent miracle story to establish a point; it is surely more difficult to say "Rise, take up your pallet and walk" than to say "Your sins are forgiven." But the fact that the "more difficult" is done (2:12) affirms that the "less difficult" is established too.

The story would have been composed and put to use in a time and place in which the primitive church, made up of 'am ha-ares, responded to its adversaries who considered its membership "sinners," persons who could not possibly stand righteous before God (2:7) because of their laxity with the Torah, yet who considered themselves forgiven by the declaration of forgiveness exercised in the church. What is important to notice is that in this place, as in others, the church does not respond to its critics on the basis of legal debate or appeal to Scripture. True, it employs the method of argument from major to minor within the story to set up a condition by which to verify the dominical saying (2:9-10). But it actually appeals to the attitude and actions of Jesus to defend its viewpoint. There is no claim made on the basis of the Torah; it is made by an appeal to Jesus. Jesus is already here, although only implicitly, the new Torah, or the replacement of the Torah, which become explicit in Paul (Rom. 10:4). It is because Jesus had associated with "sinners" in his earthly ministry that the principle is derived: "The Son of man has authority on earth to forgive sins." [35] Appeal to his unique activities in the past becomes the basis for claiming his unique authority in the present and future.[36] Such an appeal transcends the ground rules of debate.

C. Eating with Tax Collectors and Sinners
(Mark 2:15-17//Matthew 9:10-13//Luke 5:29b-32)

The issue of fellowship and its extent is dealt with in the conflict story on Eating with Tax Collectors and Sinners. The versions of the story in Matthew and Luke differ in some details from Mark's, but they are dependent on it. Our attention here will be devoted solely to Mark's account.

Although the claim has been made that in his pericope Mark reports a specific event in the life of Jesus,[37] there are problems with such a view. One problem has to do with the setting portrayed. Jesus is described as sitting in "his house" (at Capernaum?) [38] at table with tax collectors, sinners, and his disciples. But why are the Pharisaic scribes there too (within the house), as the story presupposes? Especially if Jesus was known to consort with tax collectors and sinners, it is unlikely that Pharisaic scribes would enter,[39] for the pious do not associate with such persons in table fellowship (*m. Dem.* 2:3). The scene must be considered artificial—a construction to provide a setting for the dominical saying.

From a formal point of view the story appears to have been constructed from two sayings attributed to Jesus (2:17a and 17b) and a setting, which is artificial. The two sayings consist of a proverb ("Those who are well have no need of a physician, but those who are sick," 2:17a) and an I-saying ("I came not to call the righteous, but sinners," 2:17b).

The most important point of the story for the church, for which the whole was composed and preserved, and which is the main point to be made, is the latter saying. It has been claimed that this saying is an authentic one.[40] But such a view cannot be held with confidence. The form of the saying is the verb "to come" followed by an infinitive (in this case, "to call") expressing purpose. The same form is used else-where in the gospels to indicate the purpose of Jesus (or the Son of man) in "coming" to earth. They are found in Mark (10:45), Q (Luke 12:51//Matt. 10:34), special L (Luke 19:10; 12:49), and special M (Matt. 5:17). None of them, however, can be assigned confidently to the earliest stage of the tradition. All come under suspicion of being the products of Christian reflection on the historical appearance of Jesus.[41] They are summaries of his total impact and significance for Christian faith.

That they are Christian compositions is supported in part by the fact that elsewhere such summaries (using the verb "to come" followed by an infinitive of purpose) appear where there can be no doubt that they are Christian compositions. These are at Luke 9:56 (late manu-scripts only); 1 Tim. 1:15; and in two apocryphal gospels.[42] The saying in Mark 2:17b, likewise, can be considered a summary, placed in first person, concerning the ministry of Jesus as a whole. When the early Palestinian Christians, who acknowledged that they were "sinners" in the estimation of the scribes and Pharisees, reflected upon the activities and significance of Jesus, they stated that he came to call sinners. It was they, not the righteous, who responded to him in a positive way.

The other saying ("Those who are well have no need of a physician, but those who are sick," 2:17a) has parallels elsewhere in literature of the period.[43] Because of these parallels, and because the imagery it uses—that Jesus is a physician who heals the sick (= sinners)—is especially suitable for Christian piety, it too is likely to have been a Christian composition,[44] rather than a remembered word of Jesus. Like the second saying (2:17b), it gives a general estimate of the signifi-cance of Jesus' ministry as a whole.

The entire story, then, including its dominical sayings, must have been composed and put to use in a time and place in which the church [45] was attacked by opponents on the grounds that its fellowship was suspect, that it consisted of persons for whom the phrase "tax collectors and sinners" served as a suitable epithet. But such an epithet was quite traditional. In two other places, independent of Mark, the phrase "tax collectors and sinners" is used to describe certain persons with whom Jesus associated. It appears at Luke 15:1 and in Q (Luke 7:34//Matt. 11:19). While the former is probably a Lucan editorial link, it is followed by the sentence, "This man receives sinners and eats with them" (15:2), which must be a pre-Lucan traditional say-ing.[46] The Q saying (Luke 7:34//Matt. 11:19) is, of course, a traditional saying about Jesus, and it can be assigned to critics in Jesus' own lifetime.[47] There was a basis for saying (see also Luke 19:2-10) that Jesus himself was a "friend of tax collectors and sinners" in his historical ministry.

Both the setting in Mark 2:15-16 (Jesus portrayed as sitting at table with tax collectors and sinners) and the charge against him in 2:16 ("Why does he eat with tax collectors and sinners?") were composed therefore out of general reminiscences concerning the conduct of Jesus. The primitive church in Palestine had in its fellowship persons who were looked upon with contempt. Tax collectors were considered despised (*b. Sanh.* 25b), and their trade was linked with the activities of thieves (*m. Tohar.* 7:6) and robbers (*m. Ned.* 3:4; *B. Qam.* 10:2; *b. Sebu.* 39a). Their presence in a house makes everything in it unclean (*m. Tohar.* 7:6). The term "sinners" refers to Jews who, like Gentiles, cannot or will not observe the Torah,[48] and fellowship with them was forbidden (*m. Dem.* 2:3) on the grounds that one might be drawn to accept their manner of life (*b. Ber.* 43b).

Mark 2:15-17 was composed, then, and put to use in defending the church's admission of disreputable—in the eyes of opponents—persons into its fellowship.[49] The church defended its own actions by use of traditions about Jesus. Just as he had been a "friend of tax collectors and sinners" in his historical ministry, so now the church has chosen to become such. Two summary sayings about the significance of Jesus' ministry (2:17a; 2:17b) were set within a framework giving a "typical scene" (2:15) and a "typical charge" (2:16) against Jesus. The criticism is responded to not by appeal to legal precedent, but to the attitude and activities of the Master. No other justification was considered necessary.

D. Plucking Grain on the Sabbath
(Mark 2:23-28//Matthew 12:1-8//Luke 6:1-5)

This conflict story portrays Jesus walking with his disciples on a sabbath through the grainfields, and the disciples begin to pluck grain. The Pharisees consider such an act a violation of sabbath law and therefore ask Jesus why his disciples are breaking the sabbath. Jesus responds with a counter-question (2:25-26), and then comes a pair of dominical sayings:

> The sabbath was made for man, not man for the sabbath;
> so the Son of man is lord even of the sabbath (2:27-28).

This conflict story has caused difficulties for the interpreter from the first century to the present. Already in the case of Matthew and Luke, for example, the statement "the sabbath was made for man, not man for the sabbath" (Mark 2:27) was omitted when they copied from Mark (cf. Matt. 12:8; Luke 6:5).[50] The reason for doing so may well be that for them, as actually for Mark himself, it is the Christological statement "the Son of man is lord of the sabbath" (Mark 2:28) that is the point of the whole story.[51] Matthew has highlighted the Christological significance of the story by adding 12:5-7, which contains the argument from minor to major: if the priests in the temple profane the sabbath and yet are guiltless, then how much more is it the case that Jesus' disciples are guiltless, since "something greater than the temple is here" (12:6).[52] Furthermore, Mark 2:27 may have been too extreme for Matthew. In his community the sabbath may well have been observed (cf. 24:20), and therefore Mark 2:27 was too radical. But Matthew adds that the disciples had acted as they did because "they were hungry" (12:1); furthermore, by adding the Hosea citation in 12:7 (Hos. 6:6) Matthew asserts that the sabbath commandment must be interpreted for the church in terms of "mercy," not in terms of strict, unbending demand.[53] Here "mercy" is not meant to be a "relaxing of the law," but an enacting of the commandment of love (22:34-40) and "doing good" (12:12) on the sabbath.[54]

Luke's omission of Mark 2:27 can also only be explained on the grounds that for him it is the Christological statement (Mark 2:28// Luke 6:5) which is the point of the story. By inserting the word *labōn* (6:4), Luke emphasized that David assumed authority on the sabbath; it was not a concession of the priests which allowed him and his companions to eat. So also the Son of man—who is for Luke also clearly the Son of David[55]—is lord of the sabbath. Luke records four sabbath controversies (6:1-5, 6-11; 13:10-17; and 14:1-6). In two of them (13:10-17; 14:1-6) an appeal to traditional sabbath conduct is made (i.e., that one will water his ox or rescue an animal on the sabbath) to justify Jesus' own conduct. For Luke, in sum, it is not the case that "the sabbath was made for man" (Mark 2:27). Rather, he portrays Jesus as acting on the basis of Davidic precedent (6:1-5), the principle of doing good (6:6-11), or usual sabbath conduct (13:10-17; 14:1-6).[56] In this respect, as in others, it can be said that "Luke has the most conservative outlook within the New Testament" in regard to the law.[57]

Modern interpreters have had difficulties with Mark 2:27-28 too.

Some, for example, have held that both verses must have originally—sometime before Mark wrote them—referred to either "man" or "Son of man," not both, and that a mistake was made when someone prior to Mark translated the verses from Aramaic to Greek. C. C. Torrey has translated the verses one way:

> The sabbath was made for man, and not man for the sabbath; therefore man is master of the sabbath.[58]

And T. W. Manson has suggested that originally the verses would have read the other way:

> The sabbath was made for the Son of man, and not the Son of man for the sabbath; therefore the Son of man is lord also of the sabbath.[59]

But there is another way of dealing with the two verses and with the passage as a whole.[60] That is to see that the passage has a history of development reaching far back behind Mark's Gospel into a primitive Christian community. One can remove materials which appear to have been later additions and arrive at an earlier form of the conflict story. At a bare minimum, to have a conflict story at all, the parts of the story which cannot be dispensed with are those in verses 2:23, 24, and 27.[61] Taking these verses together, we have the following:

> [23] One sabbath he was going through the grainfields; and as they made their way his disciples began to pluck ears of grain. [24] And the Pharisees said to him, "Look, why are they doing what is not lawful on the sabbath?"

> [27] And he said to them, "The sabbath was made for man, not man for the sabbath."

This is the most basic form of the story, to which the other materials in 2:25-26 and 28 are secondary. Furthermore, it can be held that this basic form corresponds to that which was originally composed in the oral period—not necessarily to its exact wording, but to its form. The materials designated secondary (2:25-26, 28) can be considered such when their function is considered. The original story ended with a statement (2:27) which would have been considered too radical for the Jewish Christian church in Palestine without some kind of qualification.[62] Because of its radical nature the allusion to David's action was added in 2:25-26.[63] This allusion tones down the statement of 2:27. There is precedent, it was shown, for breaking sabbath law.[64]

And, furthermore, the saying in 2:28 serves a complementary function, for it is a Christological assertion of the primitive community [65]
which shows that the radical statement of 2:27 is not the end of the
matter. The sabbath is for man, but that prevails only within a context in which the Son of man is lord. The freedom of the Christian is
given by the Son of man.[66] And that freedom is to realize health,
abundance, and the full possibilities of life in the new age, which the
sabbath anticipates, and which has now drawn near.[67].

It can be observed, however, that even the basic form of the pericope (2:23, 24 and 27) is non-unitary. The dominical saying in 2:27
is not dependent upon its contextual situation to be comprehensible.
It is likely to have been, prior to the composition of the story itself, a
free-floating saying for which the narrative and question of the
Pharisees (2:23, 24) were composed.[68] There are two reasons for
making this claim. First, the appearance of the Pharisees on the scene
to criticize the disciples for plucking grain appears to be contrived.
As F. W. Beare has written, "Are we to imagine them as out for a
sabbath stroll in the country, where they happen to spot the disciples
just as they are plucking a few heads of grain?" [69] And, second, the
fact that the criticism is directed against the disciples, not Jesus, indicates that the material in 2:23-24 has been composed by a Christian
community which was itself under criticism from Pharisaic opponents.[70] Since the dominical saying in 2:27 concerns the activities of
"man," not Jesus, on the sabbath, it is necessary for the setting narrated to have persons other than Jesus who are the object of criticism.

Our present pericope in Mark 2:23-28 developed, then, in two
stages. First, there was the statement concerning man and the sabbath recorded now in Mark 2:27 which, in our view, is likely to have
been a statement made by Jesus himself,[71] and which was remembered
and passed on by the earliest Christians. It was a radical statement,
not easily forgotten in a Jewish and Jewish Christian milieu. As these
early Christians came under attack by the Pharisees for failing to keep
sabbath laws prescribed by themselves, one of their members composed a conflict story, the basic form of which appears in Mark 2:23,
24, and 27. The conflict story portrayed a scene (artificial though it
may be) as a setting for Jesus' saying. The function of the story was
to defend, or justify, the "disciples" of Jesus—now his church—in response to on-going criticism. One may say, then, that its *Sitz im Leben*
was apologetics.

But the story was not left untouched. At a second stage the materials in 2:25, 26, and 28 were added. The basic function of the conflict story—that of defending Christian sabbath practice—was unchanged. But the story was developed Christologically.[72] It was no longer the earthly Jesus remembered in the community of believers to whom appeal was made. Now it was Jesus as the exalted Son of man to whom appeal was made (2:28), Jesus who as Son of man is lord of the Sabbath. The original saying (2:27) was not to be taken as license for complete freedom. Freedom of sabbath conduct was conditioned by the realization that the Son of man, not man, is lord of the sabbath, and that even his infractions, like those of David (2:25), were determined by human need and (for the church) were performed in anticipation of eschatological fulfillment, not by disregard for the essential sanctity of the day.

It is significant that outside this one incident, together with sabbath healings, there are no gospel traditions that portray Jesus and his disciples generally violating sabbath law. We do not observe them traveling, preparing food, or performing any acts of labor as deliberate challenges to established precepts. The story of Plucking Grain on the Sabbath must have been composed in a setting in which the action of Jesus' disciples, and therefore those of the church's membership, have to be justified not only outside of, but also to some degree within, the community itself. This points to a Jewish Christian setting.[73]

E. The Tradition of the Elders
(Mark 7:1-8//Matthew 15:1-9)

There developed within ancient Judaism the practice of eating one's food in a state of purity, and this was achieved by a ritual washing of one's hands. This practice is attested as existing in the second century A.D., in which it was observed by pious laymen as well as rabbis.[74] It has been argued, however, that the practice was not common in the first century, except among priests and rabbis of strict leanings in the second half of the century.[75]

This historical question must be reserved for later discussion. The issue of ritual handwashing is, nevertheless, raised in Mark (7:1-8) and Matthew (15:1-9) and debated within a conflict story.[76] The story does not appear in the Gospel of Luke.[77] Matthew's version of the story differs from that of Mark in a number of ways. Our attention here, however, will be restricted to Mark's version.

The Marcan pericope contains a great deal of material which is from the hand of Mark himself. The first four verses read as follows:

> 1 And when the Pharisees gathered together to join him, with some of the scribes, who had come from Jerusalem, 2 they saw that some of his disciples ate with hands defiled, that is, unwashed. 3 (For the Pharisees, and all the Jews, do not eat unless they wash their hands, observing the tradition of the elders; 4 and when they come from the market place, they do not eat unless they purify themselves; and there are many other traditions which they observe, the washing of cups and pots and vessels of bronze.)

Verse 1 can be considered to have been written by Mark as an introduction to the pericope, since it contains typically Marcan vocabulary and narrative style.[78] Likewise verses 3 and 4 must be considered either a Marcan parenthetical explanation for non-Jewish readers or a post-Marcan scribal gloss which was eventually worked into the text of Mark.[79] In either case the verses can be ruled out of the pre-Marcan pericope.

What remains of the pre-Marcan material is that which is relayed to us in Mark 7:2, 5-8:

> 2 [The Pharisees and the scribes] saw that some of his disciples ate with hands defiled, that is, unwashed. . . . 5 And [they] asked him, "Why do your disciples not live according to the tradition of the elders, but eat with hands defiled?"
>
> 6 And he said to them, "Well did Isaiah prophesy of you hypocrites, as it is written,
>
>> 'This people honors me with their lips,
>>   but their heart is far from me;
>> 7 in vain do they worship me,
>>   teaching as doctrines the precepts of men.'
>
> 8 You leave the commandment of God, and hold fast the tradition of men."

It is clear on further analysis that this conflict story is of a nonunitary type. For the charge against Jesus (7:5) has been created for the sake of the final verse (7:8),[80] which could ultimately be a saying of Jesus himself or, more likely, a saying composed in a Hellenistic Christian community in polemics with Pharisees (see below). As to the conflict story itself, it can be shown to have been composed in the Hellenistic church,[81] and it cannot be considered an account of an actual event (nor actual words) from the ministry of Jesus. This does not mean that the conflict story has been created out of a vacuum, of course, nor does it mean that it does not represent the attitude of Jesus on the issue. On the contrary, there is an independent tradition in Luke (11:37-41) which confirms that the attitude expressed in the conflict story, as well as Jesus' own practice of not going through the ritual washing, is essentially historical. Nevertheless, it must be concluded that the conflict story as we have it was composed in the Hellenistic church.

The reason for making this claim is based on a study of the language used. In 7:6-7 there is a quotation from Isa. 29:13. An examination of the texts shows that it is the LXX which is being quoted. The Hebrew (MT) and LXX versions are translated as follows:

MT, Isa. 29:13	LXX, Isa. 29:13
This people draws near with their mouth	This people draws near to me with their lips,
and honors me with their lips,	honoring me,
but their heart is far from me,	but their heart is far from me,
and their fear of me	and in vain do they worship me,
is a commandment of men which has been taught.	teaching precepts and doctrines of men.

Mark 7:6-7 (Isa. 29:13)

This people honors me with their lips, but their heart is far from me; and in vain do they worship me, teaching as doctrines the precepts of men.

At Mark 7:7 there is a variation from the LXX; it reads "teaching as doctrines the precepts of men," but it is not related to the Hebrew text which has "and their fear of me is a commandment of men which has been taught." The saying in Mark 7:8, then ("You leave the commandment of God, and hold fast the tradition of men"), is related to the Isaiah quotation precisely at the point where the LXX differs from the Hebrew.[82] And since the argument is based on the LXX, it must be concluded that the conflict story was composed in a Greek-speaking milieu, i.e., the Hellenistic church.

There are two other observations which confirm the same. First, it is significant to notice that it is precisely in the Hellenistic churches outside of Palestine that the passage from Isa. 29:13 is alluded to in its LXX form. In Col. 2:22 readers are chided for following Jewish customs, which are called "precepts and doctrines of men."[83] And in

Titus 1:14 readers are told not to give heed to Jewish myths and the "precepts of men." Furthermore, the second century church father Justin quotes Isa. 29:13-14 (LXX) in a dispute, indicating that it was important in his polemics with Hellenistic Judaism.[84]

Second, while it is not clear that the ritual handwashing was widely observed in first century Palestine, it has been conceded that it must have been practiced at the time among pious Jews of the Diaspora.[85] Surely the gospels themselves, as first-century documents, indicate that the practice must have been required as a cleansing ritual somewhere in the first century. Otherwise how does one explain the fact that it is debated in them as an issue at all?

Concerning the question why the conflict story (7:5-8) was composed, it must be concluded that it was formulated as an apologetic text to defend the church against Jewish criticism.[86] That it was composed in a church setting outside of Palestine is quite certain. That the church was a Hellenistic (Greek-speaking) church is obvious. That the church was made up of both Jewish and Gentile Christians is probable (e.g., only "some" disciples in 7:2 do not wash their hands). Of course, saying that the conflict story served an apologetic purpose does not mean that it gives us a transcript of a debate going on between the church and Judaism. The text would have been composed for the sake of the church's own self-understanding in response to criticism.

It should be seen, moreover, that the conflict story, while it ostensibly deals with the ritual washing of hands in particular as an issue, actually applies to the broader issue of Jewish tradition as a whole. The ritual traditions of Judaism are attacked *in toto*. Verse 8 ("You leave the commandment of God, and hold fast the tradition of men"), set in antithetic parallelism, is a general, sweeping statement against Jewish ritual practices altogether. The phrase "commandment of God" does not refer to any particular commandment in the Old Testament, nor does the "tradition of men" refer to any one custom. (The disciples' failure to observe the ritual handwashing in 7:5b has been inserted to provide an occasion for taking up the question of tradition in general within a conflict story form. Narrative requires specificity— hence the charge against the disciples in 7:5b and Mark's longer narrative additions in 7:1-4). The "commandment of God" refers to the written Torah as a whole, and the "tradition of men" refers to the entire body of Jewish tradition (cf. also 7:5a). Verse 8 affirms, then, that the Christian community itself, in contrast to Judaism, is bound to observe the will of God expressed in the Torah, but the "tradition of men" is not binding.

The community in which the conflict story was composed cannot therefore be considered to have been antinomian. It placed a positive estimate on the law in terms of its moral teachings. But in the spirit of Jesus (cf. Matt. 23:23-24; Luke 11:38-42) it rejected contemporary ritual practices. Such rejection is reflected elsewhere in the writings of the New Testament as well (Gal. 2:11-14; Col. 2:22; Titus 1:14). Hans Conzelmann has written concerning Jesus that he assumed "the law is intelligible by itself and needs no interpretation at all." [87] The same attitude came to expression in the present conflict story.

F. On Divorce

(Mark 10:2-9//Matthew 19:3-9)

The conflict story on divorce appears in Mark (10:2-9 [88]) and Matthew (19:3-9), but not in Luke.[89] It is located within a longer section of Mark which deals not only with the question of divorce, but with other matters as well: 10:13-16 affirms that children are to be admitted to church fellowship, in which the eschatological kingdom is received as a promised gift; and 10:17-27 warns the rich not to let their wealth prevent them from counting discipleship more important. The three passages have been placed together [90] in a series of duties for Christians reminiscent of the household rules in various epistles (e.g., Col. 3:18–4:1; Eph. 5:22–6:9; 1 Pet. 2:18–3:12). Of course there is a difference. In the household rules the various duties imposed are presented in paraenetic style, and it is assumed that the readers will appropriate them by their prior acknowledgment of the tradition about Christ.[91] But in the Marcan series the community is addressed by dominical sayings, and it is assumed that they will appropriate their teachings by their acknowledgment of the words of Jesus as authoritative.[92]

The Marcan pericope contains little which can be attributed to the editorial work of Mark. There are, however, two phrases which are not likely to have been in the pericope which Mark received. First, the opening words *(kai proselthontes pharisaioi,* 10:2), which appear in some important manuscripts,[93] but not in others,[94] are likely to have been added by certain scribes to the text of Mark by their harmonization of Mark to Matt. 19:3 which reads, *kai proselthon autō pharisaioi.*[95] These words are not, then, Mark's own editorial words, but words penned into the text of Mark at a later date. In this view the opponents who come to ask Jesus a question concerning divorce were originally unnamed—both in Mark's received tradition and in the original composition of Mark himself.

Second, in the same verse (10:2) there are the words "testing him," which suggest the motives of Jesus' opponents. These words are found also at the beginning of another pericope (8:11), and both can be considered Marcan redaction.[96]

Having removed these two phrases, what we have left of the material which Mark received is the following:

² They asked him, "Is it lawful for a man to divorce his wife?"

³ He answered them, "What did Moses command you?"

⁴ They said, "Moses allowed a man to write a certificate of divorce, and to put her away."

⁵ But Jesus said to them, "For your hardness of heart he wrote you this commandment. ⁶ But from the beginning of creation, 'God made them male and female.' ⁷ 'For this reason a man shall leave his father and mother, ⁸ and the two shall become one.' So they are no longer two but one.

⁹ "What therefore God has joined together, let not man put asunder."

Further analysis of the pericope demonstrates that it is a non-unitary type of conflict story. The final verse (10:9, "What therefore God has joined together, let not man put asunder") appears to be a free-floating saying which would have been independent of the foregoing material (10:2-8).[97] This can be maintained for two reasons. First, in 10:7-8 it is argued that marriage partners have become "one flesh." The words of 10:9 are therefore superfluous as an appended dominical pronouncement, and they actually have a different view of the marriage relationship, viz., that marriage is a matter of "yoking" *(syzeugnynai)* of the partners, which is hardly as binding as the "one flesh" concept. Second, the verse (10:9) is set in antithetic parallelism. Sayings in this particular pattern are generally wisdom or legal sayings (cf. Mark 2:17, 27; 3:4; 7:8; 12:17) which are not conclusions argued from the egegesis of Scripture.[98] Their authority rests not on exegetical arguments but, at least in the conflict stories, on the attitudes of Jesus as remembered by the church.

The saying in 10:9 must be considered as having originated in the Hellenistic church, not with Jesus himself. This can be maintained for three reasons. First, the form in which it is given—the use of the accusative relative pronoun *ho* to introduce the first member of the parallelism, which is itself a relative clause—is a Greek, not Semitic, construction.[99] Second, the use of the term "to yoke" *(syzeugnynai)* for marriage is current in Hellenistic culture, but has no known counterpart in non-Hellenistic Jewish literature.[100] Third, the use of *chōrizesthai* for divorce is common in Hellenistic literature, and also appears in Josephus and Paul (1 Cor. 7:10, 11, 15),[101] but it is nowhere attested as a translation for divorce terminology in the LXX, which uses instead the terms *apolyein* (1 Esdr. 9:36), *biblion apostasiou* (Deut. 24:1, 3; Isa. 50:1), *ekballō* (Lev. 21:14; 22:13; Num. 30:10), and *exapostellein* (Deut. 24:1, 3, 4; Jer. 3:8; Mal. 2:16). Within the gospels, except for this logion (Mark 10:9//Matt. 19:6), the term for divorce in dominical sayings is always *apolyein* (Mark 10:11-12; Luke 16:18; Matt. 5:32; 19:9).[102] Yet the term *chōrizesthai* is required *ad sensum* from the beginning of the formulation of this particular saying to provide the antithesis of "yoking" and "dividing." A Greek-speaking milieu is required for this set of circumstances in combination.

In content, to be sure, Mark 10:9 reflects the attitude of Jesus about divorce, i.e., that it is contrary to God's will (cf. the Q saying, Luke 16:18//Matt. 5:32, and Paul's charge "from the Lord," 1 Cor. 7:10).[103] But the verse itself must be considered an ecclesiastical ordinance that originated in the Hellenistic church concerning marriage and divorce.[104]

The rest of the pericope (10:2-8) can be seen as a Christian composition which provides an argument leading up to the final saying (10:9).[105] In verses 7 and 8 it is said, "For this reason a man shall leave his father and mother,[106] and the two shall be one flesh." The standard Hebrew text has for the latter clause, "and *they* shall be one flesh," rather than, "and *the two (hoi dyo)* shall be one flesh." The latter reading is found in the LXX (Gen. 2:24), which reads word-for-word exactly as Mark has it. Furthermore, it is essential for the argument of Mark 10:2-8 that the words of this version be used, because the conclusion is based on it: "so that they are no longer *two (hōste ouketi eisin dyo)* but one flesh" (10:8b). The upshot is that the present pericope must have been composed in a Greek-speaking Christian environment.[107] The use of Gen. 2:24 in the Epistle to the Ephesians (5:31), again in its Septuagintal form, indicates further that such an argument had force in the Greek-speaking church.

The question concerning the circumstances in which the conflict story as a whole (10:2-9) was composed can now be explored. The way that the opening question in 10:2 is stated (once the additions are removed, as indicated at the beginning of our treatment) rules out the likelihood that the conflict story originated in a debate with Jews on the issue of divorce. For the question, "Is it lawful for a man to divorce his wife?," is not a question a Jew would normally ask.[108] For the Jew divorce is indeed lawful on the part of the husband, as Deut. 24:1 makes clear. The only question for him is the grounds permitting it.[109] (This has been recognized by Matthew who adds the phrase "for any cause" in 19:3 and provides a cause in 19:9, by which the view of Jesus is conformed to that of the School of Shammai.) The conflict story reflects, rather, a setting in which converts coming into the church from Judaism are provided new teaching on the subject of divorce. This can be maintained for three reasons.

First, the question of 10:2, while not suitable for a real-life situation in a discussion with Jewish opponents, is particularly suitable for introducing a catechetical response.[110] For if indeed divorce was not permitted in the primitive church prior to the granting of exceptions (Matt. 19:9; 1 Cor. 7:12-15), so that there was a departure from both Jewish and Roman law on the issue,[111] the formulation of the question would be as it is given in Mark, calling forth either an affirmative or negative response. Converts from Judaism are taught that for the Christian community—as for Jesus himself—the real issue of divorce is no longer that of the grounds by which it can be permitted, but whether divorce is permitted at all; and it is not.

Second, the conflict story must be thought of as addressed to Jewish converts, rather than to Gentiles, because the question (10:2) is whether a man may divorce his wife (the only possibility in Jewish law; the wife could not divorce her husband [112]); there is no mention of the reverse in which a wife might wish to divorce her husband (as allowed in Roman law), although that too is implicitly ruled out.

Third, the statement of 10:5 ("For your hardness of heart [Moses] wrote you this commandment," i.e., the commandment in Deut. 24:1 that a man shall present his wife a certificate of divorce) serves to justify for converts the basis for the Christian position. Converts are to understand that while the commandment is indeed in the Torah, it stands there as a concession to the "hardness of heart" of men from Moses to the present ("you" in 10:5 applies to Judaism). But within the Christian community the commandment of Moses is relegated below the primordial word and will of God expressed at creation

(Gen. 1:27; 2:24); Moses had "allowed" (Mark 10:4) divorce as a concession to human weakness.[113] But in the new community, the restored people of God which has come into being since Jesus, the Christian is to find the will of God no longer in what "Moses allowed" (10:4), but in what God ordered "from the beginning" (10:6), and which Jesus himself taught.

Prohibitions against divorce (and subsequent marriage to another) are found elsewhere in isolated sayings, e.g., in Mark 10:11-12 and in Q, Luke 16:18//Matt. 5:32 (as well as in 1 Cor. 7:10-11). But the distinctive point about the conflict story (Mark 10:2-9) is that it gives to converts from Judaism an argued presentation for the church's position. It demonstrates a careful use of Torah citations (not an attack upon the Torah or Moses) in order to show why the church departed from Judaism on the issue of divorce. In the final analysis of course, the position of the church is based on the attitude of Jesus (hence the isolated sayings of Jesus and Paul's charge "from the Lord"). But by means of an argument from Scripture, the primitive church tried—with patience, and with respect for the Torah—to show that its own position (and even that of Jesus) was not arbitrary, but one which is based on the will of God given in Scripture.

G. On the Resurrection

(Mark 12:18-27//Matthew 22:23-33//Luke 20:27-40)

All three synoptic gospels contain a conflict story concerning the resurrection, but there are differences among them. Common to all is that certain Sadducees, who as a party deny the doctrine of the resurrection,[114] approach Jesus with a trick question. They cite a law in Deut. 25:5-6, that requires a man to take his brother's wife if the brother should die childless; and when the first son is born, that child is to perpetuate the name of the deceased.[115] Suppose, the Sadducees say, there are seven brothers who, all being childless, take the same woman as wife in succession from the death of the first to the last. Then comes the question: "In the resurrection whose wife shall she be? For the seven had her as wife" (Mark 12:23//Matt. 22:28//Luke 20:33).

At this point Mark and Matthew proceed in one direction; Luke proceeds somewhat differently. Mark and Matthew portray Jesus as establishing two points: first, that after the resurrection there is no marrying or giving in marriage; second, that the doctrine of resurrection itself can be believed on the basis of Exod. 3:6. There God spoke to Moses saying, "I am the God of Abraham, and the God of Isaac, and the God of Jacob." Although these patriarchs had long since died at the time of Moses, the fact that God speaks of himself as their God at the time of Moses indicates that they are actually living. Luke's Gospel (20:34-40) continues with a saying that "The sons of this age marry . . . but those accounted worthy . . . to the resurrection" don't (20:34). Then Luke (at 20:37) rejoins Mark in the argument for the doctrine of the resurrection, and he adds some final words which Mark does not have (20:38b-40).

Analysis of this conflict story leads to the conclusion that it has been composed from two smaller units. The first unit is contained within Mark 12:18-25 and has to do with the question of remarriage of those whose spouses have died; and the second is contained within 12:26-27, which deals with the doctrine of the resurrection proper.[116] That such is the case should become apparent after analysis of each of the two parts.

The first part (Mark 12:18-25 and par.) contains a saying which affirms that marriage does not take place in the world to come. Mark and Matthew have virtually the same saying:

Mark 12:25: For when they rise from the dead, they neither marry nor are given in marriage, but are like angels in heaven.

Matt. 22:30: For in the resurrection they neither marry nor are given in marriage, but are like angels in heaven.

But the saying in Luke (20:34-36) is longer and quite different:

The sons of this age marry and are given in marriage; but those who are accounted worthy to attain to that age and to the resurrection from the dead neither marry nor are given in marriage, for they cannot die any more, because they are equal to angels and are sons of God, being sons of the resurrection.

This version of the saying cannot be considered simply a free expansion on what Mark has written, but rather a version which had circulated independently of the conflict story, which Luke has inserted. In addition to the fact that the wording of Luke is so different from Mark's,[117] the fact that three other versions of the saying exist in non-canonical materials, which show no direct dependence on any of the three canonical gospels, leads one to this conclusion. The non-canonical versions read as follows: [118]

Justin, *Dialog with Trypho* 81, 4: Which very thing indeed our Lord said, "They shall neither marry nor be married, but shall be equal to angels, being God's children of the resurrection."

Justin, *On the Resurrection* 3: As he says, "The sons of this age marry and are given in marriage, but the sons of the age to come neither marry nor are given in marriage, but will be as the angels of heaven."

Pseudo-Titus Epistle: "In the coming age," says the Lord, "they will neither marry nor be given in marriage, but will be as the angels of heaven."

It is tempting to speculate whether all these sayings—those in Mark/Matthew, Luke, and the three non-canonical parallels—have a common origin. If so, it would appear that such a saying would be of an apocalyptic type which contrasts the activities of the present age (marrying and giving in marriage) with those of the age to come (in which there is none). The contrast is explicit in two of the versions (Luke 20:35; Justin, *On the Resurrection* 3) and at least implicit in the others. And all versions affirm that the state of non-marriage in the world to come is similar to that of the angels. Sharp contrast is made between the present state of human existence and that in the age to come.

Whether some form of the saying could have originated with Jesus is a difficult question to solve. The saying could have originated in apocalyptic Judaism just as well as with Jesus.[119] The idea of people in the age to come as being "like the angels" is found in the apocalyptic literature of the period: [120]

2 Apoc. Bar. 51:10: For in the heights of that world shall they dwell, And they shall be made like unto the angels.

1 Enoch 104:4: Be hopeful, and cast not away your hope; for ye shall have great joy as the angels of heaven.

1 Enoch 104:6: For ye shall become companions of the host of heaven.

Luke's version of the saying concerning marriage has preserved the terminology of apocalypticism in its contrast of "this age" and the age to come ("that age"[121]) and in its conception of people in the age to come as being equal to the angels. In addition, the resurrection in this version is conditional, not general; that is, only those "accounted worthy" shall rise (cf. Luke 14:14). And, finally, Luke's version expresses a negative attitude toward marriage; marrying and giving in marriage are activities of the "sons of this age" (an age considered evil in apocalyptic thought), but not of those accounted worthy of the age to come. The Marcan version (which Matthew follows) has less apocalyptic terminology and no negative attitude toward marriage. It merely indicates that after the resurrection (a general resurrection is presupposed here) there is no marrying or giving in marriage.

At this point the formation of the unit found in Mark 12:18-25 can be discussed. Mark's saying in 12:25 ("For when they rise from the dead, they neither marry nor are given in marriage, but are like angels in heaven") must be considered a Christian formulation of a current saying in apocalyptic Judaism which provides a teaching for a primitive Christian community about marital ties after the resurrection. That such a question was asked in the early church is established by 1 Cor. 7:39 in which Paul deals with the question whether widows may remarry. At that point Paul writes that a wife is bound to her husband only as long as he lives. Implicit in this affirmation is that marital ties do not continue after death. The Marcan passage deals with the same problem and provides the same answer. The dominical saying in 12:25 has been clothed with the material leading up to it (12:19-23). The material in 12:18 and 24 was added at a later time, as will be shown below.

The second unit within the conflict story, Mark 12:26-27, deals with the more general question of the resurrection as a doctrine. But it does not fit into the conditions of Palestinian Judaism. The argument it puts forth presupposes ideas current in Hellenistic Judaism, and it must have been composed in a Hellenistic Christian milieu. For it is not a clear argument for the resurrection per se, in which the dead are considered at rest awaiting the resurrection.[122]. It affirms that the patriarchs and all the dead are living. After the fashion of certain streams of Hellenistic Judaism, the doctrine of the resurrection of the dead has been swallowed up by the doctrine of the immortality of the soul.

That Hellenistic Jews often thought in this way can be established by contrasting what is written by Josephus, a Hellenistic Jew, with other writings. When he describes the teachings of the Pharisees, Josephus says that for them the souls of the dead are immortal or imperishable; yet, he says, the Pharisees teach the future resurrection of the (immortal) souls of the good: [123]

Every soul, they maintain, is imperishable, but the soul of the good alone passes into another body, while the souls of the wicked suffer eternal punishment (*J.W.* 2.8.14 §163).

They believe that souls have power to survive death and that there are rewards and punishments under the earth for those who have led lives of virtue or vice: eternal imprisonment is the lot of evil souls, while the good souls receive an easy passage to a new life (*Ant.* 18.1.3 §14).

Josephus also gives expression to a doctrine of immortality in the speech of Eleazar at the fall of Masada:

For it is death which gives liberty to the soul and permits it to depart to its own pure abode, there to be free from all calamity; but so long as it is imprisoned in a mortal body and tainted with all its miseries, it is, in sober truth, dead, for association with what is mortal ill befits that which is divine. . . .For whatever the soul has touched lives and flourishes, whatever it abandons withers and dies; so abundant is her wealth of immortality (*J.W.* 7.8.7 §344 and 348).

And when Josephus describes the beliefs of the Essenes, he also attributes to them a doctrine of immortality:

For it is a fixed belief of theirs that the body is corruptible and its constituent matter impermanent, but that the soul is immortal and imperishable. . . . Sharing the belief of the sons of Greece, they maintain that for virtuous souls there is reserved an abode beyond the ocean, a place which is not oppressed by rain or snow or heat, but is refreshed by the ever gentle breath of the west wind coming in from the ocean; while they relegate base souls to a murky and tempestuous dungeon, big with never-ending punishments (*J.W.* 2.8.11 §154-55).

Such belief in immortality as Josephus attributes to the Pharisees and the Essenes betrays a Hellenizing tendency.[124] In the Psalms of Solomon, a Pharisaic document of Palestine from the first century B.C.,[125] Pharisaic doctrine is definitely that of resurrection of the dead, and no traces of thought about the soul's immortality are present: [126]

The sinner stumbleth and curseth his life. . . .
    He falleth—very grievous is his fall—and riseth no more. . . .
But they that fear the Lord shall rise to life eternal
    And their life (shall be) in the light of the Lord, and shall come
    to an end no more (3:9-10, 16).

> Therefore [the sinners'] inheritance is Sheol and darkness and de-
> struction,
>> And they shall not be found in the day when the righteous
>> obtain mercy;
> But the pious of the Lord shall inherit life in gladness (14:9-10).

And in the Dead Sea Scrolls, which should be taken as primary sources on the Essenes (rather than Josephus), there is not found a doctrine of immortality in any sense compatible with the view which Josephus attributes to them. In fact, it is not clear whether there is even a doctrine of resurrection in the Scrolls.[127]

Besides Josephus there are other Hellenistic Jewish writers who thought in terms of immortality of the soul. In the Wisdom of Solomon, probably written in Alexandria no later than the first century B.C.,[128] nothing is said concerning the resurrection of the dead, but there are several references to immortality for the righteous (2:23; 5:15; 6:18-19; 8:17; 15:3). Moreover, Philo teaches that man is "mortal as to his body, but immortal *(athanatos)* as to his intellect" *(De Opificio Mundi* 46).[129] And 4 Macc., which has been considered the work of an Alexandrian Jew at the beginning of the Common Era, disclosing "a deeper knowledge of Greek philosophy than all other Hellenistic-Jewish writings, except Philo's work," [130] teaches a doctrine of immortality consistently for both the righteous and the wicked (7:3; 9:22; 13:15; 14:5-6; 16:13; 17:5, 12; 18:23).[131]

There is a second reason for concluding that Mark 12:26-27 presupposes ideas current in Hellenistic Judaism. That is that it is in Hellenistic Jewish literature of the period, 4 Maccabees specifically, that one finds similar allusions to the patriarchs as living in the presence of God now as immortals: [132]

> But as many as with their whole heart make righteousness their first thought, these alone are able to master the weakness of the flesh, believing that unto God they die not, as our patriarchs, Abraham and Isaac and Jacob, died not, but that they live unto God (4 Macc. 7:18-19).

> Abraham, Isaac, and Jacob shall receive us, and all our forefathers shall praise us (4 Macc. 13:17).

> With these words the mother of the seven encouraged every single one of her sons to die rather than transgress the ordinance of God; they themselves all knowing well that men dying for God live unto

God, as live Abraham, and Isaac, and Jacob, and all the patriarchs
(4 Macc. 16:24-25).

In contrast to such allusions to the patriarchs as living, there are
three sources in which the more typically Palestinian Jewish attitude
is expressed concerning the patriarchs. The first is in the *Testament
of Judah* [133] in which the patriarchs are apparently thought to be in
the abode of the dead, and Judah is made to say: [134]

> And after these things shall Abraham and Isaac and Jacob arise unto
> life, and I and my brethren shall be chiefs of the tribes in Israel
> (25:1).

Here the patriarchs are not living, as in Mark 12:26-27, but will "arise
unto life" at the resurrection of the dead.[135]

The second text is in the *Testament of Benjamin:* [136]

> And then shall ye see Enoch, Noah, and Shem,
>   and Abraham, and Isaac, and Jacob,
>   rising on the right hand in gladness.
> Then shall we also rise, each over our tribe
>   worshipping the King of heaven. . . .
> Then also all men shall rise,
>   some unto glory and some unto shame (10:6-8).

Here too the patriarchs are not thought of as immortals "living unto
God"; they await a future resurrection.[137]

The third text in which there is a reference to the deceased patriarchs is the parable of the rich man and Lazarus (Luke 16:19-31).
In this parable Abraham is not "living" as an immortal with God;
rather, he is the overseer of the righteous dead. The rich man pleads
with Abraham to release Lazarus from the abode of the righteous
dead (*apo nekrōn,* 16:30; *ek nekrōn,* 16:31).

The argument of Mark 12:26-27 must be considered, in view of the
above, as dependent on a conception of the patriarchs as living immortals with God, which is dependent on Hellenistic Jewish concep-
tions. Therefore it would have been composed by a Christian who
came out of Hellenistic Judaism. Furthermore, it would have been
composed as an apologia for the resurrection, which its introductory
formula makes clear. It begins with the words, "and concerning the
dead that they are raised" (Mark 12:26), which are strikingly similar

to the words of Paul in 1 Thess. 4:13 ("concerning those who have fallen asleep").

First century Christians were perplexed with the delay of the parousia. Would those who have died share in the salvation awaiting the living at the parousia? Paul dealt with the question at length in 1 Thess. 4:13-18 and 1 Cor. 15:18-58. In the former text Paul asserts that the dead are "asleep" awaiting the cry of command, the archangel's call, and the sound of the trumpet. In Mark 12:26-27 the same problem is treated, but somewhat differently.[138] The dead (12:26) are in fact "living" (12:27), even as the patriarchs are living.[139] The resurrection hope is based on an interpretation of Scripture (Exod. 3:6) which shows that the dead (the patriarchs as a prime example) are living already, anticipating the resurrection when they shall gain new bodies. Those who ask concerning the dead can be assured of the resurrection of the latter, and therefore reunion with them, because the dead have not perished forever.

Behind the entire conflict story in Mark 12:18-27 therefore two basic units of tradition are seen to exist (12:19-23, 25 and 12:26-27a [140]). These two units—the one addressed to the problem of remarriage in the Christian community for those whose spouses have died; the other an apologia for resurrection—contain the only synoptic sayings attributed to Jesus in which the resurrection of the dead is explicitly mentioned. It is natural that the two units would be drawn together in the process of transmission and linked. But they were not simply connected together end-to-end. Rather, they were combined into one pericope by means of juxtaposition and the addition of materials in 12:18, 24, and 27b. The controlling interest is in the argument for the resurrection. The apologetic interest predominated over that of praxis (the question of remarriage).

Those who ask the question at the outset of the pericope (12:18, "who say that there is no resurrection") are described in language similar to that of Paul (1 Cor. 15:12, "how is it that some among you say that there is no resurrection of the dead?"). They are described as Sadducees, "because it was traditional for them to deny the resurrection." [141] The words of 12:24 ("Is this not why you are wrong, that you know neither the Scriptures nor the power of God?") were added as a reply of Jesus to introduce an allusion to the Scriptures (Exod. 3:6) which is to follow (12:26). And the final saying (12:27b, "you are quite wrong"), which both Matthew and Luke omit, was added to confirm what has been said already in 12:24.

The material is presented in the form of a conflict story, and the question why that is so should be dealt with. If the pericope had to do with internal ecclesiastical concerns (the remarriage of widows and the doctrine of the resurrection), it might seem strange that it is cast in that form. But the case is actually not so strange. As indicated, the apologia for the resurrection is the dominating interest of the story once the two units had been forged together. To get the dominical words into the open, it is necessary to have someone question or challenge Jesus. The disciples, scribes, and Pharisees are not good candidates. But to have a presentation in conflict story form with the Sadducees as opponents is the most suitable, given the material available. The present form shows that the resurrection is to be affirmed; those who would deny or question it in the ecclesiastical situation would be, like the Sadducees, wrong (12:24, 27b) and ignorant of the Scriptures and the power of God (12:24).

H. Conclusions

A feature common to these seven conflict stories is that they are composed from originally independent sayings, questions, and narrative materials. The dominical saying, which is in some cases (cf. Mark 3:23-29 especially) a brief discourse, is not dependent on the opponent's question. Rather, the latter, plus narrative, has been composed for the sake of the dominical saying. The conflict stories are artificially constructed and have therefore been designated non-unitary.

Analysis of these non-unitary stories has shown that one cannot attribute to them a common *Sitz im Leben*. Even a cursory, rather uncritical reading of these seven stories indicates that they were not all formulated in debates on points of law in the style of rabbinic disputations. This is evident above all in the Beelzebul Controversy (Mark 3: 22-30//Q, Luke 11:14-15, 17-23). In this pericope there is no legal point on which Jesus is portrayed as disputing with his adversaries. Nor could all these conflict stories have been formulated with the purpose of preserving a statement of Jesus useful for preaching (either in the sense of preaching for conversion or in the sense of preaching for edification). This is clear above all in the pericope on the Tradition of the Elders (Mark 7:1-8).

The conflict stories of the non-unitary type can be divided into four categories in respect to their *Sitz im Leben*.

1. The conflict stories on the Healing of the Paralytic (Mark 2:1-12), Eating with Tax Collectors and Sinners (2:15-17), and Plucking Grain on the Sabbath (2:23-28) fit into one category. They belong to the Galilean collection of Mark 2:1—3:6 (discussed further in Chapter V), and they have two elements in common. First, they are all church compositions in which the church responds to Palestinian Jewish criticism. In each of them it has been observed that the church has grounded its response to criticism in the attitude and conduct of Jesus himself. The response is not carried on by means of legal debate but by appeal to Jesus as Master, whose attitude was, in the church's memory, that of forgiveness, eating with those considered outcasts, and overriding current sabbath proscriptions (but not the sanctity of the day) when the latter interfered with basic human considerations. Second, the setting of each can be considered a "typical scene" out of the ministry of Jesus; not typical in the sense that the actions provoking conflict "went on all the time" in sequential repetition, but in the sense that they typify those things for which Jesus was challenged, and which the church held in memory about him.

2. The conflict story on the Tradition of the Elders (Mark 7:1-8) stands by itself in a second category. It has similarities to those in the first category insofar as its setting is an action of Jesus' disciples (as in the pericope on Plucking Grain on the Sabbath), and the pericope as a whole is a defense against Jewish criticism. It could, on these grounds, be classified with those in the first category. On the other hand, it differs from them in point of origin. The Jewish criticism to which it responds is that of Hellenistic Judaism in the Diaspora. Moreover, while the response is undoubtedly based on the attitude of Jesus concerning the cultic-ritual demands of the Torah, the conclusion is essentially, as suggested above, a free-floating logion critical of Pharisaic Judaism rather than, as in the Galilean conflict stories, a saying which expresses a general attitude toward the issue at hand. It is directed against the opponents, not to the issue itself.

3. The conflict stories in the third category are those On Divorce (Mark 10:2-9) and On the Resurrection (12:18-27). These are not occasioned by activities of Jesus or his disciples, but by questions of converts concerning moral and doctrinal matters. Their settings cannot

be called "typical scenes" in the ministry of Jesus, and they did not arise out of a response to Jewish criticism. They are compositions which were formulated in the churches of the Diaspora, and they have to do with teaching converts (concerning divorce and the resurrection). And, since these have been shown to have originated in the Hellenistic church, Bultmann is incorrect when he says concerning the conflict stories as a whole,

> We can firmly conclude that the formation of the material in the tradition took place in the Palestinian Church—and that holds for those with unitary conceptions as well as for other passages. This is shown by the parallelism with Rabbinic stories, as well as by the intellectual content of problems and arguments where we can only seldom find any trace of Hellenistic influence.[142]

4. The Beelzebul Controversy (Mark 3:22-30//Matt. 12:22-32// Luke 11:14-15, 17-23) cannot be classified with any of the above. It must have been originally composed in the Palestinian church, but unlike the Galilean conflict stories it was not formulated as a response to Jewish criticism. Rather, it was composed as teaching material for use within the church when the problem arose about admitting those who had originally been hostile to Jesus in his earthly ministry, but who are now converts to the faith.

We find, then, that the origins of the non-unitary conflict stories are to be found in diverse circumstances. Those who have claimed a common *Sitz im Leben* for all conflict stories have made sweeping generalizations based on an incomplete picture. Not all arose out of typically rabbinic debates, nor the need for illustrative narratives in preaching nor the need for church pronouncements. If these suggested *Sitze im Leben* are broadly conceived, one can place certain conflict stories in each, but not all conflict stories fit into any one of them. What is common to all is their *form*, but one should not deduce *Sitz im Leben* from form alone.

NOTES

1. R. Bultmann, *Synoptic Tradition*, 47. J. Neusner (*Rabbinic Traditions*, 3.17) has made a similar observation concerning rabbinic debates.
2. Others who regard Luke's version as based solely on Q are M. Albertz, *Streitgespräche*, 166; B. H. Streeter, *The Four Gospels*, 189; F. W. Beare, *Earliest Records*, 102; and F. Hahn, *Titles of Jesus*, 292. We have left Luke

11:16 out of the pericope. It appears to be a Lucan secondary addition
(cf. Mark 8:11) to the Q material.

3. Cf. B. H. Streeter, *The Four Gospels*, 167, 203-204; and W. Kümmel, *Introduction*, 65, 132-134.

4. N. Perrin, *Rediscovering the Teaching of Jesus*, 63. Cf. also Julius Wellhausen, *Das Evangelium Marci*, 27; T. W. Manson, *The Teaching of Jesus*, 82-83; Burton S. Easton, "The Beelzebul Sections," *JBL* 32 (1913) 59; E. Schweizer, *Matthew*, 287; and E. Ellis, *Luke*, 167. For a contrary view, see C. S. Rodd, "Spirit or Finger," *ExpTim* 72 (1960-1961) 157-158. Robert G. Hamerton-Kelly ("A Note on Matthew 12:28 par. Luke 11:20," *NTS* 11 [1965] 167-169) has shown that "spirit of God" and "hand (or finger) of God" were used interchangeably in the Old Testament (Ezek. 8:1-13; 37:1; 1 Chron. 28:11-19; Exod. 7-9); therefore, he says, one cannot rule out the possibility that Luke made the change. This shows also, however, that the change from finger to spirit (by Matthew) is equally possible. Matthew, one could say, clarifies the meaning of the terminology for his readers. Why would Luke change a clearly understood term to one which would be obscure for his Gentile readers? Perrin's judgment is to be preferred.

5. Cf. R. Bultmann, *Synoptic Tradition*, 90, 327; and Charles E. Carlston, *The Parables of the Triple Tradition* (Philadelphia: Fortress, 1975) 67.

6. Cf. Günther Bornkamm, "End-Expectation and Church in Matthew," *Tradition and Interpretation in Matthew*, by G. Bornkamm, G. Barth, and H. J. Held (Philadelphia: Westminster, 1963) 34; and H. Tödt, *Son of Man*, 118-119. Cf. also M. Albertz, *Streitgespräche*, 49.

7. Luke 11:14, while differing from Matt. 12:22-23, can be assigned to Q; it is closely paralleled in Matt. 9:33, a doublet of Matt. 12:22-23. Luke 11:17//Matt. 12:25 agree over against Mark 3:23 and can be assigned to Q, although Matt. 12:25c is assimilated to Mark. Luke 11:21-22 is from Q, although it has no exact parallel in Matthew; Matt. 12:29 is from Mark 3:27, but that is simply another version of what Luke (= Q) has. Finally, Luke 11:15//Matt. 12:24; 9:34 can be assigned to Q in its Lucan form, which identifies the opponents as merely "certain men," not "Pharisees" (as Matthew has), and which has a simpler charge, as in Matt. 9:34.

8. Cf. R. Bultmann, *Synoptic Tradition*, 13, 52; W. Grundmann, *Markus*, 82-83; V. Taylor, *Mark*, 237; and C. Carlson, *The Parables*, 132.

9. Cf. V. Taylor, *Mark*, 239, who cites uses of *parakaleomai* and *parabolē* in Marcan links and compositions elsewhere; and E. Schweizer, *Mark*, 83-84.

10. The words give a direct interpretation of the meaning of the four parables which follow (3:24, 25, 26, 27). Cf. B. S. Easton, "The Beelzebul Sections," 61, who says that 3:23b is "formed out of what follows" (3:24-27). Cf. also John D. Crossan, "Mark and the Relatives of Jesus," *NovT* 15 (1973) 90-91; and R. Tannehill, *The Sword of His Mouth*, 179.

11. Ibid. (Easton), 61. The phrase destroys the formal parallelism of the rest of the verse.

12. This closing statement explains the relationship of 3:28-29 to the charge in 3:22. Cf. ibid., 67; R. Bultmann, *Synoptic Tradition*, 62, 332; V. Taylor, *Mark*, 244; and F. W. Beare, *Earliest Records*, 102.

13. The translation is my own so that exact parallels in Greek wording can be seen more clearly.

14. B. S. Easton, "The Beelzebul Sections," 67-68.

15. Ibid., 68; R. Bultmann, *Synoptic Tradition*, 13; M. Albertz, *Streitgespräche*, 49; and C. Carlston, *The Parables*, 133. V. Taylor (*Mark*, 237), while recog-

nizing that the Q form is more original in connecting the controversy with the exorcism of a dumb demon, believes that the Marcan version preserves the story with greater fidelity.

16. The Q saying, which accepts that one might be forgiven for speaking words against the Son of man, is a more difficult saying—from the standpoint of Christian piety—than the more acceptable words of Mark 3:29, which is about forgiveness and blasphemy in general. Also that the Q version is more primitive than Mark's can perhaps be vindicated by the witness of *Gos. Thom.* 44, in which (like Q) it is blasphemies against Jesus which are declared forgivable: "Jesus said: He who blasphemes against the Son will be forgiven; but he who blasphemes against the Holy Spirit will not be forgiven, either on earth or in heaven."

17. For Luke 11:19-20//Matt. 12:27-28, cf. R. Bultmann, *Synoptic Tradition*, 14, 162; F. W. Beare, *Earliest Records*, 102; and N. Perrin, *Rediscovering the Teaching of Jesus*, 63. For Luke 11:23//Matt. 12:30, cf. R. Bultmann, *Synoptic Tradition*, 14.

18. The presence of these intervening sayings does not violate the conflict story form any more than the use of Scripture does in other conflict stories (e.g., in Mark 7:1-8; and 10:2-9).

19. R. Bultmann, *Synoptic Tradition*, 162; cf. N. Perrin, *Rediscovering the Teaching of Jesus*, 64; and F. Hahn, *Titles of Jesus*, 292.

20. Cf. R. Bultmann, *Synoptic Tradition*, 14, 162; F. W. Beare, *Earliest Records*, 102; and N. Perrin, *Rediscovering the Teaching of Jesus*, 63.

21. H. Tödt, *Son of Man*, 119. Tödt discusses the passage at the level of Q, but we have argued that the verse existed in a version prior to Q, since a parallel appears in Mark 3:28-29.

22. Ibid., 119.

23. Howard C. Kee (*Jesus in History: An Approach to the Study of the Gospels* [New York: Harcourt, Brace, and World, 1970] 71) writes that A.D. 50-60 is "a reasonable conjecture"; W. Kümmel (*Introduction to the New Testament*, 71) puts A.D. 50 and 70 as the outside dates.

24. William Wrede, "Zur Heilung des Gelahmten (Mc 2.1ff.)," ZNW 5 (1904) 354-358; R. Bultmann, *Synoptic Tradition*, 14-16; Anton Fridrichsen, *The Problem of Miracle in Primitive Christianity* (Minneapolis: Augsburg, 1972) 129; M. Dibelius, *Tradition*, 66; V. Taylor, *Formation*, 66-68; idem, *Mark*, 191-192; E. Klostermann, *Markus*, 21-22; E. Lohmeyer, *Markus*, 50-54; A. Rawlinson, *Mark*, 25; R. H. Fuller, *Interpreting the Miracles*, 50-51; idem, *The Foundations of New Testament Christology*, 149; F. W. Beare, *Earliest Records*, 76-77; D. Nineham, *Mark*, 90-94; F. Hahn, *Titles of Jesus*, 35, 50; T. A. Burkill, *Mysterious Revelation*, 127-128; E. Schweizer, *Mark*, 60; H.-W. Kuhn, *Ältere Sammlungen*, 54; W. Kelber, *The Kingdom in Mark*, 18; and Thomas L. Budesheim, "Jesus and the Disciples in Conflict with Judaism," ZNW 62 (1971) 190-192.

25. M. Dibelius (*Tradition*, 66) and F. Hahn (*Titles of Jesus*, 50) designate 2:6-10 (not 5b-10) as secondary. H.-W. Kuhn (*Ältere Sammlungen*, 54) leaves the question open whether 2:5b-10 or 2:6-10 is the secondary unit.

26. Some other reasons are: (1) the narrative of Mark 2:5b-10 is not followed naturally by 2:11-12; the "scribes" mentioned in 2:6 would not be counted among the "all" of 2:12; (2) while the "faith" (2:5a) of the paralytic and his friends is important as a basis for the healing in 2:1-5a, 11-12, it has no importance in the dialogue on forgiveness of sins (2:5b-10); and (3) in

2:12 that which amazes the crowd is the miraculous healing, not the forgiveness of sins.

27. M. Albertz, *Streitgespräche*, 7-8; M. Dibelius, "Zur Formgeschichte der Evangelien," 211-212; B. Harvie Branscomb, "Mark 2:5, 'Son, thy Sins are Forgiven,'" *JBL* 53 (1935) 59; idem, *Mark*, 47; Ernest Best, "Mark 2:1-12," *Biblical Theology* 3 (1953) 52-53; A. Feuillet, "L'exousia du fils de l'homme, *RevScRel* 42 (1954) 161-192; Otto Betz, *What Do We Know about Jesus?* (Philadelphia: Westminster, 1968) 62; Richard T. Mead, "The Healing of the Paralytic—A Unit?," *JBL* 80 (1969) 348-354; and Werner G. Kümmel, *The Theology of the New Testament*, 45.

28. W. L. Knox, *Sources*, 1. 11 (footnote).

29. This view approximates those of R. Bultmann, *Synoptic Tradition*, 15; M. Dibelius, *Tradition*, 67; A. Rawlinson, *Mark*, 25; F. W. Beare, *Earliest Records*, 77; F. Hahn, *Titles of Jesus*, 35; and Howard C. Kee, *Community of the New Age: Studies in Mark's Gospel* (Philadelphia: Westminster, 1977) 36. Kee, however, thinks that it was Mark himself, rather than a predecessor, who composed the story.

30. R. Bultmann, *Synoptic Tradition*, 15; M. Dibelius, *Tradition*, 67; E. Klostermann, *Markus*, 23-24; W. Manson, *Jesus the Messiah*, 42; G. Bornkamm, *Jesus*, 229; H. Tödt, *Son of Man*, 126-130; G. H. Boobyer, "Mark II.10a and the Interpretation of the Healing of the Paralytic," *HTR* 47 (1954) 115-120; C. P. Ceroke, "Is Mark 2.10 a Saying of Jesus?," *CBQ* 22 (1960) 369-390; F. Hahn, *Titles of Jesus*, 34; R. H. Fuller, *The Foundations of New Testament Christology*, 124, 149; Lewis S. Hay, "The Son of Man in Mark 2:10 and 2:28," *JBL* 89 (1970) 71-73; H. Conzelmann, *Jesus*, 44; and H.-W. Kuhn, *Ältere Sammlungen*, 54.

Norman Perrin ("The Creative Use of the Son of Man Traditions by Mark," *A Modern Pilgrimage in New Testament Christology* [Philadelphia: Fortress, 1974] 88-89) claims that it is "to Mark that we owe the actual use of *exousia* in connection with the earthly Jesus," and that Mark 2:10 (as well as 2:28) "may not be regarded as representing a traditional use of Son of Man." Apparently Perrin thinks of these Son of man sayings as Marcan formulations. Since 2:10a, however, is the most important part of the pericope, the "punch line" to which the conflict leads, it can hardly be considered secondary, unless one is to go on to claim that the composition of 2:1-12 out of its component parts is Marcan—a claim which cannot be sustained. In another essay in the same volume ("The Son of Man in the Synoptic Tradition," 80) Perrin is more reserved. He writes concerning Mark 2:10 and 2:28, "the facts of life with regard to this use of *exousia* must be held to prove that whether Mark has created them, redacted them, or simply preserved them, they represent a characteristic emphasis of the Markan theology." But then again in still another essay in the same volume, ("The Christology of Mark: A Study in Methodology," 116, n. 24) he states that "2:10 is Markan." That 2:10 is Marcan has also been affirmed by W. Lane, *Mark*, 97-98.

31. G. Bornkamm, *Jesus*, 229-230; H. Tödt, *Son of Man*, 113-140; F. Hahn, *Titles of Jesus*, 34-37; R. H. Fuller, *The Foundations of New Testament Christology*, 124, 149; Hans Conzelmann, *An Outline of the Theology of the New Testament* (New York: Harper & Row, 1969) 133-134; idem, *Jesus*, 44.

32. So J. Jeremias, *The Parables of Jesus*, 122 (n. 31) and 209 (n. 96); idem, *New Testament Theology*, 1. 11, 114. Cf. also Luke 7:48.

33. Hans von Campenhausen, *Ecclesiastical Authority and Spiritual Power in*

the Church of the First Three Centuries (Stanford: Stanford University, 1969) 126; cf. also H. Braun, *Jesus*, 145.

34. See note 74 in Chapter III.

35. But why is the title Son of man (and not some other) applied to Jesus? H. Tödt (*Son of Man*, 129) writes that there is no indication that the Son of man forgives sins in Jewish apocalyptic nor elsewhere in the synoptics. He goes on to say that it is by the title Son of man that "authority" is ascribed to Jesus by the primitive church, and that forgiveness of sins is part of his authority: "Jesus' preaching of the coming of God's reign not only summoned men to turn round in repentance in face of this coming but also included the assurance of God's forgiveness."

36. One need not assume that the "power of the keys" in the Matthean sense (Matt. 16:19; 18:18; cf. also John 20:23) was operative at this stage of development. One can fall short of that and simply affirm, as above, that the church claimed for itself and declared openly the forgiveness of sins in the present in the name of Jesus, which is unacceptable in a Jewish milieu, since in the latter one cannot openly declare God's forgiveness in a concrete way, i.e., to a particular person on a particular occasion of repentance. For discussion of the development from the actions of Jesus to the ecclesiastical doctrine of the keys, see H. von Campenhausen, "The Power of the Keys in the Primitive Church," *Ecclesiastical Authority and Spiritual Power in the Church of the First Three Centuries*, 124-148.

37. V. Taylor, *Mark*, 203-204.

38. There are traditions elsewhere (Mark 2:1; Matt. 4:13; 9:1) that Jesus resided for a time in Capernaum.

39. I. Abrahams (*Studies in Pharisaism and the Gospels*, 1. 56) writes, "It is not at all the case that a Pharisee would have declined to receive even 'sinners' *at his own table*. But he might have refused an invitation to join them at *their* table, where the ritual and atmosphere could hardly fail to be uncongenial." Cf. also C. G. Montefiore, *Rabbinic Literature and Gospel Teaching* (London: Macmillan, 1930; reprinted, New York: Ktav, 1970) 221-224.

40. B. H. Branscomb, *Jesus and the Law of Moses*, 136; V. Taylor, *Mark*, 207.

41. Cf. H. Conzelmann, *Jesus*, 49, who writes, "On methodological grounds the words in which Jesus speaks of his 'being sent' ('I came . . .' Mark 2:17b, etc.) must be set aside, for they have been formulated in retrospect, looking back at his completed ministry." R. Bultmann (*Synoptic Tradition*, 92, 155), H. W. Kuhn (*Ältere Sammlungen*, 83), and C. Carlston (*The Parables*, 114) also consider 2:17b a church composition.

42. Since not all of these texts are readily available, they are given here: Luke 9:56 (in Koine MSS, Theta, the Vulgate, Syriac Cureton, and Marcion; but missing in other MSS considered superior), "For the Son of man came not to destroy men's souls, but to save;" 1 Tim. 1:15, "Christ Jesus came into the world to save sinners;" *Gos. Eg.* (quoted in Clement of Alexandria, *Strom.* 3.9.63), "I came to destroy the works of the woman;" and *Barn.* 5:9, "He came not to call the righteous, but sinners." See also John 18:37 (which actually has a purpose clause, rather than an infinitive expressing purpose), "For this I have come into the world, in order that I might bear witness to the truth."

43. See V. Taylor, *Mark*, 207; and W. Lane, *Mark*, 104 (n. 43), who cite various parallels.

44. Compare the statement of Ignatius (1 *Eph.* 7:2), "There is only one physician . . . Jesus Christ our Lord." Doubts about the authenticity of 2:17a

are also expressed by R. Bultmann (*Synoptic Tradition*, 105) and C. Carlston (*The Parables*, 114-115).

45. It is the disciples who are asked the question ("Why does he eat with tax collectors and sinners?"), rather than Jesus, because it is they—now (at the time of composition) the church—who are the violators of the acceptable conduct. In other conflict stories (e.g. in Mark 2:18-20; 2:23-28; and 7:1-8) this becomes more explicit. The opponents ask critical questions about the disciples. R. Bultmann (*Synoptic Tradition*, 48) writes, "It is the disciples who are attacked, i.e. it is the Church."

46. Cf. J. Jeremias, *The Parables of Jesus*, 100 (n. 42).

47. Cf. G. Bornkamm, *Jesus*, 50, 80-81; N. Perrin, *Rediscovering the Teaching of Jesus*, 119-121; and H. Conzelmann, *Jesus*, 32, 67.

48. See note 93 in Chapter III. Cf. also Joachim Jeremias, "Zöllner und Sunder," ZNW 30 (1931) 293-300; idem, *Jerusalem in the Time of Jesus*, (Philadelphia: Fortress, 1969) 267, 311. N. Perrin (*Rediscovering the Teaching of Jesus*, 94) interprets "sinners" to mean "Jews who have made themselves as Gentiles." I. Abrahams (*Studies in Pharisaism and the Gospels*, 1. 55) gives a different view. He says that "sinners" applies to "persons of immoral life, men of proved dishonesty or followers of suspected and degrading occupations." This appears to be extreme. Jacob Neusner (*From Politics to Piety: The Emergence of Pharisaic Judaism* [Englewood Cliffs: Prentice Hall, 1973] 73) thinks of the phrase "tax collectors and sinners" as "people who do not keep the law."

49. J. Neusner (*The Rabbinic Traditions about the Pharisees before 70*, 3. 287-300, 318) writes that the Pharisees were, among other things, a society for table fellowship, and (p. 297) that of 341 pericopes concerning them, 229 (or 67%) "directly or indirectly pertain to table-fellowship." Concerning the Pharisaic reproach against Jesus' fellowship recorded in the gospels, he writes (p. 288), "The obvious underlying claim is that Christian table-fellowship does not depend upon the sorts of rules important in the table-fellowship of other groups."

50. Mark 2:27 must have been in the text of Mark used by Matthew and Luke. All MSS of Mark have it except for the so-called "Western" texts of Mark, i.e. Codex Bezae (D) and some Old Latin versions (a, c, e, ff). The verse must have been integral (not a later insertion) to Mark 2:23-28, since it is impossible to account for the composition of Mark 2:23-24 without it. The saying in 2:28 does not have the "productive power" to generate 2:23-24. The latter depends on 2:27, which alludes to the activities of "man" on the sabbath. The saying in 2:28, if originally alone, would have produced material in which Jesus, rather than his disciples, breaks the sabbath law. The Western texts have probably been influenced by the readings in Matthew and Luke, i.e., harmonized. Cf. W. Lane, *Mark*, 118 (n. 94). Harmonization of the synoptic gospels is a characteristic of the Western texts noted by B. F. Westcott and F. J. A. Hort, *The New Testament in the Original Greek* (2 vols.; New York: Harper & Brothers, 1882) 2. 122-124.

It has been proposed that Matthew and Luke have conflated the text of Mark with a Q version of the conflict story, and that this Q version lacked what appears in Mark 2:27. So Hans Hübner, *Das Gesetz in der synoptischen Tradition* (Witten: Luther, 1973) 113-123. According to this proposal, the *Urform* of the pericope consisted of our Mark 2:23-24, 27-28. What appears in 2:28 originally referred to "man" (not "Son of man"), but this was transformed Christologically into "Son of man." Then the non-Christological material of 2:27 was dropped, and what appears in 2:25-26 was inserted.

The Q pericope then contained our Mark 2:23-26, 28. Matthew and Luke preferred this content to what Mark provided. The proposal is somewhat attractive, but it is finally not acceptable, since 2:28 could not have been originally in the form Hübner suggests. Would Jesus (or the early Christians attributing a saying to him) actually affirm that "man" is "lord of the sabbath"? That does not seem likely. It is better to take 2:28 as a Christological saying concerning the Son of man from its inception, and which was attached secondarily. The omission of 2:27 by Matthew and Luke can be explained on other grounds, as we attempt above.

51. Cf. Alfred Suhl, *Die Funktion der alttestamentlichen Zitate und Anspielungen im Markusevangelium* (Gütersloh: Gerd Mohn, 1965) 83; and E. Schweizer, *Matthew*, 277.

52. Cf. Krister Stendahl, "Matthew," *PCB*, 784.

53. Cf. G. D. Kilpatrick, *The Origins of the Gospel According to St. Matthew* (Oxford: Clarendon, 1946) 116; G. Bornkamm, "End Expectation and Church in Matthew" and Gerhard Barth, "Matthew's Understanding of the Law," *Tradition and Interpretation in Matthew*, 31 (n. 2) and 81; G. Strecker, *Der Weg der Gerechtigkeit*, 32-33; and O. L. Cope, *Matthew*, 67-68.

54. Cf. Reinhart Hummel, *Die Auseinandersetzung zwischen Kirche und Judentum in Matthäusevangelium* (Munich: Kaiser, 1963) 45; G. Barth, "Matthew's Understanding of the Law," 79; and David Hill, "On the Use and Meaning of Hosea VI.6 in Matthew's Gospel," *NTS* 24 (1977) 116.

55. Cf. Luke 1:27, 32, 69; 2:4; 3:31; 18:38, 39; 20:41-44.

56. Cf. Jacob Jervell, "The Law in Luke-Acts," *Luke and the People of God: A New Look at Luke-Acts* (Minneapolis: Augsburg, 1972) 140. Jervell overstates the case, however, when he writes that Luke was "concerned to show that Jesus acted in complete accordance with the law, and that the Jewish leaders were not able to raise any objections." This runs counter to Luke 6:2, 7, 11; 13:14, 17.

57. Ibid., 141.

58. *The Four Gospels: A New Translation* (trans. C. C. Torrey; New York: Harper & Row, 1933) 73. Cf. also B. H. Branscomb, *Jesus and the Law of Moses*, 144; L. Hay, "The Son of Man in Mark 2:10 and 2:28," 74; and R. Banks, *Jesus and the Law*, 122.

59. T. W. Manson, "Mark 2:27f.," *ConNT* 11 (1947) 145. Cf. also F. W. Beare, *Earliest Records*, 91; and H. Riesenfeld, "The Sabbath and the Lord's Day," 120-121.

60. For a more detailed discussion, see Arland J. Hultgren, "The Formation of the Sabbath Pericope in Mark 2:23-28," *JBL* 91 (1972) 38-43.

61. Ibid., 40. Cf. E. Klostermann, *Markus*, 29, who designates 2:23, 24, and 27 as the primitive form of the controversy dialogue; Ernst Haenchen, *Der Weg Jesu* (2nd ed.; Berlin: W. de Gruyter, 1968) 120-122; and H.-W. Kuhn, *Ältere Sammlungen*, 76.
This is contrary to the view of many who hold that the conflict story consisted first of 2:23-26, to which 2:27-28 was added: W. Bousset, *Kyrios Christos*, 78-79; Karl L. Schmidt, *Der Rahmen der Geschichte Jesu* (Berlin: Trowitzsch, 1919) 97; M. Albertz, *Streitgespräche*, 10; R. Bultmann, *Synoptic Tradition*, 16-17; M. Dibelius, *Tradition*, 64-65; A. Rawlinson, *Mark*, 33; V. Taylor, *Mark*, 218; Eduard Schweizer, "Der Menschensohn," *ZNW* 50 (1950) 199 (n. 47); idem, *Mark*, 71; A. Suhl, *Die Funktion der alttestamentlichen Zitate*, 82; and W. Lane, *Mark*, 118-119. F. W. Beare ("The Sabbath Was Made for Man?," *JBL* 79 [1960] 135, and *Earliest Records*,

90-93) offers a slight variation by suggesting that the story of the disciples in the grainfield has been composed as a framework for the saying in 2:27-28.

62. There is a close parallel, to which many commentators refer, in the statement of the second century Rabbi Simeon ben Menasya (Mek. on Exod. 31:14): "The Sabbath is delivered unto you, and you are not delivered to the sabbath." But this saying does not have the same meaning as Mark 2:27. In context it emphasizes the sabbath as a distinctive Jewish institution, i.e., as given to Israel (so Exod. 31:14). The sabbath is given to Israel as a gift, and it is understood that Israel will therefore observe it. In Mark 2:27 it is understood that the sabbath has been established for man's good. It will be kept in a Jewish milieu, of course, but what is to prevail is that which enhances human life, not sabbath casuistry—even if the intention of the latter is to make the day one of celebration.

63. That this "proof from Scripture" (2:25-26) is a secondary addition has been asserted also by K. Berger, *Die Gesetzesauslegung Jesu*, 1. 24, 197-198, 578.

64. The incident alluded to is in 1 Sam. 21:1-6. In the Old Testament there is no indication that the action of David was performed on the sabbath, although in a midrash on Samuel it is. So Str-B, 1. 618. The citations of Billerbeck are from *Yal.* on 1 Sam. 21:5 and from *b. Menah* 95b. I. Abrahams (*Studies in Pharisaism and the Gospels*, 1. 134) comments that according to the Midrash David acted to preserve life.

65. Cf. H. Tödt, *Son of Man*, 130-132; F. Hahn, *Titles of Jesus*, 35; R. H. Fuller, *The Foundations of New Testament Christology*, 124, 145-150; H.-W. Kuhn, *Ältere Sammlungen*, 73; and K. Berger, *Die Gesetzesauslegung Jesu*, 1. 584-585. W. Lane (*Mark*, 120) thinks 2:28 (like 2:10) was composed by Mark. R. Banks (*Jesus and the Law*, 120-122), on the other hand, asserts that Mark 2:28 is an authentic word of Jesus, and that it was bound together with 2:27 from the beginning.

66. Ernst Käsemann ("The Problem of the Historical Jesus," *Essays on New Testament Themes* [Naperville: Allenson, 1964] 39) writes concerning 2:27 and 2:28, "that the second saying—that about the freedom of the Son of Man—represents a distinct limitation and weakening of the first. But by now we have come very close to the hypothesis that the community embarked on this process of watering-down the saying because, while it might credit its Lord with the freedom he had assumed, it was not prepared to allow it to all men. Its members felt themselves more tightly bound by the law than he had been and, as the subsequent pericope about the healing on the sabbath shows, they exercised this freedom only in exceptional cases and not as a matter of principle; and certainly not in that spirit of unforced responsibility to God, which was Jesus' legacy to them." And F. Hahn (*Titles of Jesus*, 35) says that by the addition of 2:28, 2:27 "has been refashioned in a Christological sense: the Lord of the sabbath is not man, but the 'Son of Man.'" Cf. also Christoph Hinz, "Jesus und der Sabbat," *KD* 19 (1973) 96.

67. Cf. H. Riesenfeld, "The Sabbath and the Lord's Day," 118-119. Riesenfeld (pp. 114-118) points out that in ancient Judaism the sabbath was thought of typologically as a foretaste of the coming age, and that Jesus' symbolic actions and attitudes toward the sabbath were affirmations that the coming age had now been realized in his ministry. Cf. also R. H. Fuller, *The Foundations of New Testament Christology*, 149.

68. Cf. R. Bultmann, *Synoptic Tradition*, 16-17, and D. Nineham, *Mark*, 107.

69. F. W. Beare, *Earliest Records*, 91-92. Cf. also the statement of E. Schweizer, *Mark*, 70, "Where do these Pharisees come from, since one is permitted to go only about half a mile on the sabbath?"

70. Cf. R. Bultmann, *Synoptic Tradition*, 16; H. Braun, *Jesus*, 79.

71. Cf. E. Lohse, "Jesu Worte über den Sabbat," 84-85; E. Käsemann, "The Problem of the Historical Jesus," 38-39; E. Haenchen, *Der Weg Jesu*, 120-121; R. H. Fuller, *The Foundations of New Testament Christology*, 149; E. Schweizer, *Mark*, 71; H.-W. Kuhn, *Ältere Sammlungen*, 75; and W. Lane, *Mark*, 119-120.

72. K. Berger (*Die Gesetzesauslegung Jesu*, 1. 585) writes that in Mark 2:23-28 opposition between church and Judaism is reflected, and that for the church it is Jesus as Son of man who has authority.

73. Sabbath observance became a matter of indifference in the Hellenistic Christian churches (cf. Gal. 4:10; Rom. 14:5; Col. 2:16), but the assumption underlying Mark 2:27-28 is that the sabbath will actually be kept, albeit in a distinctive way.

74. Cf. *t. 'Abod. Zar.* 3:10 and *m. Yad.* (passim). Both refer to the second century R. Meir and his teachings concerning it.

75. Adolf Büchler, *Der galiläische 'Am-ha Ares des zweiten Jahrhunderts* (Vienna: Hölder, 1906) 134. Cf. also, for various viewpoints concerning the origins and extent of the practice, Wilhelm Brandt, *Jüdische Reinheitslehre und ihre Beschreibung in den Evangelien* (Giessen: Töpelmann, 1910) 16-25; Solomon Zeitlin, "The Halaka in the Gospels and its Relation to the Jewish Law at the Time of Jesus," *HUCA* 1 (1924) 357-373; and B. H. Branscomb, *Jesus and the Law of Moses*, 156-161.

76. K. Berger (*Die Gesetzesauslegung Jesu*, 1. 461-507) thinks of 7:1-23 (not 7:1-8) as a unit, and that the basis for the story is 7:1, 5, 15 (p. 463); the rest is secondary. He also calls 7:15 the starting point (*Ausgangspunkt*, p. 464) around which the whole is constructed. Cf. also H. Hübner, *Das Gesetz*, 159. But 7:15 hardly makes connection (as a response) to the question put to Jesus in 7:5, nor can 7:5 have been composed in light of 7:15 (7:15 would generate a question concerning clean and unclean foods, but not clean or unclean hands). It is the "tradition of the elders" which is at stake in the question (7:5), and that tradition is called the "traditions of men" in the dominical saying (7:8). That 7:1-8 is primary, and that materials in 7:9-23 have been attached to it by Mark, see R. Bultmann, *Synoptic Tradition*, 17; B. H. Branscomb, *Mark*, 123; V. Taylor, *Mark*, 338-339; D. Nineham, *Mark*, 190; A. Suhl, *Die Funktion der alttestamentlichen Zitate*, 79; Paul J. Achtemeier, "Toward the Isolation of Pre-Markan Miracle Catenae," *JBL* 89 (1970) 272-273; E. Schweizer, *Mark*, 145-147; and C. Carlston, *The Parables*, 166.

With 7:15 there is a shift "from the question of cultic purity and impurity" to the question of "the true source of impurity as man's inward disposition" (so Achtemeier) which is carried on in a private conversation between Jesus and his disciples (7:17-23). It is likely that 7:15 was an independent saying to which Mark has attached the remaining material. Cf. Charles E. Carlston, "The Things That Defile (Mark VII.14) and the Law in Matthew and Mark," *NTS* 15 (1968-1969) 92; idem, *The Parables*, 166-167.

77. The pericope (Mark 7:1-8) is part of that material (Mark 6:45-8:26) which has been called Luke's "great omission." Cf. W. Kümmel, *Introduction to the New Testament*, 61-62.

78. It begins with *kai synagontai pros auton*, which can be seen with minor

variations in editorial links at 4:1 and 6:30, and it identifies the scribes as having "come from Jerusalem," as at 3:22.

79. Cf. M. Albertz, *Streitgespräche,* 37; V. Taylor, *Mark,* 334-336; E. Klostermann, *Markus,* 67; B. H. Branscomb, *Mark,* xxxvi, 122; E. Lohmeyer, *Markus,* 139; W. Grundmann, *Markus,* 146; E. Schweizer, *Mark,* 145; W. Lane, *Mark,* 245; C. Carlston, *The Parables,* 162-163; and H. C. Kee, *Community,* 39.

80. Verse 7:8 is an anti-Pharisaic statement which charges the Pharisees with keeping "the traditions of men" in place of God's commandment(s). The saying would have been used as a response to Pharisaic criticism of the church's non-observance of certain traditions. Therefore in 7:5 the question concerns (1) the "disciples" (a surrogate for church) and (2) the "tradition of the elders." It has been composed secondarily; 7:8 can exist as a free-floating logion without 7:5.

81. Contra R. Bultmann (*Synoptic Tradition,* 18) who says that the story was composed in the Palestinian church.

82. Cf. B. H. Branscomb, *Jesus and the Law of Moses,* 162; D. Nineham, *Mark,* 195; S. Johnson, *Mark,* 131; Werner G. Kümmel, "Jesus und der jüdische Traditionsgedanke," *ZNW* 33 (1934) 122; K. Stendahl, *The School of St. Matthew,* 57-58, who indicates that the Targum agrees with the MT and that "the LXX form is a *sine qua non* for the narratives of Mark and Matthew;" Robert H. Gundry, *The Use of the Old Testament in St. Matthew's Gospel* (Leiden: Brill 1967) 15-16; E. Schweizer, *Mark,* 145; Hugh Anderson, "The Old Testament in Mark's Gospel," *The Use of the Old Testament in the New and Other Essays* (ed. James E. Efird; Durham: Duke University, 1972) 302; Henry M. Shires, *Finding the Old Testament in the New* (Philadelphia: Westminster, 1974) 83; and H. Hübner, *Das Gesetz,* 144. It is also clear that Mark 7:7 can also have been derived only from the LXX, as shown by Eberhard Nestle, "The Quotation in Matt. xv. 9; Mark vii. 7," *ExpTim* 11 (1899-1900) 330. R. Banks (*Jesus and the Law,* 134) maintains—unconvincingly—that while the form of Mark 7:8 is based on the LXX, its content can be from the Hebrew.

83. Eduard Lohse (*Colossians and Philemon* [Hermeneia Commentary; Philadelphia: Fortress, 1971] 124) writes that LXX Isa. 29:13 "was obviously quoted often in disputes with proponents of a legalistic type of piety." He refers to Mark 7:7 (//Matt. 15:9) and Titus 1:14, and says that the argument must have been traditional, since it is not introduced by the writers of Colossians and Titus as a quotation from Scripture.

84. Justin, *Dialogue with Trypho* 78:11. Cf. also *1 Clem.* 15:2.

85. G. Margoliouth, "The Tradition of the Elders (Mark 7:1-23)," *ExpTim* 22 (1910-1911) 262; C. G. Montefiore, *The Synoptic Gospels,* 1. 133-144. Cf. also D. Nineham, *Mark,* 194, who writes that Jews of the Diaspora were "constantly surrounded by Gentile 'impurity' " and may have had strict rules about handwashing earlier than the Jews of Palestine. B. H. Branscomb (*Jesus and the Law of Moses,* 156-164) reviews the issues and scholarly opinions, as does V. Taylor, *Mark,* 338-339. More recently, John Bowker (*Jesus and the Pharisees* [Cambridge: Cambridge University, 1973] 38-40) has argued that the Pharisees were "extremists" among the larger community of Hakamim (the "Sages," whom the post-70 rabbis generally speak of as their predecessors, rather than the Pharisees), and that they might well have practiced the handwashing, and enjoined the same upon others, already in the first century. If Bowker is correct this would explain why the rabbinic sources would not attest it as a widespread practice in the first century.

On the other hand, J. Neusner (*Rabbinic Traditions*, 3.288) writes, "The primary mark of Pharisaic commitment was the observance of the laws of ritual purity outside the Temple, where everyone kept them. Eating one's secular, that is, unconsecrated, food in a state of ritual purity as if one were a Temple priest in the cult was one of the two significations of party membership."

86. The attack (7:5) is against the disciples of Jesus, rather than upon Jesus himself, and undoubtedly "disciples" = "church members" at the level of composition. Cf. A. Suhl, *Die Funktion der alttestamentlichen Zitate*, 81.

87. H. Conzelmann, *Jesus*, 52.

88. Mark 10:10-12 continues the discussion, turning to the subject of the remarriage of divorced persons. It is not a part of the original conflict story, however, even though Matthew (19:9) works Mark 10:11 into the conflict story as a closing saying. See R. Bultmann, *Synoptic Tradition*, 26; E. Klostermann, *Markus*, 97; W. L. Knox, *Sources*, 1. 69; V. Taylor, *Mark*, 415, 419; Gerhard Delling, "Das Logion Mark. 10:11 (und seine Abwandlungen) im Neuen Testament," *NovT* 1 (1956) 265; E. Schweizer, *Mark*, 201; and H. C. Kee, *Community*, 155. For a contrary view, see H.-W. Kuhn, *Ältere Sammlungen*, 160-168, and David L. Dungan, *The Sayings of Jesus in the Churches of Paul: The Use of the Synoptic Tradition in the Regulation of Early Church Life* (Philadelphia: Fortress, 1971) 107-109.

89. Mark 10:2-9 is within a section of Mark's gospel (9:42—10:12) which, according to the standard two-source theory, Luke did not take over from Mark. Cf. W. Kümmel, *Introduction* 133.

90. H.-W. Kuhn (*Ältere Sammlungen*, 146-191, 229) maintains that the material in 10:2-12, 17-23, 25, and 35-45 was assembled together in a collection which Mark received. If so, Mark has broken up the collection in favor of including other materials.

91. Cf. Ernst Käsemann, "Sentences of Holy Law in the New Testament," *New Testament Questions of Today* (Philadelphia: Fortress, 1969) 75-76.

92. For references to the authority of Jesus' words for Mark's readers, see Mark 1:22, 27; 8:38.

93. The manuscripts designated B and A have "Pharisees came;" Aleph (Sinaiticus) and C have "the Pharisees came;" and W and Theta have "and the Pharisees came."

94. The manuscripts not having the phrase are all designated "Western Texts" (Greek D; Latin a, b, k, r; and the Syriac palimpsest).

95. This means that the identification of Jesus' opponents as Pharisees was made originally by Matthew, and that Mark has been edited to conform to it. There is evidence that at points the Western texts escaped revision. See Julius Wellhausen, *Einleitung in die drei ersten Evangelien* (2nd ed.; Berlin: Reimer, 1911) 9; Frederic G. Kenyon, *The Chester Beatty Papyri* (London: Walker, 1933) 16; and M. Black, *An Aramaic Approach to the Gospels and Acts*, 30. It is a generally accepted view of textual criticism that in cases where harmonization is a possibility the reading which differs is to be preferred, especially where the parallel reading is firm. See Bruce M. Metzger, *The Text of the New Testament: Its Transmission, Corruption, and Restoration* (New York: Oxford University, 1964) 217. Matt. 19:3 is firm, and the Western reading of Mark 10:2 differs, and it is to be preferred. For an opposing view, claiming that the disputed words are original to Mark, see Klyne Snodgrass, "Western Non-Interpolations," *JBL* 91 (1972) 378.

96. Cf. V. Taylor, *Mark*, 417; and W. Grundmann, *Markus*, 203. The verb

peirazein appears also in Mark 1:13 and 12:15, but in different phraseology and can be considered embedded in the tradition.

97. Cf. R. Bultmann, *Synoptic Tradition*, 81; E. Klostermann, *Markus*, 99; and A. Suhl, *Die Funktion der alttestamentlichen Zitate*, 76. K. Berger (*Die Gesetzesauslegung Jesu*, 1. 536) refers to 10:9 as the starting point in the pericope's history of tradition. For a contrary view, see H. Dibelius (*Tradition*, 221), who says that Mark 10:9 is deduced from 10:2-8.

98. Mark 7:8, like 10:8, is set at the conclusion of a Scripture quotation, but (see Part E above) it too was a free-floating saying (a caricature of the Pharisees).

99. Cf. Klaus Beyer, *Semitische Syntax im Neuen Testament* (SUNT 1; 1 vol. to date; Göttingen: Vandenhoeck & Ruprecht, 1962) 167-168.

100. Xenophon, *Oeconomicus* 7.30; Josephus, *Ant.* 6.13.8 §309; both are cited in BAG, 783. The closest parallel in rabbinic literature (so Str-B, 1.803-804) is in *Pesiq. Rab Kah.* 11b, in which it is stated that God, since creation, has been matching couples for marriage. But this has to do with the arranging of marriages, not their establishment ("yoking").

101. Josephus, *Ant.* 15.7.10 §259; for references to Hellenistic literature and papyri, see BAG, 898; J. H. Moulton and G. Milligan, *The Vocabulary of the Greek Testament*, 696; Boaz Cohen, *Jewish and Roman Law: A Comparative Study* (2 vols.; New York: Jewish Theological Seminary, 1966) 1. 394 (n. 83); and Donald W. Shaner, *A Christian View of Divorce According to the Teachings of the New Testament* (Leiden: Brill, 1969) 38-43, 57-63.

102. Cf. also Matt. 1:19; 19:3; Mark 10:2, 4.

103. Matt. 19:9 has the exception "except for unchastity," which is generally considered Matthew's own insertion into the saying (cf. Matt. 5:32). Cf. R. Bultmann, *Synoptic Tradition*, 27; B. H. Branscomb, *Jesus and the Law of Moses*, 149-156; Günther Bornkamm, "Die Stellung des Neuen Testaments zur Ehescheidung," *EvT* 7 (1948) 283-285, and *Jesus*, 98-99, 205, who writes that the early church abandoned the more rigorous view of Jesus, as Matthew (5:32; 19:3-9) shows for the Jewish Christian church, and Paul (1 Cor. 7:12-16) for the Hellenistic Church. Cf. also T. W. Manson, *The Teaching of Jesus*, 200 (n. 5), 292-294, 304 (n. 2); Heinrich Greeven, "Zu den Aussagen des Neuen Testaments über die Ehe," *ZEE* 1 (1957) 109-125; G. Kilpatrick, *The Origins of the Gospel According to St. Matthew*, 106; R. Schnackenburg, *The Moral Teaching of the New Testament*, 135-141; G. Barth, "Matthew's Understanding of the Law," 95; W. D. Davies, *The Setting of the Sermon on the Mount* (Cambridge: Cambridge University, 1964) 388; G. Strecker, *Der Weg der Gerechtigkeit*, 132; Reinhart Hummel, *Die Auseinandersetzung*, 51; W. Kümmel, *Introduction*, 112-113, and *Theology of the New Testament*, 52; H. Conzelmann, *Jesus*, 66; J. Jeremias, *New Testament Theology*, 1. 224-225; David R. Catchpole, "The Synoptic Divorce Material as a Traditio-Historical Problem," *BJRL* 57 (1974) 93-110; Joseph A. Fitzmyer, "The Matthean Divorce Texts and Some New Palestinian Evidence," *TS* 37 (1976) 203, 207-211, 221-223; and Bruce Vawter, "Divorce and the New Testament," *CBQ* 39 (1977) 530, 535.

For a contrary view (that Matthew preserves the teaching of Jesus) see M. Lehmann, "Gen. 2:24 as the Basis for Divorce in Halakhah and New Testament," *ZAW* 72 (1960) 266; Abel Isaksson, *Marriage and Ministry in the New Temple* (ASNU 24; Lund: Gleerup, 1965) 75-115; and D. Dungan, *The Sayings of Jesus*, 102-131.

104. On other grounds, D. Daube (*The New Testament and Rabbinic Judaism*, 73)

considers the verse an insertion into the pericope—either by Mark or by a predecessor, but secondary in any case. Daube (pp. 73-74, 368-369) gives further lexical treatment of "to yoke" and "to divide," but he refrains from tracing the verse back as an authentic statement of Jesus.

105. Cf. A. Suhl, *Die Funktion der alttestamentlichen Zitate*, 76; and K. Berger, *Die Gesetzesauslegung Jesu*, 1. 536.

106. Some manuscripts insert here, "and be joined to his wife," which the RSV and NEB have, but these words do not appear in the best manuscripts.

107. The variation given in the LXX, however, is also found in the Jerusalem (Pseudo-Jonathan) Targum, Samaritan Pentateuch, and Peshitta, as well as in the Vulgate and Philo. Nevertheless, Mark 10:7, 8a is surely based on the LXX (Gen. 2:24). Cf. D. Daube, *The New Testament and Rabbinic Judaism*, 81; K. Stendahl, *The School of St. Matthew*, 59-60; R. Gundry, *The Use of the Old Testament in St. Matthew's Gospel*, 16-17; E. Haenchen, *Der Weg Jesu*, 339; H.-W. Kuhn, *Ältere Sammlungen*, 190-191; K. Berger, *Die Gesetzesauslegung Jesu*, 1. 539, 547-549, 575; and Kenneth J. Thomas, "Torah Citations in the Synoptics," *NTS* 24 (1977) 86-87.

108. This is mentioned in spite of the very fine survey of materials by J. Fitzmyer, "Matthean Divorce Texts," 197-226. Fitzmyer claims that certain Qumran texts (11QTemple 57:17-19; CD 4:12b-5:14a) indicate prohibition of divorce among the Essenes. He concludes that the question brought to Jesus implies: "Do you side with the Essenes or with the Pharisees?" (pp. 222-223) and that it could have been brought by a Pharisee during Jesus' ministry (p. 222). Yet it is not clear that these texts (which Fitzmyer provides) actually proscribe divorce. What is certain is that they proscribe polygamy (taking a second wife in that sense only). See G. Vermes, "Sectarian Matrimonial Halakhah in the Damascus Rule," *JJS* 25 (1974) 197-202; and B. Vawter, "Divorce and the New Testament," 533. But even if Fitzmyer is correct concerning the Essenes, it is by no means certain that the Essene view would have been a known option for Jesus or his questioners or that it was a point of dispute between the Essenes and the Pharisees. Who would raise such a question to Jesus? We have already indicated above that the term "Pharisees" is not original to Mark, and therefore not to the pre-Marcan tradition. It is more likely that the question is raised for the sake of providing Christian teaching—rather than a real question from the lifetime of Jesus—and composed for the sake of the dominical saying in 10:9, for which we are prepared by the use of Gen. 2:24 (LXX) in 10:7-8.

109. Cf. the debate in *m. Git.* 9:10: "The School of Shammai say: A man may not divorce his wife unless he has found unchastity in her, for it is written, Because he hath found in her indecency in anything. And the School of Hillel say: [He may divorce her] even if she spoiled a dish for him, for it is written, Because he hath found in her indecency in anything. R. Akiba says: Even if he found another fairer than she, for it is written, And it shall be if she find no favour in his eyes;" quoted from the *Mishnah* (H. Danby), 321. The parties to the discussion refer to Deut. 24:1 as that which "is written." For discussion of divorce in Judaism, see G. F. Moore, *Judaism*, 2. 122-126; J. Jeremias, *Jerusalem in the Time of Jesus*, 370-371; and especially I. Abrahams, *Studies in Pharisaism and the Gospels*, 1. 66-78; for discussion of Jesus' views on divorce in relationship to those in Judaism, see T. W. Manson, *The Teaching of Jesus*, 292-295.

110. It has been held by many that Mark 10:1-27 (or 10:1-31) makes up a catechetical document employed by Mark. Whether that is the case or not,

the catechetical interests of this section have long been noticed. It can be concluded, furthermore, that a catechetical interest existed from the time that 10:2-9 was composed. Cf. A. Isaksson, *Marriage and Ministry*, 111-115.

111. Roman law permitted divorce on the part of either party to a marriage. See B. Cohen, *Jewish and Roman Law*, 1. 377-408. See also the Deed of Divorce from a woman to her husband in the first century B.C. recorded in *The New Testament Background: Selected Documents* (ed. C. K. Barrett; New York: Harper & Row, 1961) 39. In Mark 10:2-9 (as well as in Matt. 19:3-9) it is a man's divorcing his wife which is at issue.

112. Cf. Josephus, *Ant.* 15.7.10 §259. I. Abrahams (*Studies in Pharisaism and the Gospels*, 1. 66-78) provides details and quotes from *m. Yebam.* 14:1, "A woman may be divorced with or without her will, but a man only with his will." Occasionally, says Abrahams, a wife was able to persuade the court to compel her husband to write her a Bill of Divorce, so that "by a legal fiction . . . the act would still be described as voluntary on the husband's part" (p. 75). Cf. also Z. W. Falk, "Jewish Private Law," *The Jewish People in the First Century* (*Compendia Rerum Iudaicarum ad Novum Testamentum;* 10 vols.; ed. S. Safrai and M. Stern: Philadelphia: Fortress, 1974-) 1. 517-18; and J. Fitzmyer, "Matthean Divorce Texts," 203-205.

113. K. Berger (*Die Gesetzesauslegung Jesu*, 1. 542) writes that the reproach of *sklērokardia* (10:5) is in keeping with Mark's "hardening theory." If so, it is possible that this conflict story (10:2-9) is a Marcan composition altogether. Berger's conclusion, however, that the conflict story originated with Mark in polemics with Judaism (intending to show Judaism's apostasy) is not convincing. The fact that the pericope is located in a catechetical series (10:1-27) indicates that for Mark the thrust was catechetical, not polemical.

114. Josephus (*J. W.* 2.8.14 §164-166) describes the Sadducees. He says that "as for the persistence of the soul after death, penalties in the underworld, and rewards, they will have none of them." Acts 23:8 has, "the Sadducees say that there is no resurrection." Cf. also Acts 4:1-3. Additional texts are cited by W. Lane, *Mark*, 427 (especially n. 37).

115. Actually in Deuteronomy this law applies only when two brothers live together.

116. For the view that Mark 12:26-27 is an addition to the rest of the pericope, see R. Bultmann, *Synoptic Tradition*, 26; B. H. Branscomb, *Mark*, 218-219; F. W. Beare, *Earliest Records*, 213; A. Suhl, *Die Funktion der alttestamentlichen Zitate*, 70; and E. Schweizer, *Mark*, 245. For the view that 12:26-27 was a unit with 12:18-25 from the beginning, see E. Lohmeyer, *Markus*, 257; and V. Taylor, *Mark*, 480.

117. Vincent Talyor (*Behind the Third Gospel* [Oxford: Oxford University, 1926] 99-100) has written that while the Lucan passage as a whole (20:27-40) has 63.8% of the words given in Mark 12:18-27 (almost verbatim agreement in Luke 20:27-33; and 70.5% agreement in 20:37-38), the percentage is just under 24 in Luke 20:34-36. F. W. Beare (*Earliest Records*, 212-213) concurs that Luke 20:34-36 is based on a non-Marcan source.

118. The quotations from Justin Martyr are translated from the Greek texts published in *Synopsis Quattuor Evangeliorum* (ed. Kurt Aland), 385. The quotation from the *Pseudo-Titus Epistle* is from *NT Apocrypha* (eds. Hennecke-Schneemelcher/Wilson), 2. 155.

119. There is also a saying in rabbinic literature, attributed to Rab (a teacher of the third century A.D.), which indicates again that the saying was independent and circulated in different versions: "Rab used to say, In the world

to come there is no eating or drinking or marrying or envy or hate; but the pious rest with crowns upon their heads, and are satisfied with the glory of God" *(b. Ber. 17a;* reference in Str-B, 1. 890); quoted from *The Babylonian Talmud* (I. Epstein).

120. These quotations are taken from *APOT,* 2. 509 and 276.

121. The phrase *ho aiōn ekeinos* appears nowhere else in the New Testament.

122. Cf. Hugh Anderson, "The Old Testament in Mark's Gospel," *The Use of the Old Testament in the New* (ed. J. Efird) 300, who writes, "The argument is of course a plea for life beyond death as a life of unbroken communion with God and not for resurrection strictly speaking." On the other hand, E. Earle Ellis ("Jesus, the Sadducees, and Qumran," *NTS* 10 [1963/64] 274-279, and *Luke,* 234-246) sees in the passage an argument for resurrection. According to him, the passage presupposes the notion of a "living God" who, in keeping with his covenant with the patriarchs, resurrects them (and therefore others). But, contra Ellis, the point of the passage is that the *patriarchs are living,* not that God is the "living God" who keeps his covenant. The same criticism applies to D. H. van Daalen, "Some Observations on Mark 12, 24-27," *SE* 4 (1968) 241-245; and W. Lane, *Mark,* 429-430.

123. The four quotations from Josephus are from translations by H. St. John Thackery in *Josephus* (LCL; 9 vols.; Cambridge: Harvard University, 1926-65) 2. 385, 387; 9. 13; 3. 601, 603; and 2. 381, 383.

124. For the view that Josephus has attributed a Hellenistic understanding of the soul and immortality to the Pharisees, see Norman Bentwich, *Josephus* (Philadelphia: Jewish Publication Society of America, 1940) 116-117. For the view that he attributed the same to the Essenes, see Frank M. Cross, *The Ancient Library of Qumran* (rev. ed.; Garden City: Doubleday & Company, 1961) 92; Helmer Ringgren, *The Faith of Qumran* (Philadelphia: Fortress, 1963) 151; and Matthew Black, "The Account of the Essenes in Hippolytus and Josephus," *The Background of the New Testament and Its Eschatology* (ed. W. D. Davies and D. Daube; Cambridge: Cambridge University, 1964) 172.

125. Cf. G. B. Gray in *APOT,* 2. 630, who writes that "it is the Pharisaic piety that breathes through the Psalms." Cf. also Robert H. Pfeiffer, *History of New Testament Times with an Introduction to the Apocrypha* (New York: Harper and Row, 1949) 63, and Leonhard Rost, *Judaism Outside the Hebrew Canon: An Introduction to the Documents* (Nashville: Abingdon, 1976) 119.

126. These quotations are from the translation by G. B. Gray in *APOT,* 2. 635 and 646.

127. Those who claim that there is a doctrine of resurrection include Matthew Black, *The Scrolls and Christian Origins* (London: Charles Scribner's Sons, 1961) 173-191; and Manahem Mansoor, *The Thanksgiving Hymns* (Leiden: E. J. Brill, 1961) 84-89. R. B. Laurin ("The Question of Immortality in the Qumran Hodayot," *JSS* 3 [1958] 344-355) finds no such doctrine, nor does Eduard Lohse, *The New Testament Environment* (Nashville: Abingdon, 1976) 195. For a comprehensive discussion, see George W. E. Nickelsburg, Jr., *Resurrection, Immortality and Eternal Life in Intertestamental Judaism* (HTS 26; Cambridge: Harvard University, 1972) 144-159.

128. So R. Pfeiffer, *History of New Testament Times,* 326-327, and L. Rost, *Judaism Outside the Hebrew Canon,* 59.

129. "Throughout his writings Philo speaks of the immortality of the soul, rather than the resurrection of the body." So writes Henry A. Wolfson, *Philo: Foundations of Religious Philosophy in Judaism, Christianity, and Islam*

(2 vols.; Cambridge: Harvard University, 1947) 1. 404. Wolfson provides several references. He also writes (p. 396) that "Resurrection of the body and immortality of the soul are the two forms which [beliefs about the hereafter] took, the former primarily among Palestinian Jews, the latter primarily among Hellenistic Jews."

130. R. Pfeiffer, *History of New Testament Times*, 215. Cf. L. Rost, *Judaism Outside the Hebrew Canon*, 110, who also attributes the work to a Hellenistic Alexandrian Jew in the first half of the first century A.D.

131. Cf. G. Nickelsburg, *Resurrection, Immortality, and Eternal Life*, 109-111.

132. Quotations are from *APOT*, 2. 674-675, and 682. It has been suggested that within these three passages (at 7:19; 13:17; and 16:25) there are "perhaps Christian interpolations;" so Israel Abrahams, "Books of Maccabees," *JE*, 8. 244. But Abrahams gives no reasons for his assertion, nor does he indicate specifically the extent of the interpolations which may, in his view, exist.

133. The origins of the *Testaments of the Twelve Patriarchs* are obscure. It is widely affirmed that, whatever their origins, they have been edited by Christians who supplied their own interpolations. Nevertheless, that they were written in Palestine is quite certain. So L. Rost, *Judaism Outside the Hebrew Canon*, 145. R. Charles (*APOT*, 2. 282) concluded that the older traditions of the *Testaments* were written by a Pharisee expressing anti-Hellenistic Jewish piety of Maccabean times. Cf. also R. Pfeiffer, *History of New Testament Times*, 65. Surveys of critical opinion (in addition to Rost's discussion) are given by Morton Smith, "The Testaments of the Twelve Patriarchs," *IDB*, 4. 575-579; M. E. Stone, "The Testaments of the Twelve Patriarchs," *IDBSup*, 877 (with bibliography); and H. Dixon Slingerland, *The Testaments of the Twelve Patriarchs: A Critical History of Research* (SBLMS 21; Missoula: Scholar's Press, 1977).

134. Quotation from translation by R. Charles, *APOT*, 2. 324.

135. For resurrection doctrine in *T. Judah*, see G. Nickelsburg, *Resurrection, Immortality, and Eternal Life*, 34-35.

136. Quotation from *APOT*, 2. 359.

137. For resurrection doctrine in *T. Benj.*, see G. Nickelsburg, *Resurrection, Immortality, and Eternal Life*, 141-142.

138. Cf. A. Suhl, *Die Funktion der alttestamentlichen Zitate*, 71-72.

139. Luke (20:38b) adds "for all live unto him," which is similar to statements in the Hellenistic work 4 Macc. 7:19 ("they [the patriarchs] live unto God") and 16:25 ("men dying unto God live unto God").

140. Mark 12:27b ("you are quite wrong") reiterates material in 12:24 ("you are wrong") which is considered an addition, as maintained above.

141. R. Bultmann, *Synoptic Tradition*, 26.

142. Ibid., 48.

Part Three
The
Collection and Use
of the Conflict Stories
in the Primitive Church

V. Five Conflict Stories (Mark 2:1-3:6): Their Collection and Setting in the Primitive Church

Within Mark 2:1–3:6 there are five conflict stories: the Healing of the Paralytic (2:1-12); Eating with Tax-Collectors and Sinners (2:15-17); the Question about Fasting (2:18-20); Plucking Grain on the Sabbath (2:23-28); and Healing on the Sabbath (3:1-5). The last is followed by a comment (3:6).

Various scholars have held, for some time now, that these five stories had been collected together into a written source prior to Mark, and that the latter took up the collection and placed it into his gospel.[1] Certain others have held that while 2:1–3:6 does indeed constitute a collection, the collection was made by Mark himself.[2] Finally, H.-W. Kuhn has argued recently that the collection does not span 2:1–3:6, but 2:1–2:28, and that the collection was compiled in written form in Mark's community in the decade prior to Mark's writing of his gospel.[3]

Kuhn's argument that the collection consisted of 2:1-28 only deserves some attention before proceeding further. He argues that the pericope in 3:1-5 (the healing of a man with a withered hand on the sabbath) was added by Mark himself to the collection in 2:1-28.[4] It differs from the other four conflict stories, he says, and therefore did not exist with them in a collection, in the following ways: (1) it does not contain a Christological logion, while the others do (2:10, 17b, 19-20, 28); (2) the opponents of Jesus are not identified, while they are identified in the others (2:6, 16, 18, 24); and (3) no challenge is given to Jesus in spoken form, contrary to the others (2:7, 16, 18, 24); the opponents merely "watched" Jesus (3:2) to see whether he would heal the man on the sabbath.

To conclude on the basis of these points, however, that 3:1-5 does not belong to the earlier collection is not convincing. The points he makes are themselves debatable. First, while there is no Christological assertion in 3:1-5 in the manner of the other conflict stories, the peric-

ope as a whole is surely Christological; for the primitive community
the dominical words "to do good" and "to save life" refer to the
saving action of the Messiah.[5] Second, while the opponents of Jesus
are not identified in 3:1-5, it is naturally assumed that the persons
referred to in the words "they watched him" (3:2) are the Pharisees
of the previous pericope (2:24). Moreover, there is another conflict
story in which the opponents are not identified. At 2:18-20 (the
Question about Fasting) it is only certain unnamed persons who
come to ask of Jesus a question (2:18a). Finally, Kuhn is correct in
saying that, contrary to other conflict stories, there is no charge given
in verbal form against Jesus in 3:1-5. However, it must be seen that
in this case the dominical saying, a question (3:4), does not lend itself
to a verbal attack and, as R. Bultmann has written, "the lurking silence
of the opponent (3:2)" can have the significance of a statement.[6]

There are reasons outside of this discussion for holding that all of
2:1–3:6 is a literary unit. First, 2:1–3:6 interrupts the sequence of the
Gospel of Mark.[7] Chapter 1 ends with Jesus healing a leper, after
which it is written that "Jesus could *no longer* openly *enter a town,*
but was out in the country; and people came to him from every quarter" (1:45b). Chapter 2 opens with the words, "And when he returned
to Capernaum," thereby having Jesus *enter* into a *town.* At 3:7, however, following upon 2:1–3:6, Jesus withdraws with his disciples to
the sea, and people "from every quarter" (1:45b) come to him; they
come from Galilee, Judea, Jerusalem, Idumea, the Trans-Jordan, and
Tyre and Sidon. The section 2:1–3:6 therefore interrupts the narrative
sequence of 1:45b and 3:7. Second, the five conflict stories have the
same form (as conflict stories) and motif (opposition against Jesus on
points of law in Pharisaic understanding). And, finally, 3:1-5 fits together with the previous story (2:23-28) as a "complex of tradition." [8]
As a result of the first sabbath conflict in 2:23-28, Jesus is portrayed
as under observation (3:2) in the second instance by the same opponents as in the first. And while in the first the Pharisees tell him "it is
not lawful" for his disciples to act as they do (2:24), in the second
Jesus asks them whether "it is lawful" to heal (3:4). Having been
placed on the defensive (2:23-28), Jesus places the Pharisees in the
same position (3:1-5) by a question concerning healing, and thereby (for the Christian reader) gets the better of his opponents: Is it
lawful to do good and save life?

Although it is sometimes argued to the contrary, the collection of
stories in 2:1–3:6 must be regarded as a pre-Marcan composition.

This will be supported with more detail below, but here two points can be made. First, the section closes with a saying (3:6, "The Pharisees went out, and immediately held counsel with the Herodians against him, how to destroy him") which goes nowhere; Jesus is not put to death by these opponents (Pharisees and Herodians) either soon or later. It has been debated pro and con whether 3:6 comes "too soon within Mark's plan," as Albertz has put it.[9] Some writers have argued that 3:6 is a redactional sentence written by Mark himself, so that it does not come too soon.[10]

We shall argue in the next section, however, that arguments for Marcan composition of 3:6 are not compelling, and that it would have been written prior to Mark. Here it need only be said that while the "shadow of the cross" falls back upon the ministry of Jesus from time to time in Mark's Gospel (1:22; 2:20; 8:31; 9:31; 10:33; 11:18; 12:12; and, we should add, 3:6) prior to the passion narrative, 3:6 is more explicit in content. It is not a general summary of, nor an allusion to, the way set before Jesus, but a statement in which certain named opponents (Pharisees and Herodians) are said to have entered into collusion against him. The statement must have had meaning for its author and his readers. But, although these opponents reappear in the narrative again (12:13), where Mark introduces a series of conflict stories once more, it is clearly not these who (for Mark and his readers) figure into the arrest, trial, and death of Jesus in the passion narrative. In fact 12:13 neutralizes 3:6. Because of 3:6, Mark is compelled to reintroduce the Pharisees and Herodians in 12:13. But he does not have them carry out their alleged purposes of 3:6. He has them merely enter into debate with Jesus again. The weight of the passion tradition (in which it is the chief priests, scribes, and elders who act against Jesus) prevents him from having the Pharisees and Herodians enter into the proceedings leading to Jesus' death. In short, 3:6 causes a problem for Mark, and it must be considered pre-Marcan in origin.

A second consideration for holding that 2:1–3:6 has a pre-Marcan origin is that the term "Son of man" appears twice (2:10, 28) in the section (and the term is essential to the argument of the two pericopes in which it occurs, so its use is surely not redactional), but does not appear again until 8:28 and thereafter; this indicates that Mark has taken over a block of material which has the titles in it already.

On the basis of the foregoing, it is our purpose in the following paragraphs to pursue further the question of the origin and setting

of Mark 2:1–3:6. We shall attempt to determine the setting in which
2:1–3:6 would have been composed, and that will be the church of
Galilee in the first part of the decade A.D. 40-50. In doing so, we shall
add further considerations to the claim for a pre-Marcan composition
of the section, and we shall press toward conclusions which stand over
against those articulated by H.-W. Kuhn.

A. The Setting of the Collection

One of the most important indicators for the setting of 2:1–3:6 is
the material in 3:6. Although H.-W. Kuhn has argued on stylistic
grounds that 3:6 is a Marcan editorial link, this does not hold up,[11]
and what was said in the previous section militates against it. Virtually every commentator has admitted that the reference to the
Herodians contained in the verse is problematic. Apart from this reference in 3:6 (which is not reproduced in Matt. 12:14 and Luke
6:11), there is only one other reference to the Herodians in the New
Testament, viz., Mark 12:13 and its parallel in Matt. 22:16.[12] As to
the question of who the Herodians were, various commentators have
identified them as friends and supporters of Herod Antipas, and it has
thus been held that the Pharisees and Herodians—the religious and
political leaders together—conspired against Jesus.[13]

But ancient sources which refer to the Herodians [14] (aside from the
gospels) do not support this identification. It is not clear from these
sources that Herodians existed in the time of Jesus,[15] and therefore one
cannot demonstrate on external evidence that the references to them in
3:6 and 12:13 reflect events in the ministry of Jesus. The question
arises as to why Herodians would be found in a Jerusalem setting
(12:13), since Herod Antipas, a Galilean king, had no authority
there; Judea was a Roman imperial province.

The problem can be solved on the basis of a suggestion by B. W.
Bacon.[16] Bacon says that Mark has lapsed into an anachronism in
his reference to the Herodians. The Herodians, he says, were those
Jews identified by Epiphanius who took Herod as a ruler promised in
messianic prophecy. Epiphanius writes concerning the "Herodians"
that they "considered Herod the Messiah, having thought that Herod
himself was the Messiah expected in all the writings of the law and
the prophets," and that they applied to him the prophecy (Gen.
49:10) that "the sceptre shall not depart from Judah." [17] But this
Herod was not Herod Antipas (King of Galilee, 4 B.C.-A.D. 40).

Rather, Epiphanius has Herod Agrippa I in mind, to whom Claudius restored sovereignty in Galilee in A.D. 40 and Judea in A.D. 41, thus uniting all of Palestine under his rule.[18] Bacon says that the messianic prophecy represented precisely the hope of Jewish nationalists of the Pharisaic party, such as Josephus, in the time of Agrippa I.

Bacon's suggestion gains a high degree of probability when seen in light of first century history and various texts. The earlier rulers of the Herod family (Herod the Great and Herod Antipas), being of Idumean ancestry, were not considered genuinely Jewish. But Agrippa I, the grandson of Herod the Great, was a Hasmonean through his grandmother Mariamne. With him as king it was possible that the "sceptre" would "not depart from Judah."

In addition to the words of Epiphanius, in which it is said that the "Herodians" believed Herod (Agrippa I) to be the Messiah, there is a reference to the same in a second text. That is in (pseudepigraphal?) Tertullian's *Against All Heresies*, I, where the Herodians are spoken of as persons "who said that Herod was the Christ." [19] Which Herod is meant is not said, but it is nevertheless a second tradition in which an identification of the Herodians is made along the lines of that given by Epiphanius.

That Agrippa I gained the favor of the Jews, and of the Pharisees in particular, is widely attested. Josephus (a Hellenistic Pharisee) speaks of him in glowing terms:

> He scrupulously observed the traditions of his people. He neglected no rite of purification, and no day passed for him without the prescribed sacrifice.[20]

And in the Mishnah the popular attitude toward him is expressed as warm. A scene is related in which Agrippa, as King of the Jews, reads a portion of the Torah in the Temple court at the Feast of Tabernacles. After receiving the scroll from the high priest, Agrippa sat down and read:

> And when he reached [the words of the law; Deut. 17:15], "Thou mayest not put a foreigner over thee which is not thy brother," his eyes flowed with tears; but they called out to him, "Our brother art thou! our brother art thou! our brother art thou!" [21]

As Bacon has suggested, it is with Agrippa I, known for his pro-Pharisaic policies,[22] that a coalition of Herodians and Pharisees could exist for the first time. Furthermore, it is Agrippa I who is referred to in the book of Acts as a persecutor of the church in concert with "the Jews":

> About that time Herod the king laid violent hands upon some who belonged to the church. He killed James the brother of John with the sword; and when he saw that it pleased the Jews, he proceeded to arrest Peter also (12:1-3).

> And Peter came to himself, and said, "Now I am sure that the Lord has sent his angel and rescued me from the hand of Herod and from all that the Jewish people were expecting" (12:11).

But Bacon's assertion that it was Mark who lapsed into an anachronism at 3:6 is doubtful. One cannot produce evidence that Herodians existed at the time he wrote his gospel (presumably in the late seventh or early eighth decade A.D.). Matthew and Luke, on the contrary, omit the reference to the Herodians in their parallels (Matt. 12:14; Luke 6:11), because the term is apparently meaningless to readers toward the end of the first century. With the death of Agrippa I in A.D. 44 there was no further question of using the Herodian dynasty "to solve the problem of Palestine." [23]

It is more likely that the reference to the Pharisees as conspiring with the Herodians (Mark 3:6) was made during the time of the coalition between the Herodian supporters of Agrippa I and the Pharisees, i.e., the early part of the fifth decade, when Agrippa carried on his persecution of the Palestinian Christians.[24] This gives a terminus ante quem for the collection of the five conflict stories in Mark 2:1—3:6 as A.D. 44. The place of collection would most likely be Galilee, as we shall go on to establish. The collector would have been a member of the Christian community who in his own day knew the opponents of the church to be the Pharisees and Herodians, the supporters of the Herodian dynasty who believed in Agrippa as the promised Messiah who would restore the sceptre to Judah. The collector who penned the words of Mark 3:6 looked back on the ministry of Jesus as opposed by the same type of opposition he knew—that of Galilean Pharisees essentially—but in anachronistic fashion, and writing for his own time, he portrayed the Herodians as opposed to the true Messiah Jesus, as well. Not writing history in the strict (modern) sense, he charged the present opposition with collusion "from the beginning." [25]

If such a reconstruction can be accepted, it means that we have in Mark 2:1—3:6 a source behind Mark's gospel that fixed primitive traditions within some fifteen years or less after the death of Jesus.[26] Furthermore, we have asserted that this source comes from the home-land of Jesus, Galilee. Such an assertion can be maintained by giving attention to two questions: Did such a church exist in Galilee, and do the traditions themselves appear to be Galilean?

1. A Galilean Church?

It has been held by various writers that there was a Christian community in Galilee, perhaps headquartered at Capernaum, soon after the death and resurrection of Jesus.[27] The evidence for the existence of such a community is fragmentary, but it rests on some fair certainties:

First, it was in Galilee that Jesus recruited disciples (Mark 1:16, 19; 3:14-19; John 1:43-45) and attracted other followers (Mark 1:45; 3:7, 13). These, or at least some of them, one can assume, would naturally have formed the nucleus of a primitive community in Gali-lee after the resurrection,[28] aside from the larger question whether the disciples fled there immediately after the crucifixion in anticipa-tion of resurrection appearances and/or the parousia.[29]

Second, although the evidence from the ancient period is indeed small, there is reference to a Christian community in Galilee at Acts 9:31 at the time of Paul's call as an apostle (early part of the fourth decade). There are also the traditions of John 21 and the apocryphal *Gospel of Peter* (14) that the apostles themselves returned to their occupations in Galilee.

Third, the evidence of one later writer seems to indicate that there were Christians residing in Galilee at least in the latter part of the first century, if not earlier. Eusebius records the statement of Hege-sippus (fl. A.D. 180) that grandsons of Jude, the brother of Jesus, lived in Palestine in Domitian's time (A.D. 81-96). These men, who were Christians, owned a farm in Palestine of 25 acres which they worked themselves. They "ruled the churches" there also.[30] It is not indicated, but we would assume that their farm and therefore the churches they ruled were in Galilee, the homeland of Jesus' family.[31]

2. Galilean Traditions?

That the traditions contained in the conflict stories of 2:1–3:6 are Galilean appears certain. Not only are the conflict stories set in Galilee by their place references (Mark 2:1, 13, 15). There are other indicators within them pointing to a Galilean origin and final editing of them as well.

a. The Galilean Milieu

The five conflict stories presuppose a Galilean milieu, as can be seen in three ways. First, the conflict stories deal with interpretation of the law and its observance, not with matters related to the temple or Judean interests, which are evident, for instance, in the Jerusalem conflict stories of Mark 11:27-33 and 12:13-37.[32] Pharisees and scribes would have been found in the villages of Galilee, and the issues debated in the conflict stories of 2:1—3:6 presuppose the oral traditions of Pharisaic interpretations of the Torah, rather than the more conservative legislation of the Sadducees and priests, for whom oral tradition was not binding.

Second, at least three of the conflict stories almost certainly presuppose Galilee as their setting on the basis of the activities which provoke conflict. The Plucking of Grain on the Sabbath (2:23-28) presupposes such. While some grains have been grown sparsely in certain valleys of Judea, it is primarily in Galilee that there are plains upon which grains have been grown abundantly. In ancient times crops were so plentiful that grains were exported from there.[33] The tradition of Jesus' disciples as having been criticized for plucking grain on the sabbath is most likely to have originated in Galilee.[34] The setting of the Healing of the Paralytic (2:1-12) is also Galilean, for it is there that the mud-thatched roof (2:4) was characteristic of houses generally in this period.[35] And the setting for Eating with Tax Collectors and Sinners (2:15-17), it has been said, "naturally belongs to Galilee, for Jesus would more likely come in contact with tax-collectors in Capernaum than anywhere else." [36]

Finally, as a third observation as to why the collection of conflict stories as a whole draws on Galilean traditions, the Galilean place references themselves (2:1, 13, 15) cannot all be attributed to Mark. The reference in 2:13 may well be Marcan.[37] But within 2:1 there are two references to the Galilean setting of the first conflict story (2:1-12). The first reference ("Capernaum") may be Marcan,[38] but the second ("it was reported that he was at home," i.e., Capernaum; Nazareth is not likely to be meant, but even that is in Galilee) belongs to the tradition.[39] The place reference in 2:15 ("he sat at table in his house") can also be considered a part of the pre-Marcan tradition. There is no need to assign it to Mark, since its wording is not typical of that found elsewhere in Marcan editorial links, and one is hard pressed to give any reason why Mark would want to locate the conflict story in Jesus' home.

Taking these three observations together, it is not likely that it was Mark who first placed the "Galilean" conflict story section into a Galilean setting. The section contains traditions that originated in Galilee, and it appears in Mark's Gospel within the Galilean ministry of Jesus not by Mark's design alone, but because internal, traditional references to a Galilean setting require it.

b. The Galilean Opponents

The opponents of Jesus in this collection of conflict stories are scribes (2:6, 16) and Pharisees (2:16, 18, 24; 3:6), plus the Herodians in 3:6. In contrast to the Jerusalem conflict stories (cf. 11:27; 12:18), his opponents are never chief priests, elders, and Sadducees. If the Galilean collection of conflict stories contains genuine historical information, one would naturally expect that these latter figures peculiar to Jerusalem would not be given as his opponents. It is questionable, however, whether in the earliest stage of their development the stories should even contain references to scribes and Pharisees as opponents. In two of them the opponents are not identified as such at all. In 2:18 it is simply "they come" to Jesus to ask a question, and in 3:2 it is simply "they watched him." Who these opponents were is not indicated. Bultmann has suggested that at the earliest stage of the conflict stories "the questioners were for the most part unspecified persons, but that as the tradition developed they were characterized as opponents, Pharisees or scribes." [40] There is, he says, "an active tendency seeking always to present the opponents of Jesus as scribes and Pharisees." [41]

It is of great interest to notice that there are pericopes within the collection of 2:1–3:6 in which the opponents are not identified by name (scribes, Pharisees, or whatever). This would indicate, if Bultmann is correct, that the collection is indeed primitive. It contains indicators of the transition being made, i.e., the transition from presenting the opponents (or questioners) of Jesus as unidentified to presenting them as full-blown representatives of "official Judaism." One of the purposes of 3:6 is to identify the Pharisees as the opponents of Jesus for the whole collection, thereby completing the transition at the level at which the collection was completed. In Galilee

of the early fifth decade the scribes and Pharisees would be the representatives of Judaism who would have opposed the church there.
That they would also have been actual opponents of Jesus in matters of law cannot be denied (cf. the Q passage Matt. 23:23//Luke
11:42 showing division between Jesus and the Pharisees). But the
fact that they are identified in 3:6 as the opponents of Jesus as a
conclusion to all of the conflict stories in 2:1–3:5 indicates that the
collector (for his own purposes) used the five to show that "official
Judaism" conspired in the death of Jesus on the grounds that he
violated Pharisaic law.

It has been recognized that there is a disagreement between the
early part of Mark and the latter part as to who the Jewish opponents
of Jesus were.[42] In Chapters 2 through 13 Jesus' opponents are usually
the scribes (2:6, 16; 9:14; 12:38), Pharisees (2:18, 24; 3:6; 8:11; 10:2;
12:13), or both (7:1, 5). In four cases the opponents are the chief
priests and scribes (8:31; 10:33; 11:18, 27), and twice the elders are
mentioned along with the chief priests and scribes (8:31; 11:27).
But in Chapters 14 and 15 the Pharisees are not mentioned at all.
There the chief priests are the enemies of Jesus, and the scribes and
elders are mentioned only in connection with them.[43] Joseph C. Weber,
Jr., has concluded that

> . . . there is no definite historical connection between Jesus' oppo-
> nents in the pre-Passion tradition and those in the Passion material.
> . . . Jesus encounters opposition on the part of some scribes and
> Pharisees over the question of Torah interpretation, but there is no
> historical evidence of an open break or of any progressively increas-
> ing hostility during Jesus' Galilean ministry. The historical relation-
> ship between Jesus and his opponents in the pre-Passion material does
> not serve to explain Jesus' execution. Both the opponents and the
> crucial issues are different in the two bodies of material.[44]

But if the section 2:1–3:6 is in fact a collection of conflict stories
made in the Galilean church, references to the scribes and Pharisees
as opponents of Jesus and the closing statement of 3:6 that the
Pharisees sought Jesus' death can be readily understood. The church
in Galilee would have been quite remote from the representatives of
Judaism who were the actual enemies of Jesus, i.e., the chief priests of
Jerusalem.[45] The representatives of Judaism whom they knew, who
opposed the Christian movement, would have been the scribes and
Pharisees.

B. Mark's Editorial Work

The editorial links within 2:1–3:6 are largely, with a few exceptions, non-Marcan (pre-Marcan). Typical Marcan connecting words [46] are "again" at 2:1, 13; 3:1; "he went out" in 2:13; [47] and the phrase "beside the sea" in 2:13.[48] Generally the introductions to the five conflict stories are relatively free of editorial links.[49] The introductory words are brief and, for the most part, are imbedded in the tradition; they provide settings which would have been formulated in a stage of transmission prior to Mark's use of them.

Nevertheless, in addition to the words and phrases already mentioned, there are longer portions of the section in which the hand of Mark the evangelist can be detected. Some consist of clauses and sentences. There are four: (1) 2:1a ("and when he returned to Capernaum after some days"); [50] (2) 2:2b ("and he was speaking the word to them"); [51] (3) 2:18a ("and John's disciples and the Pharisees were fasting"); [52] and (4) 3:5a ("and having looked around at them with anger, grieved at their hardness of heart").[53]

There are also two longer additions to 2:1–3:6 which Mark made. The first is at 2:13-14. Marcan editorial words abound in 2:13 (see above); and 2:14, the call of Levi, while perhaps traditional in content, is modelled on the call of the four disciples (Peter, Andrew, James, and John) in 1:16-20.[54] It appears that Mark has introduced the material in 2:13-14 as an introduction to the conflict story of 2:15-17 in which Jesus eats with tax collectors and sinners.

Finally, the two little sayings on patches and wineskins in 2:21-22 appear to have been added by Mark.[55] They have nothing to do with the question at hand, that of fasting, but function to emphasize further the difference between Christian practices and those of Judaism. They break up the sequence of an otherwise uninterrupted series of conflict stories, and it is likely that Mark added them for the sake of Gentile Christian readers, for whom it was impossible to express their religious life through the old forms of Judaism.[56]

C. Results

Our analysis leads to the conclusion that Mark has taken over material from a written source consisting of the following: 2:1b-2a, 3-12, 15-17, 18b-20, 23-28; 3:1-4, 5b-6. Furthermore, we conclude that this source was formulated as a collection of conflict stories in the Galilean church of the fifth decade (ca. A.D. 40-44), and that it served as a response to Pharisaic criticism. The conflict stories are not to be considered transcripts of actual debates of Christians with Pharisees, nor as sources for carrying on debate, but as a body of material by which the church's own way of thinking and acting could be informed in response to criticism from outside.

More must be said about this. But it is necessary first to deal with the position of H.-W. Kuhn, which has been argued so persuasively, and which differs from my own. Kuhn maintains that the *Sitz im Leben* of the individual stories and of the collection as a whole (2:1-28 only) is polemics between primitive Christianity and Judaism.[57] However, he says, the "Judaism" at stake is not Judaism *outside* the primitive community; it is Jewish Christianity *within*. The stories individually and as a collection were composed "by teachers for teachers" in a mixed community of Jews and Gentiles, probably in Syria, and were composed specifically by the latter as a response to the former.[58] The Jewish Christians, in this view, attempted to maintain certain Jewish practices, which the Gentile Christians repudiated. The collection, he says, was composed as a written source in the decade prior to the writing of Mark's gospel.[59]

Kuhn bases his position on several points. He thinks, first, that the question of table fellowship (Jesus' eating with tax collectors and sinners, Mark 2:15-17) has to do with the relationship between Jewish and Gentile Christians, particularly in regard to table fellowship.[60] This appears to be Kuhn's major point. He goes on at great length to show that it was a problem in primitive Christianity elsewhere (Gal. 2:11-21; Rom. 14; Acts 11:3); and he claims that "sinners" is a cipher for "Gentiles" in Mark 2:15-17, so that table fellowship between Gentile and Jewish Christians is the issue dealt with in the conflict story. Second, he argues that the collection was composed in a Greek-speaking community, and that it therefore is not likely to have been composed in Palestine; Syria is more probable.[61] Here he maintains that certain word usages are typically Greek and impossible in Aramaic.[62] And finally, he says that the argumentation of the collection would have been completely unintelligible for Jews outside of the Christian community. The persons addressed must have been Christians who had come out of Judaism. They must be considered Christians because the argumentation is filled with Christological sayings; such sayings would have had no authority in polemics with Judaism.[63]

Objections can be raised to each of these points. That the conflict story on eating with tax collectors and sinners (2:15-17) speaks to the issue of table fellowship between Jewish and Gentile Christians is not satisfactory for two reasons. First, the identification of "sinners" with Gentile Christians appears forced. The phrase "tax collectors and sinners" is found in Q (Luke 7:34//Matt. 11:19), and one would not insist that for the Q community "sinners" would designate Gentiles (or Gentile Christians). Neither does the term "sinners" have such a connotation in Luke 15:2 ("This man receives sinners and eats with them"), nor does the term refer to Gentiles elsewhere (e.g., Simon Peter at Luke 5:8; the sinful woman at 7:37, 39; the Galileans at 13:2; the tax collector at 18:13; and Zacchaeus at 19:7; cf. also 15:7). The phrase "tax collectors and sinners" must be considered a stylized formulation which describes in a general way certain persons with whom Jesus had fellowship, which is attested in three streams of tradition (Mark, Q, and L).[64] Second, the question asked in the conflict story (2:16, "Why does he eat with tax collectors and sinners?") is directed at the disciples. At the level of composition it must be concluded that "disciples" is a surrogate for "church," and that it is the church which violates acceptable conduct.[65]

And finally, the dominical saying ("I came not to call the righteous, but sinners," 2:17b) concerns the saving influence of Jesus *pro nobis*. It is the familiar form of the verb "to come" followed by the infinitive of purpose.[66] All such sayings are summaries of the Christian community concerning the soteriological function of Jesus known in the church itself. The saying would not have been used for polemics within the church, but as a Christian affirmation within a non-Christian environment.

Nor do Kuhn's other claims hold up to criticism. The fact that there are certain word usages which cannot be expressed in Aramaic does not mean that the individual stories and the collection as a whole were first composed in a Greek-speaking milieu, as Kuhn himself acknowledges.[67] These consist of three items which could have been introduced at the level of translation or further editing. [68] Finally, Kuhn's point that the argumentation of the collection would have been unintelligible (and, by implication, ineffective) in debate with Jews outside of the Christian community carries no weight if one holds that the collection was for use in the Christian community to help shape the latter's way of thinking and acting in response to the larger Jewish environment. Saying that the collection was written as a response to Jewish criticism does not mean that it was written for Jewish readers.[69]

For example, Matthew carries on polemics against the Pharisees, but that does not mean that Matthew wrote his gospel (or parts of it) for Pharisaic opponents to read; and the Gospel of John portrays controversies with "the Jews," but again this does not mean that it was written for a Jewish readership. Neither gospel was written with the assumption that its assertions are effective in debate with Jewish opponents; assertions made are for Christian self-consciousness over against Judaism, and they are effective only for believing Christians. It can be held that the collection of conflict stories was likewise addressed to Christians, not Jews, who live as a small minority in Galilee within a Jewish majority environment (not a sealed-off community within), and who were attempting to work out a way of life (thought and action) in response to the larger social setting.

But Kuhn's position is untenable on other grounds as well. First, it must be seen that certain conflict stories preserve within themselves ordinances which would have been brought into the church by Jewish Christians, and a *positive* evaluation is placed upon these "Jewish" practices. For example, fasting is not rejected; it is merely transferred to another day (2:20). And the sabbath is not rejected; it is to be observed, although in a new way (2:28; 3:4).[70] This points to a controversy between Jewish Christianity and Judaism, not a controversy carried on by a Gentile majority (or power group) against a Jewish minority (or faction) in a given church setting.

Second, the first conflict story (2:1-12), which establishes that forgiveness of sins is a present reality in the church ("on earth") given through the Son of man (2:10), hardly deals with an inner-Christian controversy (between Jewish and Gentile Christians). It is difficult to imagine that a Jewish Christian would take issue with such a claim in the decade (A.D. 60-70) prior to the writing of Mark's Gospel. Certainly the claim of forgiveness in the name of Jesus as an issue must reflect a Christian self-understanding over against Judaism.[71] Furthermore, the passage is not likely to have been composed in a Hellenistic milieu; verse 2:7 has an Aramaic background, which points to an earlier Semitic origin of the story.[72]

Third, as indicated previously, the setting of each story and of the collection as a whole is Galilee, and the stories relate vivid scenes from Jesus' ministry in that locale. Kuhn has nothing to say on this point. But a conclusion concerning the setting of these stories in the collection as a whole must take the question of Galilean interest into account. Would Hellenistic Gentile Christians of Syria in the decade of A.D. 60-70 provide the wealth of Galilean detail which the stories provide? It is not likely.

Fourth, it is significant that the opponents are designated in various ways in the individual stories: scribes (2:6), scribes of the Pharisees (2:16), Pharisees (2:24), and unnamed opponents (2:18; 3:2). There is no highly-stylized and uniform designation. The final verse (3:6) clears up the matter so that all the opponents are to be taken as Pharisaic. But one gets the impression that in certain instances vivid memory is at work; this is particularly the case in 2:18 and 3:2 (both verses are contained within unitary stories).

In sum, the stories reflect a setting in the 40s in Galilee more than the 60s in Syria by their vivid twin portrayal of Galilean surroundings and of the attitude, words, and actions of Jesus as remembered by the first generation of Jewish Christians there.

We have argued, prior to and during this critique of Kuhn, that the collection of conflict stories in Mark 2:1–3:16 was formulated in the Galilean church in the fifth decade (ca. A.D. 40-44). This claim rests, first, on our discussion of the historical allusion in 3:6 to the Herodians conspiring with the Pharisees. It rests, second, on the fact that the traditions are specifically Galilean, and one can maintain that it is in Galilean Christianity that such traditions of Jesus would be remembered, treasured, and put to use. And, finally, the opponents of Jesus are, whenever they are named, the scribes and Pharisees—the representatives of Judaism which were known to the church in Galilee.[73]

There is another factor which adds further weight to this proposal. First-century Galilee does not have a good reputation in rabbinic literature. Its people, who had been converted to Judaism only about 120 B.C. and following, are cast in a bad light, and surely the Galilean Christians, who came out of such a background, were objects of the same negative estimation that the Pharisees expressed toward the Galileans generally in the first century. During the early decades of the first century A.D., the Pharisees were beginning their infiltration into Galilee, and eventually Tiberias became the Pharisaic capital of Galilee and the center of Palestinian Judaism in the second and third centuries.[74] But during the first century there was no easy accommodation. The Jews of Galilee did not admire the Pharisees,[75] and the Pharisees considered the Galileans crude, undisciplined, and even contemptuous of learning.[76] For example, Rabban Johanan ben Zakkai (ca. A.D. 1-80), on leaving 'Arav of Galilee after 18 years of efforts there in the first half of the first century A.D., is reported to have exclaimed:

> O Galilee, Galilee! You hate the Torah!
> Your end will be to be besieged! [77]

Such is the assessment of at least one Pharisee concerning the Galileans.

But what is striking about the Galilean conflict stories, in contrast, is that they preserve traditions in which there are words of approval by Jesus concerning the Galilean *'am ha-ares* who followed him.[78] They preserve traditions which show that Jesus considered his Galilean followers approved before God (presumably because they accepted his preaching of the coming of God's reign), in spite of Pharisaic judgment to the contrary. This is especially apparent in 2:15-17 (Eating with Tax Collectors and Sinners), but it is also seen in those pericopes on Forgiveness (2:1-12), on Fasting (2:18-20), and the two on sabbath observance (2:23-28; 3:1-5). The conflict stories of 2:1– 3:6 are not simply concerned with *Jesus,* nor with questions of doctrine (which are so much more important in other conflict stories, e.g., in 3:22-30; 10:2-9; 11:27-33; 12:13-17, 18-27); their concern is to a large extent with *Jesus' disciples,* who came out of the ranks of the Galilean *'am ha-ares,* and they seek to establish their approval before God, regardless of their inability or lack of desire to measure up to Pharisaic standards of religious observance. It is the Galilean church to which we should naturally look as the milieu in which these traditions were preserved and collected.

The question remains, however, whether Mark 2:1–3:6, as a pre-Marcan collection, could have existed as a unit apart from a larger gospel framework. Granted that 2:1–3:6 appears to be a self-contained unit, could it have been composed, and could it have been used, apart from the rest of Mark's Gospel? This question is taken up in the next chapter.

NOTES

1. These include M. Albertz, *Streitgespräche,* 5; K. L. Schmidt, *Der Rahmen der Geschichte Jesu,* 103-104; R. Bultmann, *Synoptic Tradition,* 349; B. S. Easton, "A Primitive Tradition in Mark," 85-101; R. H. Lightfoot, *History and Interpretation in the Gospels* (New York: Harper, 1934) 110; B. H. Branscomb, *Mark,* xxiii, 41; C. H. Dodd, "The Framework of the Gospel Narrative," *New Testament Studies* (Manchester: Manchester University, 1953) 4, 10-11;

D. Nineham, *Mark*, 89; V. Taylor, *Formation*, 68, and *Mark*, 191 (but on p. 92 he says that Mark himself may have compiled the collection); T. A. Burkill, *Mysterious Revelation*, 123; F. Hahn, *Titles of Jesus*, 34; Willi Marxsen, *Introduction to the New Testament* (Philadelphia: Fortress, 1968) 130; and W. Lane, *Mark*, 91. W. L. Knox (*Sources*, 1. 8) holds that the collection is pre-Marcan, but he suggests that the collection may begin at 1:40, not 2:1.

2. Included here are M. Dibelius, *Tradition*, 219; Étienne Trocmé, *Jesus as Seen by His Contemporaries* (Philadelphia: Westminster, 1973) 52; but he is less certain in his book, *The Formulation of the Gospel According to Mark* (Philadelphia: Westminster, 1975) 34-36; and P. Mourlon Beernaert, "Jésus controversé. Structure et theologie de Marc 2, 1-3, 6," *NRT* 95 (1973) 129-149. As indicated in the previous note, V. Taylor (*Mark*, 92) indicates that Mark may have been the collector, but he does not so affirm elsewhere.

3. H.-W. Kuhn, *Ältere Sammlungen*, 18-24, 53-98.

4. Ibid., 80.

5. Cf. R. H. Fuller, *Interpreting the Miracles*, 52-53; and H. Riesenfeld, "The Sabbath and the Lord's Day," 118, who writes that "deeds of healing on Sabbath days must be interpreted as signs that in the person of Jesus was being realized something of what the Sabbath had pointed forward to in the eschatological expectation of the Jewish people."

6. R. Bultmann, *Synoptic Tradition*, 390-391.

7. Cf. Joanna Dewey, "The Literary Structure of the Controversy Stories in Mark 2:1–3:6," *JBL* 92 (1973) 394.

8. J. Jeremias, *New Testament Theology*, 1. 279.

9. M. Albertz, *Streitgespräche*, 5.

10. M. Dibelius, *Tradition*, 219; C. G. Montefiore, *The Synoptic Gospels*, 1. 82; E. Schweizer, *Mark*, 74; H.-W. Kuhn, *Ältere Sammlungen*, 19-20; N. Perrin, "The Son of Man in the Synoptic Tradition," 80; T. Weeden, *Mark—Traditions in Conflict*, 20-21; and W. Kelber, *The Kingdom in Mark*, 21.

11. Kuhn's argument (*Ältere Sammlungen*, 20) proceeds as follows: First, the words *hopōs auton apolesōsin* express the Marcan introduction to the passion, as at 11:18 (*pōs auton apolesōsin*). But, contra Kuhn, the introductory words *hopōs* (3:6) and *pōs* (11:18) are quite different. Verse 11:18 reads clearly, "and they sought *how* they might destroy him," but in 3:6 *hopōs*—a word which never reappears in Mark—functions in the way of *hōste* with an infinitive; they "consulted *with a view* to destroy him;" cf. BAG, 580. Second, he says, the opening words *kai exelthontes* are a common redactional link. On this Kuhn is correct. One can also add, in addition to what Kuhn has, that the word *euthys* is typically Marcan. The verse has undoubtedly, in my view, been stylized by Mark in his customary ways. However, Kuhn overlooks the fact that there are traditional materials within the verse. First, why is it that it is with the Herodians that the Pharisees conspire? Such a connection must antedate Mark and have some basis. It cannot be shown why Mark would have introduced the Herodians. Second, the phrase "held counsel" (*symboulion edidoun*) is unusual. It is not used by Mark elsewhere (in 15:1 he writes *symboulion hetoimasantes*, or *symboulion poiēsantes* as some texts have it); Matthew substitutes *elabon* for the verb (12:14); and Luke has *dielaloun pros allēlous* (6:11). V. Taylor (*Mark*, 224) writes that the words in Mark were considered strange to the evangelists and to later copyists, and therefore alterations were made. The phrase may have an origin in Aramaic (so Wellhausen and Lohmeyer, cited by Taylor). The verb *didōmi* used in the sense of "to make" (*poieō*), which some texts of 15:1 have (*poiēsantes*), as well as some texts of 3:6 (including Sinaiticus and

Ephraemi, which have *epoiēsan,* and Bezae, which has *poiountes),* has a basis in Aramaic. See M. Black, *An Aramaic Approach to the Gospels and Acts,* 132-133.

12. They are also mentioned in some texts of 8:15, i.e., a reading of "the leaven of the Herodians" rather than "the leaven of Herod." But these MSS are for the most part relatively late (except p45), and it is to be considered a correction influenced by Mark 3:6 and 12:13, as V. Taylor *(Mark,* 366) suggests.

13. Cf. Eduard Meyer, *Ursprung und Anfänge des Christentums* (2 vols.; Stuttgart and Berlin: Cotta, 1921) 1. 107; C. G. Montefiore, *The Synoptic Gospels,* 1. 83; H. H. Rowley, "The Herodians in the Gospels," *JTS* 41 (1940) 14-27; V. Taylor, *Mark,* 224; S. Johnson, *Mark,* 72; Bo Reicke, *The New Testament Era: The World of the Bible from 500* B.C. *to* A.D. *100* (Philadelphia: Fortress, 1968) 104, 124; F. F. Bruce, *New Testament History* (Garden City: Doubleday, 1971) 185. Typical is the statement of W. P. Armstrong, "Herodians," *A Dictionary of Christ and the Gospels* (2 vols.; ed. James Hastings; New York: Charles Scribner's Sons, 1906) 1. 723, that the origin of the Herodians was in the time of Herod the Great (37-4 B.C.), and that "after the death of Herod the Great, the deposition of Archelaus, and the establishment of Roman rule in Judaea, the aims and purposes of the party would naturally centre in Antipas. . . . Members of the party which wished to see Antipas set upon the throne of his father may have been in Galilee as well as Jerusalem."

It has also been suggested that the Herodians were the Boethusians, persons of the house of Boethus, who were allied with the house of Herod politically and with the Sadducees theologically. So Harold W. Hoehner, *Herod Antipas* (SNTSMS 17; Cambridge: Cambridge University, 1972) 331-342. Basic to Hoehner's proposal is that one reading of Mark 8:15 (p45, W, and Theta) speaks of "the leaven of the Herodians" (rather than "the leaven of Herod," which is found in other witnesses), which Hoehner takes to be original, and which Matthew (16:6) has altered to "the leaven of the Sadducees." The implication drawn by Hoehner is that the Herodians were Sadducees of the Boethusian line. There are several problems with this proposal.

First, the term "Herodians" (rather than "Herod") may or may not have been in the text of Mark which Matthew used; apart from p45, other significant witnesses (including Sinaiticus, B, and A) speak against it, and its existence is most probably due to alteration in light of 3:6 and 12:13.

Second, from a redaction critical point of view, it is more likely that Matthew placed the term "Sadducees" here as he does elsewhere in his gospel to create his stock phrase "Pharisees and Sadducees" (as opponents in concert against Jesus), as at three other places close at hand (in the same chapter), 16:1, 11, and 12, as well as at 3:7.

Third, if "Herodians" did in fact appear in Matthew's text of Mark 8:15, it is probable that the term carried no meaning for him or his readers, so that he removed it (as at 12:14) and placed "Sadducees" in his text to create his stock phrase.

Finally, if Matthew consciously equated Herodians with Sadducees, why did he not substitute "Sadducees" for "Herodians" at 22:16, since he tended elsewhere to place the term Sadducees into his text? This would have provided another occasion for collusion of Pharisees and Sadducees. Hoehner maintains that Matthew would not make a change here because in this instance a political question (on tribute) was being raised, so "Herodians" is natural (p. 339). That may be so, but it assumes the identity of the

Herodians and Sadducees; it does not actually help to establish it. For another line of argument against Hoehner's position, see W. J. Bennett, Jr., "The Herodians of Mark's Gospel," *NovT* 16 (1975) 10-11.

14. Josephus, *Ant.* 14.15.10 §450; *J. W.* 1.16.6 §319; Epiphanius, "Against the Herodians," *Against Heresies;* and Tertullian, *Against All Heresies,* 1.

15. Cf. F. J. Foakes-Jackson and Kirsopp Lake, "Varieties of Thought and Practice in Judaism," *The Beginnings of Christianity,* 1. 119; E. Lohmeyer, *Markus,* 67.

16. B. W. Bacon, "Pharisees and Herodians in Mark," 102-112; idem, *The Gospel of Mark,* 74-76. Cf. also E. Lohmeyer, *Markus,* 67 (n. 2).

17. Epiphanius, "Against the Herodians;" my translation from *Epiphanii Opera,* 1. 330.

18. For discussion of the rise and reign of Herod Agrippa I, see E. Schürer, *The History of the Jewish People* (rev. ed.), 1. 444-445; and M. Stern, "The Reign of Herod and the Herodian Dynasty," *The Jewish People in the First Century* (ed. S. Safrai and M. Stern), 1. 288-300.

19. Tertullian, *Against All Heresies,* 1 (ANF, 3. 649). On p. 14 of the same volume this work is called spurious by the editors. If not by Tertullian, it is said that it might have been written by Victorinus Petavionensis, who died in A.D. 303.

20. Josephus, *Ant.* 19.7.3 §331; translation by Louis H. Feldmann (LCL; Cambridge: Harvard University, 1965) 369-371.

21. *M. Sota* 7:8. Quoted from *Mishnah* (H. Danby), 301. Cf. also *m. Bik.* 3:4, in which he participated in the festival of firstfruits by going into the Temple Court.

22. Cf. also Hugo Mantel, *Studies in the History of the Sanhedrin* (Harvard Semitic Studies 17; Cambridge: Harvard University, 1965) 73, who gives further references, as well as M. Stern, "The Reign of Herod," 243-300.

23. W. L. Knox, *Sources,* 1.10. Cf. H. G. Wood, "Interpreting This Time," *NTS* 2 (1956) 262-263.

24. The additional reference to the Herodians as co-conspirators with the Pharisees in Mark 12:13 can be considered a Marcan addition (cf. R. Bultmann, *Synoptic Tradition,* 26) for two reasons. First, the verse can be removed, and there is still an introduction to the pericope in 12:14. Second, the verb *apostellousin* refers back to members of the Sanhedrin (chief priests, scribes, and elders) in 11:27. The existence of 12:13 is dependent on Mark's narration containing 11:27-33; without the latter 12:13 has no antecedent. For further discussion of 12:13, see Chapter III, Part B, 1.

That Herodians would have been in Jerusalem during the final events of Jesus' life cannot be considered a likely historical or geographical-political possibility. It was not until A.D. 37 that Agrippa became a serious political figure on his appointment by Caligula as "king" (actually tetrarch) of the tetrarchy of Philip. The Lucan pericope on Herod's presence in Jerusalem during the trial (23:6-13), probably a non-historical legend, cannot be cited as evidence that Herodians were present in Jerusalem during Jesus' ministry there. The reference to the Herodians in Mark 12:13 is not reproduced in Luke 20:19-20.

25. It is interesting to notice that, concerning Mark 3:6, H. C. Kee, F. W. Young, and K. Froehlich (*Understanding the New Testament* [2nd ed.; Englewood, Cliffs: Prentice-Hall, 1965] 267) have written, "It may be that the enmity toward Herod Agrippa is recalled by the Church in reporting the alleged conflict between Jesus and 'the Herodians,' of whom we otherwise know nothing." The idea, however, is not developed, nor is there an attempt

to determine when or where 3:6 was composed, except that "by the time Mark wrote, the Herodian family had vanished from the Palestinian scene."

26. W. Marxsen *(Introduction to the New Testament,* 130) has written, without giving a basis for his claim, "The controversies source [in Mark 2:1–3:6] probably came into being in the 40s of the first century and was meant to help the Church in the confrontation with its opponents."

27. B. H. Streeter, *The Four Gospels,* 233; Ernst Lohmeyer, *Galiläa und Jerusalem* (Göttingen: Vandenhoeck & Ruprecht, 1936) 51-52, 97; Frederick C. Grant, *The Earliest Gospel* (New York: Abingdon-Cokesbury, 1943) 125-147; L. E. Elliott-Binns, *Galilean Christianity* (Chicago: Allenson, 1965) 43-53; Sherman E. Johnson, *Jesus in His Homeland* (New York: Charles Scribner's Sons, 1957) 7-9; W. L. Knox, *St. Paul and the Church of Jerusalem* (Cambridge: Cambridge University, 1925) 7, 87-89; F. W. Beare, "Sayings of the Risen Jesus in the Synoptic Tradition: An Inquiry into their Origin and Significance," *Christian History and Interpretation: Studies Presented to John Knox* (ed. W. R. Farmer, C. F. D. Moule, and R. R. Niebuhr; Cambridge: Cambridge University, 1967) 164-166.

28. Cf. Rudolf Bultmann, *Theology of the New Testament* (2 vols.; New York: Charles Scribner's Sons, 1951) 1. 52; and Morton S. Enslin, *Christian Beginnings* (New York: Harper & Row, 1938) 169-170.

29. This discussion has been summarized in Kirsopp Lake, "The Command Not to Leave Jerusalem and the 'Galilean Tradition,'" *The Beginnings of Christianity,* 5. 7-16. The issue has been dealt with further by E. Lohmeyer, *Galiläa und Jerusalem;* Willi Marxsen, *Mark the Evangelist* (Nashville: Abingdon, 1969) 75-92; and Hugh Anderson, *Jesus and Christian Origins* (New York: Oxford University, 1964) 195-199.

30. Eusebius, *Ecclesiastical History,* 3.20.

31. Cf. Floyd V. Filson, *A New Testament History* (Philadelphia: Westminster, 1964) 300.

32. The conflict stories in Mark 11:27-33 and 12:13-27 would not have had a Galilean origin. These presuppose a Judean or specifically Jerusalem setting. Mark 11:27-33 is related to the Temple Cleansing (see Chapter III, Part A, 2). Mark 12:13-17—the first in the Jerusalem collection—refers to the tax paid by residents living in the imperial province of Judea; see note 33 of Chapter III. Finally, 12:18-27 has Sadducees as opponents, who would be found in Jerusalem, not Galilee.

33. Cf. the discussion by Gustaf Dalman, *Sacred Sites and Ways: Studies in the Topography of the Gospels* (New York: Macmillan, 1935) 1 -14. On p. 191 Dalman suggests that the setting of this pericope could be just outside the village of Jebel ed-Dahi, which is near Nain in Galilee. Ernest W. G. Masterman *(Studies in Galilee* [Chicago: University of Chicago, 1909] 137) indicates that in both ancient and modern times Galilee is characterized by "miles of hillside and valley . . . waving with grain." Cf. also the articles by Kenneth W. Clark, "Galilee" and "Judea," *IDB,* 2. 344-347 and 1011-1012.

34. Cf. Sherman E. Johnson, "Jesus and First-Century Galilee," *In Memoriam Ernst Lohmeyer* (ed. Werner Schmauch; Stuttgart: Evangelisches Verlagswerk, 1951) 70, who maintains that the pericope originated in "an early stage of Galilean tradition."

35. Ibid., 79.

36. Ibid., 79. G. Dalman *(Sacred Sites and Ways,* 148-152) indicates that there was a customs office at Capernaum. Capernaum was both a border town and the northern entrance to the Sea of Galilee.

37. See note 24 above; Marcan editorial words are plentiful in the verse.

38. W. Marxsen (*Mark the Evangelist,* 62) says that the place reference to Capernaum was in the pre-Marcan tradition. For the view that it was added by Mark, see R. Bultmann, *Synoptic Tradition,* 64, 340-341; F. W. Beare, *Earliest Records,* 77; and note 50 below.
39. See note 50 below. Cf. also S. Johnson, "Jesus in First-Century Galilee," 79.
40. R. Bultmann, *Synoptic Tradition,* 66.
41. Ibid., 52.
42. A. F. J. Klijn, "Scribes, Pharisees, Highpriests, and Elders in the New Testament," *NovT* 3 (1959) 259-267; and Joseph C. Weber Jr., "Jesus' Opponents in the Gospel of Mark," *JBR* 34 (1966) 214-222.
43. Ibid. (Weber), 214.
44. Ibid., 222.
45. That the Sanhedrin had authority outside of Judea is improbable. See the discussion of this by W. L. Knox, *St. Paul and the Church of Jerusalem,* 58. Cf. Also *m. Ned.* 5:5.
46. So R. Bultmann, *Synoptic Tradition,* 339-340.
47. See the frequency of this verb (or *apelthein*) in 1:29, 35; 6:1, 32, 34, 46; 7:24, 31; 8:13, 27; 9:30; 11:12.
48. Cf. 3:7; 7:31.
49. Cf. V. Taylor, *Mark,* 92.
50. Cf. R. Bultmann, *Synoptic Tradition,* 64, 340-341; and F. W. Beare, *Earliest Records,* 77. The words *palin eis Kapharnaoum* refer back to 1:21. But a sufficient setting for the story is simply (2:1b), "It was reported that he was in a house," as similarly at 2:15.
51. The sentence appears twice more in Mark (4:33; 8:32a), and these are most certainly Marcan compositions. Cf. E. Schweizer, "Anmerkungen zur Theologie des Markus," 42; idem, "Die theologische Leistung des Markus," 344; T. A. Burkill, *Mysterious Revelation,* 172; and H.-W. Kuhn, *Ältere Sammlungen,* 133.
52. The conflict story would have begun at 2:18b, "And people came and said to him. . . ." See discussion in Chapter III, Part C.
53. Cf. discussion in Chapter III, note 70. Cf. also K. Berger, *Die Gesetzesauslegung Jesu,* 1. 578.
54. In vocabulary and style there are striking similarities: (1) the word *paragōn* in 2:14 and 1:16; (2) "he saw Levi . . . sitting" (2:14), "he saw Simon and Andrew . . . casting" (1:16), and "he saw James . . . and John . . . mending" (1:19); (3) "and he said to him, 'Follow me'" (2:14) and "and he said to them . . . 'Come after me'" (1:17); and (4) "and he rose and followed him" (2:14) and "and . . . they left . . . and followed him" (1:18).
55. Cf. R. Bultmann, *Synoptic Tradition,* 19; W. Grundmann, *Markus,* 66; F. W. Beare, *Earliest Records,* 79; and C. Carlston, *The Parables,* 125-129. M. Dibelius (*Tradition,* 65) and H.-W. Kuhn (*Ältere Sammlungen,* 72, 89) leave the question open whether 2:21-22 was added by Mark.
56. Cf. A. Rawlinson, *Mark,* 32. For the view that they may reflect the substance of Jesus' preaching on repentance at a pre-Marcan stage, see H. C. Kee, "The Old Coat and the New Wine," 13-21.
57. H.-W. Kuhn, *Ältere Sammlungen,* 84.
58. Ibid., 85, 97-98, 222, 229, 232. On p. 98 Kuhn writes that, from the standpoint of the history of tradition, the individual units contained in the collection are specifically Gentile Christian responses. Generally, however, he thinks of them as reflecting polemics between the "church" (Jewish and Gentile?) and (certain persons of?) its Jewish membership. There is some lack of clarity in his presentation. W. Kelber (*The Kingdom in Mark,* 22 and 64) has taken

the same position; for him too the conflict stories in Mark 2:1–3:6 reflect an "internal Christian situation," not a "Jewish-Christian struggle."

59. Ibid. (Kuhn), 98.

60. Ibid., 61, 83, 92-95, 228.

61. Ibid., 91, 95, 98, 232-233.

62. The use of the word *kai* (as "also") in 2:28 ("so the Son of man is lord also of the Sabbath") is not possible in Aramaic; ibid., 91. And the phrases *kai ginetai* (2:15) and *kai egeneto* (2:23), he says (p. 92), are used in a typically Greek way.

63. Ibid., 83, 96, 229. So also W. Kelber, *The Kingdom in Mark*, 22.

64. Cf. discussion in Chapter IV, Part C.

65. This implies that it is precisely a community made up mainly (or entirely) of Jewish Christians who have table fellowship with disreputable persons, and it is necessary for them to defend their conduct in response to criticism from outside. It is impossible (contra Kuhn) that Gentile Christians alone would have generated such a story to defend their fellowship with Jewish Christians, or to convince the latter to have fellowship with themselves. If such were the case, the Gentile Christians would be designating the Jewish Christians as "disciples" (2:15, 16) and themselves as "tax collectors and sinners" (2:15, 16, 17). Such would assume that the former make up the dominant "power group" in the community of composition, and the latter are those knocking at the door for entry. Yet Kuhn thinks that it is Gentile Christians who have the upper hand in the community and who instruct the Jewish Christians by appeal to the Jesus tradition. One cannot have it both ways. It is more likely, as indicated, that in 2:15-17 it is the church which defends its table fellowship with persons who do not measure up to current standards of righteousness in a Palestinian milieu.

66. See Chapter IV, Part C (including notes 41 and 42).

67. H.-W. Kuhn, *Ältere Sammlungen*, 92.

68. The phrases in question at 2:15, 23 (see note 62 above) appear after Marcan insertions (2:13-14; 2:21-22) and can be attributed in their present form to Mark himself. As to the use of *kai* in 2:28, it can be due to editing in a Greek-speaking milieu. Its use (as "even") heightens the significance of the statement ("Nowhere else does Jesus claim personal lordship over the Sabbath," V. Taylor, *Mark*, 220.), although 2:28 can make perfect sense without it (hence, its editorial significance). Kuhn interprets the *kai* as "also" (*auch;* pp. 73, 91) and rejects the meaning "even" (*sogar;* p. 73). He does so to maintain that 2:28 is a Christological saying which concludes the whole section 2:1-28, and to claim that by use of it the collector stated that the Son of man is lord in all the issues debated (forgiveness, table fellowship, fasting, and *also* sabbath conduct). We have argued earlier, however (Chapter IV, Part D), that 2:28 is a Christological conclusion to 2:23-27.

69. Contra W. Kelber, *The Kingdom in Mark*, 22, who takes the same position as Kuhn and writes, "The Markan argument is not set up in such a way that it could meet the Jewish position in any meaningful manner. Above all, it is the christological logic which must remain foreign to *Jewish readers*" (emphasis mine).

70. Interestingly, H.-W. Kuhn (*Ältere Sammlungen*, 84-85) recognizes this.

71. Cf. discussion in Chapter IV, Part B.

72. Cf. M. Black, *An Aramaic Approach to the Gospels and Acts*, 65, 122.

73. Helmut Koester ("Gnomai Diaphoroi: The Origin and Nature of Diversification in the History of Early Christianity," *Trajectories Through Early Christianity* [James M. Robinson, coauthor; Philadelphia: Fortress, 1971] 119-120)

writes that a large portion of the synoptic "controversy paradigms" were written in an environment in which the church dealt with non-Christian Judaism. D. Daube (*The New Testament and Rabbinic Judaism,* 172-175) takes a similar view; he writes that the conflict story form was employed by a church in "controversy with the Pharisees" (p. 172) and which was defending its own "revolutionary actions" (p. 175). K. Berger (*Die Gesetzesaus-legung Jesu,* 1. 577) concludes that the "primary *Sitz im Leben* of the *Streit-gespräche* is a response to Pharisaic confrontation," and that they represent a decisive break with Judaism on the part of the church" (p. 578). Finally, M. Smith ("The Jewish Elements in the Gospels," 96) has written that passages showing Jesus disputing with the scribes and Pharisees "show a concern to answer Jewish criticisms."

74. Cf. G. F. Moore, *Judaism,* 1. 93-94; and Jacob Neusner, *A Life of Yohanan ben Zakkai Ca. 1-80 C. E.* (2nd ed.; SPB 6; Leiden: Brill, 1970) 24-26.

75. Louis Finkelstein (*The Pharisees: The Sociological Background of Their Faith* [3rd ed.; 2 vols.; Philadelphia: The Jewish Publication Society of America, 1962] 1. 97) attributes this to the provincial character of the inhabitants of Galilee and their failure to appreciate the urbanity and love of learning characteristic of the Pharisees. Cf. also Wilhelm Bousset, *Die Religion des Judentums im neutestamentlichen Zeitalter* (Berlin: Reuther & Reichard, 1903) 110; and A. Büchler, *Der galiläische 'Am-ha Ares des zweiten Jahr-hunderts,* 1-2. J. Neusner (*A Life of Yohanan ben Zakkai,* 25) writes, "The Pharisaic party . . . never solidly established itself in Galilee before the second century A.D. The religious beliefs of recently converted people could not have encompassed ideas and issues requiring substantial study, elaborate schooling, and a well-established pattern of living," and (p. 57) that the Galileans' faith was "an open, primitive, unlettered faith, pure and all-embracing, but more enthusiasm than discipline."

76. The memory of Pharisaic attitudes toward the Galileans is preserved in the *Babylonian Talmud:* "Rab Judah stated in the name of Rab: The Judeans who cared for [the beauty of] their language did not retain their learning. But does this depend on whether one cares [for linguistic beauty] ?—Rather say: The Judeans who were exact in their language, and who laid down mnemonics for their aid, retained their learning; but the Galileans who were not exact in their language, and who laid down no mnemonics as an aid, did not retain their learning. . . . Rabina said: The Judeans who made their studies accessible to the public retained their learning, but the Galileans who did not make their studies accessible to the public did not retain their learning;" quoted from *Babylonian Talmud* (I. Epstein), *'Erub.* 53a.

77. Quoted from J. Neusner, *A Life of Yohanan ben Zakkai,* 51. The saying is attributed to Johanan by 'Ulla (a third century Amora). Neusner (pp. 47-53) maintains that Johanan lived at 'Arav in Galilee ca. 20-40 C.E. Tradition has it that during this time only two cases were brought to him in Galilee. Neusner writes elsewhere (*Development of a Legend: Studies on the Traditions of Yohanan ben Zakkai* [SPB 16; Leiden: Brill, 1970] 133-134) that 'Ulla's saying may be pseudepigraphic, and that it may be a famous maxim about the Galileans put into Johanan's mouth. In *y. Šabb.* 16:8 Johanan's saying is also recorded, but with some variation: "O Galilee, Galilee, thou hatest the Torah; hence wilt thou fall into the hands of robbers!'

78. G. H. Boobyer ("Galilee and Galileans in St. Mark's Gospel," *BJRL* 35 [1953] 334-348) asserts that the Galilean followers of Jesus would have been chiefly Gentiles. But Albrecht Alt (*Where Jesus Worked: Towns and Villages of Galilee Studied with the Help of Local History* [London: Epworth, 1961]

7-12, 24) calls attention to the fact that Jesus' ministry in Galilee was limited to villages which are known from ancient sources to have been inhabited by masses of Jewish peasantry. Jesus seems to have avoided the "Hellenistic" cities bordering on Galilee (e.g., Tarichea, Sepphoris, and Tiberias) which contained a large foreign element mixed with the old Israelite population.

VI. The Use of the Conflict Stories in the Primitive Church and by the Evangelists

The task remains to trace the history of the use of the conflict stories from their beginnings to their appearance in the synoptic gospels. This history falls into four areas of study: (1) the use of the conflict stories in the period prior to the writing of the gospels; (2) Mark's use of them; (3) Matthew's; and (4) Luke's.

A. The Period Prior to the Evangelists

This period must be divided into two parts. It has been recognized in previous chapters that certain conflict stories have their origins in a Palestinian setting (hereafter called Palestinian conflict stories), while others have their origins at the level of their composition (as distinguished from traditional material within them) in the Hellenistic church (hereafter called Hellenistic conflict stories). We shall give attention to both groups of stories separately. However, we shall also have to see whether the Palestinian stories underwent any changes in the Hellenistic milieu, through which they were transmitted prior to the writing of the gospels.

1. The Palestinian Conflict Stories

The Palestinian conflict stories include the following: the Healing of the Paralytic (Mark 2:1-12); Eating with Tax Collectors and Sinners (2:15-17); the Question on Fasting (2:18-20); Plucking Grain on the Sabbath (2:23-28); Healing on the Sabbath (3:1-5); the Question about Authority (11:27-33); Paying Taxes to Caesar (12:13-17); the Beelzebul Controversy (Mark 3:22-30; Q, Luke 11:14-15, 17-23); and the Sinful Woman in Simon's House (parts of Luke 7:36-50).

There are several characteristics common to these stories. First, most are characterized by brevity; two exceptions are the Beelzebul

Controversy (Mark 3:22-30; Q, Luke 11:14-15, 17-23) and the Sinful Woman in Simon's House (within Luke 7:36-50). Second, each gives a vivid portrait of Jesus as he was remembered in the Palestinian community. It has been suggested that some of these stories preserve reminiscences of actual conflicts between Jesus and his adversaries, which ended with a decisive saying of the historical Jesus (Mark 11:27-33; 12:13-17; perhaps 3:1-5 and the original special Lucan pericope behind present Luke 7:36-50), although secondary materials have been added in the process of transmission. Those which do not preserve reminiscences of actual conflicts, however, without exception either preserve a saying which can be attributed to Jesus (although not always in its present version)—e.g., Mark 2:19a in 2:18-20; the Q saying of Luke 11:20 (//Matt. 12:28) in Luke 11:14-15, 17-23; and Mark 2:27 in 2:23-38—or they preserve a memory of the attitude of Jesus on the issue at stake—e.g., in Mark 2:1-12 and 2:15-17 (both deal with Jesus' attitude toward sinners, and that attitude is paralleled in the Q saying of Luke 7:34//Matt. 11:19).

What is most characteristic of the Palestinian conflict stories, however, is that they are all, with one exception,[1] *apologetic.* Hence their use in the Palestinian situation was that of an apologetic response to Jewish criticism against the church for its belief and conduct. As such, of course, they are not pronouncement stories (Taylor); they do not *prescribe* conduct or belief, but rather *defend* it in the face of opposition at the earliest level of composition and use. By means of these stories the Palestinian church defended its own conduct and belief by appealing to the conduct and attitudes of Jesus. The traditions about Jesus became a vehicle to show "how it all started;" [2] his conduct and attitudes were displayed as the prototype of Christian conduct and belief. There is no attempt in the various stories to argue a Christian position in terms of contemporary Judaism's presuppositions for argumental procedure; they lack appeal to Scripture and/or hermeneutical rules of procedure. Nor do they contain new law for Christian conduct. They center not in law, but in the person of Jesus —his conduct, words, and attitudes.

As indicated in the previous chapter, not all of the conflict stories circulated independently without interruption. Five of them were collected together (Mark 2:1–3:6). And the question arises, What use did the collection serve?

The suggestion has been made by W. L. Knox that the collection would originally have served (by means of 3:6) "as an introduction to a full Passion story."[3] This, however, seems unlikely. For it is impossible to make a smooth transition from 2:1–3:6 to any passion narrative which would contain the features, even in a rudimentary form, of the passion narratives which exist in the gospels. The geographical transition (from Galilee to Jerusalem) would be awkward without some narration that would place Jesus in the Jerusalem setting. Moreover, it is impossible to make a smooth transition from 3:6, where the Pharisees are said to plot with the Herodians to kill Jesus, to a passion narrative in which the chief priests, scribes, and elders would be the enemies of Jesus.

H.-W. Kuhn has suggested another function. He has maintained that the collection (Mark 2:1-28 only) was formulated "by teachers for teachers" to combat Jewish Christian practices in the church.[4] His position has been discussed and dismissed earlier.

In the previous chapter it was concluded that Mark 2:1–3:6 was formulated as a collection in the Galilean church in the fifth decade. Whether such a collection could exist independently of a larger gospel framework remains a problem, but there are reasons for holding that it could. First, from the standpoint of literary and form criticism, it has been held that, prior to the writing of Mark's Gospel, there were other collections made up of materials sharing a common form, such as the collection of parables contained in Mark 4:1-32 and the collection of miracle stories contained in Mark 4:35–5:43.[5] Second, the existence of the Q document shows that traditions about Jesus were collected together and preserved in written form apart from a larger gospel framework, and that such a collection could serve a purpose in the (presumably) Palestinian church prior to the composition of the gospels.

On principle, then, the existence of a pre-Marcan collection of conflict stories is not an unusual phenomenon. Connected together, the five stories portray an immense breach between Jesus and his opponents—a breach too wide to be closed; a breach which could only end in Jesus' death (so 3:6). The collection would not only have provided apologetic material—the individual stories—but would have provided also an answer to the question (from the Galilean church perspective) of why Jesus was put to death. It "explains" his death without narrating the events in Jerusalem.

But could a block of material exist which served to explain Jesus' death, but which did not contain a passion narrative? Analogies from Acts show that indeed that is possible. In certain speeches within Acts

the death of Jesus is explained as due to the hostility of Jewish officials in Jerusalem (2:36; 3:13-15; 4:10; 5:30; 7:52; 10:39; 13:28), but
no narrative is given. Similarly, Mark 2:1–3:6 portrays hostility against
Jesus on the part of Galilean adversaries, and it ends with a notice of
his coming death as due to that hostility. The fact that it is opponents
of the Galilean church in the fifth decade (i.e., Pharisees essentially,
but also Herodians) who are mentioned (anachronistically) indicates
that the collector wanted to show that the contemporary opposition
in Galilee was rooted "in the beginning." The shadow of the cross falls
in two directions—back upon the Galilean ministry of Jesus, and forward upon the Galilean community. The locale (Galilee), the opponents (Pharisees and Herodians), and the ones opposed (Jesus and
his Galilean followers) remain unchanged.

2. *The Hellenistic Conflict Stories*

The conflict stories that originated (in the *form* of conflict stories)
in a Hellenistic church setting include three in Mark's gospel: the
Tradition of the Elders (7:1-8); On Divorce (10:2-9); and On the
Resurrection (12:18-27).

There are several characteristics common to them. First, they are
non-unitary compositions. That is, they are stories in which the opponents' questions and the narrated scenes are secondary, i.e., composed
to give a setting for a dominical saying that had circulated independently prior to the composition of each story.[6] Each of these three
stories has been constructed out of traditional materials which may
likely reflect the attitude of Jesus on the particular issue at hand. But
actually none contains a specific saying which can be definitely attributed to Jesus on the basis of the various criteria commonly used to
test authenticity.

A second characteristic of the Hellenistic stories is that they are
longer and more complex than most of those from the Palestinian
setting. While the latter (excluding the Beelzebul Controversy and
the Sinful Woman in Simon's House, which are longer than the rest)
average four and one-half verses, the Hellenistic stories average
slightly over eight verses.

A third characteristic is that each of the Hellenistic stories makes
use of Old Testament citations, whereas only one of the Palestinian
conflict stories (Mark 2:23-28) does, and that (2:25-26) has been
designated a secondary addition. It is evident that while in the

Palestinian conflict stories appeal is made to the conduct and attitude of Jesus as the decisive element in the defense of Christian conduct and belief, such an appeal is not determinative in the Hellenistic conflict stories. Instead, arguments are presented on the basis
of Scripture. It is not Jesus as a free agent in his conduct and attitude
who is authority, but Jesus as a scribe. The description of Jesus as
one who teaches "as one who had authority, and not as the scribes"
(Mark 1:22) applies exactly to the Jesus of the Palestinian conflict
stories, but not so well to the Jesus in those stories that originated
in the Hellenistic church.

A fourth characteristic is that each of these stories provides a text
for teaching converts and regulating life in the community. Less apologetic than the Palestinian stories, they are essentially *catechetical*. They
contain teaching on the Christian's stance toward the cultic-ritual legislation of Judaism (Mark 7:1-8), teaching on marriage from the Christian viewpoint (10:2-9), and teaching on the resurrection and the
subordinate question of whether widows/widowers may remarry
(12:18-27). The teaching on the resurrection was not a departure from
that of Pharisaic Judaism in the Diaspora, but it was a new doctrine
for Christians coming out of a Gentile background.

The other two pericopes, however, convey teachings which are distinctive departures from Judaism. The teaching concerning the Tradition of the Elders (7:1-8) is especially apologetic on that account, and
like the Palestinian conflict stories it is a defense of Christian conduct
against Jewish criticism in the Diaspora. As indicated earlier (Chapter
IV, Part E), 7:8 is most likely an anti-Pharisaic saying current in the
church. But this pericope is not only apologetic. It is a Christian scribal
composition, making use of an Old Testament citation, in which a
position is worked out for Christian practice: converts to Christianity
are not obligated to "walk according to the tradition of the elders"
(7:5), for the "tradition of the elders" did not originate in the revealed
will of God, but is in fact merely the "tradition of men" (7:7-8). Insofar as the pericope was a basis for a policy taught to converts, it can be
considered a catechetical text used for regulation of life in the community. That the pericope on marriage (10:2-9) also established Christian teaching on the basis of a Scriptural argument is even more clear.

The Palestinian conflict stories reached Mark and—in the case of the
Q (Luke 11:14-15, 17-23) and special Lucan (Luke 7:36-50) pericopes
—Luke in the Greek language, having passed through a Hellenistic
church milieu. Therefore the question arises whether any of the char-

acteristics found in the Hellenistic stories are found in these because
of their transmission in this milieu. Fundamentally it is clear that they
did not undergo significant changes. Most of the pre-Marcan additions
to them have been traced in previous chapters to the Palestinian
church itself. There is one possible exception. That is the use of a
Scripture reference at Mark 2:25-26, which has been designated
(Chapter IV, Part D) a later addition to the pericope on Plucking
Grain on the Sabbath (Mark 2:23-28). But Mark 2:25-26 would not
have been added in the Hellenistic church; it belongs to the Palestinian
milieu. The use of Scripture in this story differs from its use in the
Hellenistic stories. It is not used as a basis for an exegetical argument
leading to a conclusion. The conclusion is based on the dominical word
(2:27) apart from the allusion to 1 Sam. 21:1-6 (Mark 2:25-26). It has
been argued (Chapter IV, Part D) that Mark 2:23-24, 27 is complete
apart from (and prior to) the Old Testament allusion. The allusion
merely shows precedent for the conduct of Jesus' disciples at a secondary level of composition.

It can be concluded, then, that the transmission of the Palestinian
conflict stories in the Hellenistic church prior to their use in Mark and
Q did not have an effect on them in terms of either form or editorial
expansion. It is certain, on the contrary, that the form of the Palestinian
conflict stories was the model upon which the Hellenistic ones were
formed, allowing for the greater complexity of the latter.

B. Mark's Use of the Conflict Stories

The designation of the gospels by Martin Kähler as "passion narratives with an extended introduction"[7] has been widely accepted, at
least in the case of Mark.[8] Mark, it has been said, composed his gospel
"in backward direction"[9] in light of the conclusion.

The question of the function of the conflict stories in Mark must be
dealt with in terms of this general characterization of the gospel.
According to W. L. Knox, the function of the conflict stories in Mark
2:1-3:6 is that of indicating to Mark's readers the reason why Jesus'
own people would want to kill him: he was put to death because of
his conflicts with representatives of Judaism on points of law.[10] Likewise, according to M. Albertz, both the Galilean (Mark 2:1-3:6) and
the Jerusalem (Mark 11:15-17, 23-33; 12:13-40) conflict stories serve
to show why Jesus was put to death.[11] It is our purpose here to test
whether this is the function which all or any of the conflict stories serve.

At the outset caution is necessary. While it can be accepted that Mark was not simply a collector of traditions, but an author in his own right,[12] it is also the case that some materials available to him had already been joined together (e.g., the conflict stories in 2:1-3:6; the parable collection in 4:1-32; the collection of miracle stories in 4:35-5:43; and perhaps the passion narrative), and Mark incorporated these materials with relatively few changes. Even if we do not accept the view of C. H. Dodd that Mark had a "meager outline" of the career of Jesus before him, but allow the possibility that the outline was Mark's own, Dodd's statement can be accepted that "where groups of narrative units came down to him already arranged topically, he allowed the arrangement to stand, relating the first member of the group (e.g., 2:1-12, the first conflict story) to what appeared to be its most suitable point in the outline scheme. When he was left with wholly disconnected units on his hands, he found place for them as best he could." [13]

This means that a priori it is possible that the conflict stories have been placed in the framework of Mark's narrative out of purely pragmatic and topical considerations, and that one should not exaggerate their importance as preludes to the passion. Perhaps they do not serve the framework in leading up to the passion any more than, say, collections of parables or miracle stories. It may be that he simply had the conflict stories "on his hands," and that he placed them in his gospel outline wherever they seemed to fit best.

But, having allowed for that, there are indications that Mark interpreted the conflict stories for his readers. It cannot be assumed that Mark simply had the conflict stories before him and had to work them into his gospel. Each of the evangelists was certainly selective with materials available—taking some pericopes and collections into his gospel; and, on the other hand, rejecting others—and, furthermore, there are redactional clues as to how Mark intended his readers to understand parables, miracle stories, and the conflict stories.

The most striking datum arising out of our survey of the conflict stories is Mark's identification of Jesus' opponents. In many of the conflict stories the opponents of Jesus had been identified already in the pre-Marcan stages of transmission, e.g., in 2:1-3:6 (at 2:6, 16, 18, 24; 3:6);[14] 11:27-33;[15] and 12:18-27.[16] But in three other cases it is Mark who identifies the opponents of Jesus:

(1) In 3:22-30, Mark identifies the opponents as "the scribes who came down from Jerusalem." [17]

(2) In 7:1, Mark identifies the opponents as "Pharisees" and "scribes, who had come down from Jerusalem." [18]

(3) In 12:13, Mark prefaces the originally nameless opponents of 12:14 with the statement that "they"—which is to be understood as the "chief priests and the scribes and the elders" of 11:27—sent some Pharisees and Herodians "to entrap him" in his talk.[19]

In the only remaining conflict story in Mark, 10:2-9, the identification of the opponents was made in a post-Marcan gloss.[20]

Within the passion narrative the enemies of Jesus are the chief priests, with whom the scribes and elders are associated (14:1; 15:31; cf. 11:18). Likewise, in two passion predictions it is the "elders and the chief priests and the scribes" (8:31) or the "chief priests and the scribes" (10:33) who are indicated as those under whom Jesus must suffer. What emerges from the three instances given above is that Mark's identification of the opponents of Jesus, when he received conflict stories in which the opponents were not identified, is in keeping with a view toward the passion narrative and the traditional passion predictions; i.e., he identifies them as Jerusalem scribes. Likewise, in 9:14, which can be considered a Marcan composition,[21] it is said that "the scribes" disputed with the disciples. For Mark it is "the scribes"— meaning scribes from the Jerusalem Sanhedrin—who enter into the controversies with Jesus along with Pharisees, scribes of the Pharisees (2:16), Sadducees, and Herodians. In instances in which the opponents are identified in the traditions as these latter groups, Mark does not make changes. But Mark has the Jerusalem scribes enter into controversies, even in the Galilean period (3:22; 7:1) of Jesus' ministry, to anticipate his suffering and death at the hands of the Sanhedrin. He thereby links up the earlier ministry with the passion, and it can be said that certain conflict stories are preludes to it.

But not all conflict stories function as preludes to the passion. There is a second series of redactional indicators which shows how Mark understood certain other conflict stories in relationship to his gospel as a whole. The redactional notations, without comment here, are:

(1) In 2:2, Mark adds, "and he was speaking the word to them" (the crowds).[22]

(2) After the conflict story of 2:18-20, Mark attaches two little similitudes (2:21-22).[23]

(3) In the conflict story of 3:1-5, Mark describes Jesus as grieved at the "hardness of heart" of his opponents (3:5).[24]

(4) At 10:2, Mark indicates that the purpose of the question of the Pharisees to Jesus was to "test him," as also in their request for a sign from heaven (8:11).[25]

The first three Marcan additions are in the collection of 2:1-3:6. By means of these additions Mark interprets the significance of the collection for his readers. In Mark's view Jesus arrives on the scene at Capernaum having impressive accomplishments behind him already. He has taught with authority (1:22) and has cast out unclean spirits with authority (1:27). He has healed many diseases, has silenced many demons (1:32-34), and has cleansed a leper with a brief utterance (1:40-45). The conflict stories are placed here by Mark (as the term "authority" at 2:10 in the first conflict story of 2:1-3:6 suggests, recalling 1:22 and 1:27) to indicate that the struggle of Jesus with his adversaries is a continuation of his struggle with hostile powers that were first represented by the demons in Chapter 1.[26] The exorcism of 1:21-28 is described as "a new teaching," since it had been accomplished by an utterance in 1:25 (cf. also 1:41).

Mark intends to have his readers understand that in the disputes in 2:1-3:6, in which Jesus is victor over sin, disease, and the opposition of his adversaries on points of law, Jesus acts by sovereign power. His victories are indications of the eschatological powers at work in his ministry. It is to the "many" (2:2) or the "crowd" (2:4) gathered at the door at Capernaum that Jesus "preaches the word" (2:2). They listen to his word, and in their presence he forgives sins and heals by his word of authority (2:5, 11). But he is opposed by adversaries who represent, in Mark's view, history prior to Jesus, the old age of Israel, a period of history which has come to a decisive end with the appearance of John as the forerunner of Jesus,[27] but which continues to be represented anachronistically by its "old guard" in Judaism. Nevertheless, Jesus is victor over his adversaries. Mark inserts the two similitudes of 2:21-22 into the conflict story collection to illustrate more clearly the clash of two epochs of history. In the present era, in which Jesus teaches with authority, the conventions of the old age (which is compared to an old garment and old wineskins) are no longer applicable. And in 3:5 Mark indicates that Jesus' adversaries would not recognize his authority because of their "hardness of heart." Their stance toward Jesus is to "test him" (8:11; 10:2) rather than to recognize him as the Son of God/Messiah.

The two series of redactional additions by Mark indicate that there is no single function of all conflict stories in his gospel. The first series indicates that certain conflict stories function to show a continuity between the conflicts of Jesus with his adversaries in his earlier ministry and the final conflict in Jerusalem. The second series indicates that certain other stories function to show a continuity between the victories of Jesus over his adversaries in verbal combat and his victory over the supernatural hostile powers.

C. Matthew's Use of the Conflict Stories

Matthew's use of the conflict stories can be dealt with under three headings: (1) the location of the conflict stories in the plan of his gospel as a whole; (2) the formulation of additional conflict stories out of Marcan, special Matthean, and Q materials; and (3) the editorial additions and omissions of words, phrases, and clauses by Matthew in the conflict stories he received from Mark.

(1) The location of the conflict stories in Matthew's Gospel has been determined largely by their location in Mark. The conflict stories which were placed by Mark and his predecessors in a Galilean setting, for example, remain in that setting in Matthew's Gospel, and those in the Jerusalem setting remain there. Furthermore, the sequence of the stories in Matthew follows that of Mark; never is there a reversal of their order of presentation. Nevertheless, Matthew has placed the conflict stories in his presentation by a conscious choice of location, and he breaks up the Galilean collection (Mark 2:1–3:6) in order to insert materials of his own.

The Galilean collection is not encountered in Matthew's Gospel until Chapter 9. But even here only three of the five appear. They are the Healing of the Paralytic (9:1-8 from Mark 2:1-12), Eating with Tax Collectors and Sinners (9:10-13 from Mark 2:15-17), and the Question on Fasting (9:14-17 from Mark 2:18-22). The other two stories appear in Chapter 12 (12:1-8, 9-14).

The reason for Matthew's placing the Galilean conflict stories in two different locations can be seen in light of his arrangement of material in general. The first three have been placed into a section (Matt. 8-9) which follows the teaching discourse of Matt. 5-7 (the Sermon on the

Mount). In the Sermon on the Mount Jesus is portrayed as a second Moses in his giving the new law. In Chapters 8 and 9 Matthew has collected miracle stories, showing Jesus again as a second Moses-Messiah, but this time as such a figure in action. Just as Moses brought about ten plagues (Exod. 7–12), Jesus as a second Moses performs ten miracles.[28] The first conflict story in Mark (2:1-12) consists mainly of a healing narrative. And although for Matthew the point is that "persons" (9:8, i.e., the church) have authority on earth to forgive sins,[29] he has placed this story among the other nine miracle stories, thereby providing a series of ten miracles as "deeds of the Messiah" (11:2). The other two stories follow the Marcan order.

But the last two conflict stories in the Galilean collection—Plucking Grain on the Sabbath (12:1-8 from Mark 2:23-28) and Healing on the Sabbath (12:9-14 from Mark 3:1-6)—come later. They fall within a section of the gospel (Matt. 11 and 12) which portrays a growing opposition against Jesus on the part of his critics. Both stories have to do with the breaking of sabbath law and serve to demonstrate the growing hostility between Jesus and the Pharisees.[30] Matthew adds to the first a couple of sayings (12:6-7) which heighten the cleavage, and the second contains the reference to the plot of the Pharisees (the Herodians are not mentioned) against Jesus (12:14), which was already in Mark (3:6), and which marks the irreparable breach between Jesus and his adversaries. Closely thereafter Matthew places the Beelezbul Controversy (12:22-32) and the Refusal of a Sign (12:38-42), which also illustrate the hostility.

Matthew does not change the location of the remaining conflict stories vis-à-vis Mark's location of them. While the stories concerning the Tradition of the Elders (15:1-9) and on Divorce (19:3-9) are altered somewhat by Matthew, their location corresponds to that of Mark. The same can be said concerning the three Jerusalem conflict stories: the Question About Authority (21:23-27 from Mark 11:27-33), Paying Taxes to Caesar (22:15-22 from Mark 12:13-17), and On the Resurrection (22:23-33 from Mark 12:18-27).

(2) One of the most distinctive features of Matthew's Gospel in regard to the conflict stories is that three additional conflict stories have been formulated by Matthew out of Marcan, special Matthean, and Q materials. In 12:38-42 there is the Refusal of a Sign. Here Matthew has taken Q (12:39-42//Luke 11:29-32) and Marcan (Mark 8:11-12) materials, and he has presented the whole in the form of a

conflict story portraying debate between Jesus and the scribes and
Pharisees. The words narrated by Mark (8:11, "The Pharisees came
and began to argue with him, seeking from him a sign from heaven,
to test him") are reformulated into direct discourse by Matthew
(12:38, "Then some of the scribes and Pharisees said to him, 'Teacher,
we wish to see a sign from you.'"). Thereupon—with face-to-face
debate—the materials are presented in the form of a conflict story.

Second, in 22:34-40 the discussion on the Double Commandment of
Love is given in the form of a conflict story. It is not presented so by
Mark (12:28-34). In Mark the material is presented in the form of a
scholastic dialogue, and its tone as a whole is amiable; the questioner
(a scribe) and Jesus are portrayed as in agreement. It has been argued
elsewhere [31] that in this case Matthew has based his pericope on
material in his own special tradition (22:37-40), to which he has added
Marcan (Mark 12:28//Matt. 22:36) and Q (Matt. 22:35//Luke
10:25a) materials. It is from the latter that Matthew gets the motif of
"testing," which sets the tone as polemical. Furthermore, the questioner
is no longer an amiable scribe; he is now a lawyer from among the
Pharisees: "a lawyer [of the Pharisees] asked him a question to test
him" (22:35). The result is a conflict story in which the Double Commandment of Love is established as the key for right interpretation of
the law and the prophets in the Matthean community over against the
position of the Pharisees.[32] And, finally, in 22:41-46 the Question
About David's Son has been composed as a conflict story through the
transformation of a Marcan saying (Mark 12:35-37a) into a dialogue
between Jesus and the Pharisees, which is polemical in tone.[33]

In the first of these three conflict stories (Refusal of a Sign, 12:38-42)
the opponents of Jesus are named as Pharisees already in Mark (8:11).
But in the latter two stories (Double Commandment of Love, 22:34-40;
and David's Son, 22:41-46) it is Matthew who has so identified them.
And these latter two lead, furthermore, directly into the long discourse
of Jesus against the scribes and Pharisees (Matt. 23:1-36). The identification of the opponents in these conflict stories formulated by Matthew undoubtedly reflects the conditions of Matthew's own time and
place.[34] He creates conflict stories—modeled on the traditional form—
out of sources available to him as part of his polemical program against
the Pharisees.

(3) Matthew also makes extensive editorial changes in the conflict
stories. Not all of them need to be dealt with here, however. Our atten-

tion will focus on those changes that demonstrate his purposes in using the conflict stories.

What is most characteristic about the conflict stories in Matthew is that they portray Jesus as interpreter of the law for the church.[35] This can be seen in its twofold aspects: (1) in terms of form, there are some conflict stories in which sayings of Jesus have been shaped into halachic statements for the community;[36] and (2) in terms of teaching, there are instances in which the conflict stories are altered by Matthew to apply interpretations of the Torah to questions in the church. Of course the conflict stories had always been used, broadly speaking, to address questions within the primitive church. But in Matthew's Gospel one can observe that the process is guided by a more overt concern to deal with questions of Torah interpretation than was previously the case.

The formal changes can be seen in three of the conflict stories. In the discussion of Healing on the Sabbath (12:9-14) Matthew has altered Mark's account (3:1-6) so that the question "Is it lawful on the sabbath to do good or to do harm, to save life or to kill?" (Mark 3:4) has become a halachic decision by Jesus in Matt. 12:12b, "so it is lawful to do good on the sabbath." The debate about the Tradition of the Elders (15:1-9) has been expanded to include the Qorban pericope (Mark 7:9-13) to demonstrate how the scribes and Pharisees "transgress the commandment of God" (Matt. 15:3) in the Torah (Exod. 20:12; 21:17) for the sake of "your tradition." The charge of the Pharisees, "Why do your disciples transgress the tradition of the elders?" (15:2), is countered by the question, "Why do you transgress the commandment of God?" (15:3). This serves to reject the binding force of the tradition,[37] but at the same time it affirms the abiding validity of the Mosaic Torah. Matthew adds the halachic decision for the church in 15:20, "to eat with unwashed hands does not defile a man." And, finally, in the Question about Divorce (19:3-9), the Marcan material is reworked so that the question has become, "Is it lawful to divorce one's wife *for any cause?*" (19:3), whereas in Mark (10:2) the question had been a general one ("Is it lawful for a man to divorce his wife?"). Matthew reformulates the final word of Jesus into a halachic decision ("And I say unto you," 19:9), with its exception ("except for unchastity," 19:9), by which the issue of divorce and remarriage is decided for the community in keeping with the halachah of the School of Shammai.[38]

By such additions and formal alterations of the sayings of Jesus it is evident that Matthew found the conflict stories useful for expounding

and clarifying Christian teaching for the church. The stories lend themselves well to Matthew's purposes of providing a manual of Christian
teaching, since many contain within themselves conventional Jewish
(mainly Pharisaic) teaching over against which peculiarly Christian
teaching can be clarified and given authority. This use of the conflict
stories to expound and clarify church teaching is seen not only when
the saying of Jesus is given in a halachic formulation, but in various
other ways. In the Healing of the Paralytic (9:1-8) the teaching that
the authority to forgive sins has been given to the church is expressed
in Matthew's alteration of Mark's choral ending (Mark 2:12b) into a
summary report which brings out, to Matthew, the true significance
of the pericope (Matt. 9:8).[39] Matthew omits the Marcan saying of
Jesus concerning sabbath observance that "the sabbath was made for
man, not man for the sabbath" (Mark 2:27). The saying is too radical
for Matthew, in whose congregation the sabbath was probably kept
(cf. 24:20), although certainly not in the same strict sense as in the
rabbinate.[40] Matthew explains why the disciples acted as they did by
adding "they were hungry" (12:1). By adding the Hosea citation in
12:7 (Hos. 6:6) Matthew asserts that the sabbath commandment,
although it is to be observed, must be interpreted for the church in
terms of mercy, not in terms of strict, unbending demand,[41] and in
fulfillment of the commandments of love (22:34-40) and "doing good"
(12:12) on the sabbath.[42]

Furthermore, by inserting the materials in 12:5-7, containing the
argument from minor to major, Matthew is able to show that, if it is
the case that the priests in the temple profaned the sabbath and yet
were guiltless, then it is the case that Jesus' disciples are guiltless, since
"something greater than the temple is here" (12:6). The pronouncement follows that "the Son of man is lord of the sabbath" (12:8), and
therefore the sabbath will be observed in Matthew's community under
the aspect of obedience to Christ, not in uncritical obedience to tradition alone. The same Hosea citation (6:6) is used again in connection
with the conflict story of Eating with Tax Collectors and Sinners (9:10-
13). While according to the Pharisaic-rabbinic understanding strict
separation from sinners is required, Matthew interprets Jesus' association with them as a paradigm of the mercy that God wills (9:13), and
therefore the church is to have this same attitude toward sinners,
rather than the attitude of the Pharisees.

Finally, as already indicated, Matthew uses his ("his," because it
is not a conflict story in Mark) conflict story on the Double Command-

ment of Love (22:34-40) for establishing the way of scriptural interpretation in the church. Over against the Pharisees, whose interpretations miss the true meaning of Scripture (cf. 23:23-24, 13; 15:3), the
Double Commandment of Love is to be taken as the starting point
from which interpretation is to proceed.

The remaining Matthean redactional additions and omissions serve
to identify the Pharisees as the opponents of Jesus and to broaden
the gulf between them and Jesus. At 12:2 Matthew has the Pharisees
level a direct charge against Jesus' disciples (contrast the interrogative
form of Mark 2:24). Matthew omits mention of the scribes as opponents of Jesus (although they had been identified as such in Mark) in
9:11 (against Mark 2:16); 21:23 (against Mark 11:27); 22:35 (against
Mark 12:28); and 22:41 (against Mark 12:35). Matthew substitutes
the Pharisees for them in three cases (9:11; 22:35; and 22:41; in 21:23
he allows "the chief priests and the elders" to remain). Matthew may
have removed the reference to the scribes, as R. Hummel has suggested, [43] because Christian "scribes" are important in Matthew's
church (cf. 13:52; 23:34). Matthew also designates the Pharisees as
those who are behind the delegation to Jesus in 22:15.[44] There is a
heightened hostility between Jesus and the Pharisees, compared with
Mark, especially in the Jerusalem conflict stories. The Pharisees are
called "hypocrites" (22:18), who are possessed with "malice" toward
Jesus, and one of them "tests him" (22:35; Matthew also takes over
the Marcan "testing him" in 19:3 from Mark 10:2 [45]).

In summary, the conflict stories have been developed by Matthew
into important materials for his ecclesiastical book. By his transposi-
tions, by his formulations of additional conflict stories, and by his
editing of others, Matthew makes use of conflict stories to draw out
important insights and teachings for his readers. They are used in the
service of presenting Jesus as Teacher to the church in which Matthew
worked, a church which had to develop its own doctrinal self-consciousness apart from the contemporary rabbinate. Generally it can be
said that the conflict stories in Matthew serve the structure of the
gospel narrative as preludes to the passion narrative less than in Mark,
although his identification of the Pharisees as opponents in certain
conflict stories, especially in the Jerusalem setting, is evidence that
Matthew did use them to portray growing hostility against Jesus prior
to the passion narrative. But even in these instances the interest of
Matthew is not so much to write an "extended introduction" to the
passion narrative as to provide a Pharisaic position, often correspond-

ing to a position current in the rabbinate in his own time, from which it can be seen that the Teacher departs, as should his disciples, the church.

D. Luke's Use of the Conflict Stories

Two Marcan conflict stories do not appear in Luke, viz., the Tradition of the Elders (Mark 7:1-8) and On Divorce (Mark 10:2-9). These two pericopes are in larger sections of Mark which are not taken over by Luke into his gospel (Mark 6:45–8:26 and 9:42–10:12). For the Marcan Beelzebul Controversy (Mark 3:22-30), Luke has substituted a Q version (Luke 11:14-15, 17-23) in his so-called "great interpolation" (9:51-18:14), apparently making no use of Mark at all (see Chapter IV, Part A), and in his so-called "small interpolation" (6:20-8:3) he has included the conflict story of the Sinful Woman in Simon's House (7:36-50) from his own special materials. Elsewhere, however, Luke makes use of each of the remaining Marcan conflict stories, and he follows Mark's sequence.

Luke has two additional conflict stories (13:10-17; 14:1-6) not found in Mark which have to do with sabbath healings. These have been considered variants of Mark 3:1-5, however, and the main thing they are said to accomplish is to introduce further sayings concerning sabbath practices (13:15; 14:5).[46]

Luke's use of the story on the Sinful Woman in Simon's House (7:36-50) is typical of those special Lucan traditions in which he expresses God's love for the despised through Jesus' conduct and message (Chapter 15; 18:9-14; 19:1-10). But more important for our study is his use of the Marcan conflict stories. It can be said that generally when Luke incorporated these into his gospel he did so without major changes, virtually taking over blocks of material entirely. One does not get the impression that for Luke the Marcan conflict stories could be developed consciously to deal with live issues of the day; the issues dealt with in the conflict stories belong essentially to the past.

Nevertheless, Luke does place three conflict stories (all non-Marcan; see below) within the so-called travel section of his gospel (9:51-19:44),[47] and these serve an important function there. Throughout this section attention is focused on Jerusalem as Jesus' goal (9:51, 53; 13:22, 33-34; 17:11; 18:31; and 19:11) so that the cross, resurrection, and ascension are anticipated. Moreover, the section sets forth thematic motifs which fall basically into two categories:[48] instruction for Jesus' disciples as forerunners of the new community (hence, consolidation) and disputation with opponents (hence, division). The section is almost entirely didactic and polemical. It contains, for didactic purposes, parables and sayings having to do with discipleship (9:60, 62; 11:2-4, 28; 12:8-13, 14-15, 22-34; 14:25-27; 16:10-13, 18; 17:1-6, 20-21; 18:15-17, 24-34); and, for polemical purposes, it contains harsh sayings against Jesus' opponents (10:13-15; 11:29-32, 37-52; 12:1-3; 16:14-15) as well as three conflict stories that show division between Jesus and his adversaries. These are the Beelzebul Controversy from Q (11:14-15, 17-23) and two conflict stories concerning healing on the sabbath (13:10-17; 14:1-6), which are peculiar to Luke, but which appear to be variants of Mark 3:1-5. The theme of division in this section anticipates the crucifixion and the ultimate separation of Jesus' disciples (the church) from Judaism, and the theme of instruction shows Jesus equipping his disciples for carrying on his work after his death and resurrection.

Although Luke incorporated the Marcan conflict stories in Marcan sequence, he made certain alterations in three of them in such a way that they help portray his redemptive-historical outlook. To the conflict story on Fasting (Mark 2:18-20//Luke 5:33-35), which had two similitudes attached to it already in Mark (2:21-22//Luke 5:36-38), Luke adds an additional saying (5:39), "And no one after drinking old wine desires new; for he says, 'The old is good.'" By means of this saying Luke interprets the pericope in such a way that the disciples of John and those of the Pharisees are placed within the course of redemptive history. While the "old and the new," as in Mark, are incompatible, Luke concedes to the old world (i.e., the Old Testament-Judaic era up to the Christ event) a validity and importance of its own.[49] "The old" as an epoch of redemptive history "is good" insofar as it was an era in which the promises of salvation, now being realized, were given.[50]

The second Marcan conflict story which Luke has altered in keeping with his view of redemptive history is the Question of Authority (Mark 11:27-33//Luke 20:1-8). In Luke's Gospel the connection between this pericope and the Temple Cleansing (19:45-46) is closer than in Mark (see Chapter III, Part A). The Temple Cleansing is not an eschatological sign, as it is in Mark, but a means by which Jesus "takes possession"[51] of a place in Jerusalem for his work. Luke portrays Jesus as "teaching the people" (20:1) and "preaching the gospel" (20:1) in the temple, whereas the chief priests, scribes, and elders oppose him. The term "the people" in Luke refers to the people of God who stand within the saving events, i.e., Israel and the church.[52] Luke makes use of the conflict story to show that the message of salvation to the world goes out programmatically not only from the apostles in Jerusalem (Acts 1:8), but initially from Jesus himself within the temple.

Finally, in the Healing of the Paralytic (Mark 2:1-12//Luke 5:17-26) Luke adds at the beginning that "the power *(dynamis)* of the Lord was with [Jesus] to heal" (5:17). For Luke, *dynamis* is the "*dynamis* of the Spirit*" (4:14), and its work in the ministry of Jesus points ahead to that of the church in which the "power of the Spirit" is operative as well.[53]

In addition to this use of three conflict stories in depicting redemptive history, Luke also found opportunity for political apologetic in another.[54] In the question about Tribute to Caesar (Mark 12:13-17// Luke 20:20-26), Luke makes it clear that there is a plot to find cause for bringing Jesus before the Roman governor (20:19-20). But the plot fails. They are unable to catch him in what he said (20:26). Yet ironically the main charge against Jesus before Pilate (23:1-2) is based on a perversion of this very incident. The conflict story is documentation that there was no substance to the charge before Pilate.[55] Additional apologetic may be seen in Luke's portrayal of Jesus' favor among the people (20:1, 19, 26).

Luke, in sum, made his own distinctive use of the conflict stories in two major ways. First, he used a Q story (11:14-15, 17-23) and two of his own stories (13:10-17; 14:1-6) for a thematic purpose within his so-called travel narrative (9:51-19:44). And, second, he altered certain stories received from Mark for the purposes of his redemptive-historical and political-apologetic purposes. Outside of these two major ways there is only Luke's alteration of the Plucking Grain on the Sabbath (6:1-5) which remains significant. By omitting Mark 2:27 and by inserting the word *labōn* in connection with David (6:4), Luke has allowed the final saying (6:5 from Mark 2:28) to give the whole story a Christological emphasis, which, however, is hardly a radical step, since it had such an emphasis already in Mark even with 2:27 included.

Aside from the changes registered above, Luke left the other stories that he received and employed from Mark unaltered, except for stylistic changes. In writing his orderly account (1:3) he considered the conflict stories important for his narrative and certain thematic concerns. Yet it must be concluded that, although Luke is generally considered the most literary and artistic of the gospel writers, the conflict story form *as form* did not have the significance for him that it had for Mark, Matthew, and the formulaters of the conflict stories in the pre-Marcan and pre-Q periods.

NOTES

1. The Beelzebul Controversy (Mark 3:22-30; Q, Luke 11:14-15, 17-23) might be considered an exception. As indicated earlier (Chapter IV, Part A), it served to affirm that those who became disciples only after the resurrection are forgiven.

2. Cf. the use of this phrase by C. F. D. Moule, "The Intention of the Evangelists," *New Testament Essays* (ed. A. J. B. Higgins; Manchester: Manchester University, 1959) 167; idem, *The Birth of the New Testament* (New York: Harper & Row, 1962) 87, 91.

3. W. L. Knox, *Sources*, 1. 12. M. Dibelius (*Tradition*, 45) writes that Mark 3:6 serves to connect 2:1–3:5 with the passion. More recently it has been argued that Mark 3:1-6 serves as a bond between 2:1-3:6 and the passion by Anitra B. Kolenkow, "Healing Controversy as a Tie Between Miracle and Passion Material for a Proto-Gospel," *JBL* 95 (1976) 623-638.

4. H.-W. Kuhn, *Ältere Sammlungen*, 97-98.

5. Cf. R. Bultmann, *Synoptic Tradition*, 325, 348-349; V. Taylor, *Mark*, 90-104; Helmut Koester, "One Jesus and Four Gospels," *Trajectories Through Early Christianity*, 164-165; P. Achtemeier, "Toward the Isolation of Pre-Markan Miracle Catanae," 265-291; and W. Kümmel, *Introduction*, 85 (with additional references).

6. Cf. R. Bultmann, *Synoptic Tradition*, 47.

7. Martin Kähler, *The So-Called Historical Jesus and the Historic, Biblical Christ* (Philadelphia: Fortress, 1964) 80 (n. 11).

8. Cf. the statement of W. Marxsen (*Introduction to the New Testament*, 132), "We can really say this only of Mark, for Matthew and Luke had their Passion story 'with introduction' before them."

9. W. Marxsen, *Mark the Evangelist*, 209; cf. 30-31.

10. W. L. Knox, *Sources*, 1. 8.

11. M. Albertz, *Streitgespräche*, 6, 16, 18.

12. Cf. W. Marxsen, *Mark the Evangelist*, 15-29.

13. C. H. Dodd, "The Framework of the Gospel Narrative," *New Testament Studies* (Manchester: Manchester University, 1953) 11. Cf. also, for a similar viewpoint, H. Riesenfeld, "On the Composition of the Gospel of Mark," *The Gospel Tradition*, 70-74. For a critique of Dodd's thesis of an "outline scheme," see David E. Nineham, "The Order of Events in St. Mark's Gospel —An Examination of Dr. Dodd's Hypothesis," *Studies in the Gospels: Essays in Memory of R. H. Lightfoot* (ed. D. E. Nineham: Oxford: Basil Blackwell, 1955) 223-239.

14. See Chapter V, Part A, 2, b; also Chapter IV, Part B, c; Chapter III, Part C; Chapter IV, Part D; and Chapter V, Part A.

15. See Chapter III, Part A.

16. See Chapter IV, Part G.

17. See Chapter IV, Part A. Contrast the Q pericope in Luke 11:14 in which the opponents are not identified.

18. See Chapter IV, Part E.

19. Cf. V. Taylor, *Mark*, 478; D. Nineham, *Mark*, 316; and W. Grundmann, *Markus*, 242.
20. See Chapter IV, Part F (including notes 93, 94, and 95).
21. Cf. R. Bultmann, *Synoptic Tradition*, 52; and V. Taylor, *Mark*, 396.
22. See Chapter IV, Part B; and Chapter V, Part B.
23. See Chapter III, Part C; and Chapter V, Part B.
24. See Chapter III, note 70; and Chapter V, Part B.
25. See Chapter IV, Part F.
26. This is essentially the viewpoint expressed by J. M. Robinson, *The Problem of History in Mark*, 43-51. Cf. also H. C. Kee, *Community*, 36-38. Robinson says that the decisive parallel to the conflict stories is to be found in the exorcisms, not in rabbinic debate (p. 44). While this may be true for Mark, it is not necessarily the case for the conflict stories in the pre-Marcan stages of transmission, nor in the Q and special Lucan stories. Robinson makes his conclusion with the whole of Mark in view, not the history of transmission of the conflict stories nor their use at the beginnings of that history.
27. Cf. ibid., 23-24; W. Wink, *John the Baptist*, 5-6; and A. Suhl, *Die Funktion der alttestamentlichen Zitate*, 133-137, for the view that Mark conceived history essentially in terms of two epochs: prehistory (the Old Testament period) and the present history begun with the preaching of John.
28. Cf. R. H. Fuller, *Interpreting the Miracles*, 77-78.
29. Cf. Adolf Schlatter, *Der Evangelist Matthäus* (Stuttgart: Calwer, 1929) 301; R. Bultmann, *Synoptic Tradition*, 15-16; B. W. Bacon, *Studies in Matthew* (New York: Holt, 1930) 189-190; Heinrich Greeven, "Die Heilung des Gelähmten nach Matthäus," *Wort und Diesnst* N. S. 4 (1955) 70; and H. J. Held, "Matthew as Interpreter of the Miracle Stories," *Tradition and Interpretation in Matthew* (G. Bornkamm, G. Barth, H. J. Held), 175-177, 273-274. For a contrary view, see Wolfgang Schenk, " 'Den Menschen' Mt 9:8," *ZNW* 54 (1963) 272-275.
30. Cf. B. W. Bacon, *Studies in Matthew*, 86.
31. A. Hultgren, "The Double Commandment of Love in Mt 22:34-40," 373-378.
32. Ibid., 376, 378. Cf. also V. Furnish, *The Love Command in the New Testament*, 32-33; and G. Barth, "Matthew's Understanding of the Law," 77, who writes, "The whole law and the prophets can be exegetically deduced from the command to love God and the neighbor, they 'hang' exegetically on these."
33. Cf. R. Bultmann, *Synoptic Tradition*, 51; and Joseph A. Fitzmyer, "The Son of David Tradition and Mt 22:41-46 and Parallels," *Essays on the Semitic Background of the New Testament* (Missoula: Scholars, 1974) 114.
34. Cf. R. Hummel, *Die Auseinandersetzung*, 13-17. For recent discussions of anti-Pharisaism in Matthew, see Georg Strecker, *Der Weg der Gerechtigkeit*, 137-143; Wolfgang Trilling, *Das wahre Israel: Studien zur Theologie des Matthäus-Evangeliums* (Munich: Kösel, 1964) 198-202; W. D. Davies, *The Setting of the Sermon on the Mount*, 290-292 et passim; and Douglas R. A. Hare, *The Theme of Jewish Persecution of Christians in the Gospel According to St. Matthew* (SNTSMS 6; Cambridge: Cambridge University, 1967) 85-96.
35. Cf. the discussion of the *Streitgespräche* in Matthew by R. Hummel, *Die Auseinandersetzung*, 36-56.
36. For discussion of the halachic form in Matthew, see W. Trilling, *Das wahre Israel*, 116-117. J. Neusner (*The Rabbinic Traditions about the Pharisees before 70*, 3. 5) defines the form as used in rabbinic materials: "A legal, or *halakhic*, tradition is a saying or story about the *way* something is to be done, a statement intended to have practical effect and carry normative authority, or an inquiry into the logic or legal principle behind such a rule."

37. G. Barth, "Matthew's Understanding of the Law," 87.
38. See *m. Git.* 9:10. Cf. J. Fitzmyer, "Matthean Divorce Texts," 205-211.
39. Cf. H. J. Held, "Matthew as Interpreter of the Miracle Stories," 175-177, 273-274.
40. Cf. G. Bornkamm, "End-Expectation and Church in Matthew," and G. Barth, "Matthew's Understanding of the Law," 31 (n. 2); and 81.
41. Ibid. (G. Barth), 81; G. Strecker, *Der Weg der Gerechtigkeit*, 32-33.
42. Cf. D. Hill, "On the Use and Meaning of Hosea VI. 6 in Matthew's Gospel," 116.
43. R. Hummel, *Die Auseinandersetzung*, 17-18. In 7:29 Matthew identifies the scribes as "their" (= the Jews') scribes (against Mark 1:22), and in 2:4 it is "scribes of the people" in distinction from Christian scribes.
44. It was suggested above (Chapter IV, Part F) that Matthew also designated the Pharisees as opponents at 19:3, and that originally in Mark 10:2 the questioners were undesignated.
45. Cf. also Matt. 16:1 (from Mark 8:11).
46. R. Bultmann, *Synoptic Tradition*, 12-13. Although these pericopes are to be classified as conflict stories, they are not given treatment in our study, since that would give a disproportionate emphasis to sabbath conflict stories. Also to be noted are certain other passages in Luke which have similarities to the conflict story form, but which are finally not to be classified as such. These are at 11:37-41; 15:2-7; and 16:14-15. The first of these (11:37-41) opens with recording the amazement of a Pharisee (that Jesus did not wash before dinner, 11:38), but this is followed by an anti-Pharisaic statement (11:39-41) which begins an anti-Pharisaic discourse (11:39-44) which has parallels in Matt. 23:25-26, 23, 6-7, 27, and which may be based partly on Q material. The second (15:2-7) opens with a charge against Jesus (15:2), to which Jesus responds with a parable (15:3-7). The third (16:14-15) records scoffing at Jesus by the Pharisees (16:14), to which Jesus responds with a polemical saying against them (16:15).
47. Various commentators have disagreed concerning the extent of this section. It clearly begins at 9:51, but where does it end? The following have been suggested by various scholars: 18:14; 19:10, 27, 28, 44, 46, and 48. The first suggestion (18:14) has nothing to commend itself except that at 18:15 Luke resumes his use of Mark (cf. Mark 10:13). Other places (19:10, 27, 28) short of 19:44 must be rejected, since each is followed by a resumption of travel (19:11, 28, 41). The last two (19:46, 48) fall within the ministry of Jesus in the temple. The section closes at 19:44. For further discussion, and an overview of Luke's structure as a whole, see Arland J. Hultgren, "Interpreting the Gospel of Luke," *Int* 30 (1976) 353-368.
48. Cf. Bo Reicke, "Instruction and Discussion in the Travel Narrative," *SE* 1 (1959) 206-216; idem, *The Gospel of Luke* (Richmond: John Knox, 1964) 38-39; E. Ellis, *Luke*, 146-150; I. Howard Marshall, *Luke: Historian and Theologian* (Grand Rapids: Zondervan, 1970) 152-153.
49. Cf. Walter Grundmann, *Das Evangelium nach Lukas* (Berlin: Evangelische Verlaganstalt, 1964) 133; and Helmut Flender, *St. Luke: Theologian of Redemptive History* (Philadelphia: Fortress, 1967) 20-21.
50. Cf. Jervell, *Luke and the People of God*, 43.
51. Hans Conzelmann, *The Theology of St. Luke* (New York: Harper & Brothers, 1960) 77-78.
52. Ibid., 164; and H. Flender, *St. Luke*, 133.
53. Cf. C. K. Barrett, *The Holy Spirit and the Gospel Tradition* (New York:

Macmillan, 1947) 69-78; and H. Conzelmann, *The Theology of St. Luke*, 183-184.

54. For a discussion of "political apologetic" in Luke-Acts as a whole, see H. Conzelmann, *The Theology of St. Luke*, 138-144; in Acts alone, Burton S. Easton, *Early Christianity: The Purpose of Acts and Other Papers* (ed. Frederick C. Grant; Greenwich: Seabury, 1954) 33-41; and Erwin R. Goodenough, "The Perspective of Acts," *Studies in Luke-Acts* (ed. Leander E. Keck and J. Louis Martyn; Nashville: Abingdon, 1966) 51-59.

55. Cf. H. Conzelmann, *The Theology of St. Luke*, 139.

Conclusions

The synoptic conflict stories were formulated at various stages in the history of the synoptic tradition. The process of formation had its beginning in the Palestinian church. But, contrary to R. Bultmann,[1] the process was not limited to that milieu. It continued in the Hellenistic churches of the Diaspora, and it took place also in the church of Matthew, in which materials were taken over from Mark, Q, and special Matthean traditions and formulated as conflict stories.

That the conflict stories were formulated in such diverse circumstances calls into question the assumption that one can assign them all to a common *Sitz im Leben* as R. Bultmann and M. Dibelius have done. A comparative study of the conflict stories within the context of ancient dialogue forms (Chapter I) leads to the conclusion that the conflict stories do not share the form of rabbinic debates presented in the Jewish sources. Nor do they share the form of the Hellenistic chriae. The use of rabbinic disputations and chriae as analogies to the conflict stories has short-circuited the study of the latter as a unique form, and it has resulted in premature judgments as to their *Sitz im Leben*.

The conflict stories formulated in the Palestinian church have a *Sitz im Leben* in apologetics (except for the Beelzebul Controversy); the community appeals to the attitude, conduct, and sometimes authentic words of Jesus in response to Jewish criticism. Christian conduct and belief are justified not by debate after the fashion of the rabbis but, rather, by going behind the rules of juristic procedure to the spirit of the Master himself regarding the oral interpretation of the Torah.

The conflict stories formulated in the Hellenistic church, however, have a different *Sitz im Leben*. They are catechetical, serving the needs of teaching converts and regulating the life in the community. Within these stories Scripture is used, and the teaching given is presented as

197

an exegetical conclusion. The function of the adversaries is to state a position over against which Christian teaching departs.

Finally, the conflict stories which Matthew formed out of Marcan, Q, and special Matthean traditions have a *Sitz im Leben* in the teaching activities peculiar to that setting. The evangelist presents Jesus as Teacher over against the Pharisaic position on the details of the law by identifying the opponents frequently as Pharisees. The Christians are instructed in the spirit of the Teacher himself to depart from the Pharisaic position.

The question as to how far the conflict stories are historically trust-worthy concerning the life of Jesus of Nazareth has not been a major object of this study, but the question is inescapable, and it may be touched on here. Certainly the judgment of M. Albertz that all the synoptic conflict stories contain within themselves (in what he calls the "original dialogues") reports of actual conflicts in the ministry of Jesus[2] cannot be accepted, since it has been observed that the conflict stories were formulated at various stages in the history of the tradition to serve the needs of the Christian communities.

However, one should not conclude that the process of formation has its impetus merely in the attitude of early Christians vis-à-vis con-temporary Judaism. To be sure, all of the conflict stories are Christian compositions; they cannot be attributed to Jesus (i.e., Jesus did not compose conflict stories). But what is common to them is that they portray vividly Jesus' relationship to current thought and practice, and this portrayal exists very early in the tradition. (We have traced the collecting of Mark 2:1–3:6 back into the early 40s in Chapter V, but this means that the composition of individual stories could have been even earlier.) Some of the conflict stories contain traditional sayings of Jesus concerning the issues of his time; a few of them, fur-thermore, present vivid scenes out of his ministry. Others, in which no traditional sayings of Jesus can be found, have nevertheless been shown to express the attitude of the historical Jesus (concerning fel-lowship with sinners, tradition, divorce, and resurrection, for example). Therefore it cannot be said that the creative impulse for the conflict story form of presentation originated purely in the conflicts of church and synagogue. Behind the process of conflict story formation stands the personality of Jesus himself as it was remembered by those who knew him, and as it was made known to others incorporated into their fellowship.

Beyond our study lies the broader question of the place of Jesus and the early church within and (for the latter) outside of ancient Judaism. Certainly the conflict stories portray but one aspect of the whole. It has been suggested, for example, that it was only certain types of Pharisees with whom Jesus would have entered into polemics, and that other Pharisees were quite close in spirit to him.[3] In any case, it is certain that Jesus and those who composed the Palestinian conflict stories did not work "outside of" Judaism but, as children of Abraham, made decisions "from within" (a particular strain of) Jewish tradition (which Jesus represented) concerning certain teachings and practices. These decisions were developed and strengthened in the developing communities (but also revised, such as in Matthew's classic revision of teaching on divorce, 19:3-9) as they moved "outside of" Judaism toward their own self-consciousness as Christian communities within the larger environment, both Jewish and Gentile. What is distinctive about all the conflict stories, however, is their constant reference to Jesus [4]—his words, attitude, and conduct—by whom it was claimed, God's gracious call to the kingdom was realized among his children.

NOTES

1. R. Bultmann, *Synoptic Tradition*, 48. Bultmann says concerning the conflict stories that "we can firmly conclude that the formulation of the material in the tradition took place in the Palestinian Church," and that "we can seldom find any trace of Hellenistic influence." In "The Study of the Synoptic Gospels," 41, he writes, "One may safely infer that these narratives have almost all been formulated in a Jewish environment and do not belong to the later Hellenistic period of development."
2. M. Albertz, *Streitgespräche*, vi, 57-80.
3. Asher Finkel, *The Pharisees and the Teacher of Nazareth: A Study of Their Background, Their Halachic and Midrashic Teachings, the Similarities and Differences* (Leiden: Brill, 1964; reprinted and corrected, 1974) 134. Finkel thinks that the polemics were with the House of Shammai's disciples only, and that the disciples of Hillel's House would have been well disposed. Such a view is probably extreme. For example, tradition has it (Acts 22:3) that Paul, prior to his call as an apostle, was a disciple of Gamaliel of the House of Hillel, and yet he was an opponent of Christianity from the start (even through Gamaliel himself is said to have been tolerant in Acts 5:34-39). Second, the teaching of Jesus on divorce (Mark 10:2-9) is certainly not in harmony with that of Hillel. In short, the situation is complex, and one must conclude that in first century Christianity there was no consciousness of an affinity between the spirit of Jesus and that of Hillel. Nevertheless, Finkel's point that Pharisaism was not monolithic, and that certain Pharisees might not have taken offense at Jesus is well taken.
4. Cf. W. D. Davies, "The Moral Teaching of the Early Church," *The Use of the Old Testament in the New and Other Essays* (ed. J. Efird) 314-315.

Afterword: Christians and Jews in Light of the Conflict Stories

The conflict stories appear in gospels that the church has come to consider a part of canonical Scripture. On certain occasions therefore they will be read during public worship, in the classrooms of the church school, and privately. From time to time they will be the subject of preaching and teaching.

It is important for the interpreter to know the circumstances surrounding the origins of the conflict stories. They reflect ways in which the church dealt with issues and made some important judgments and conclusions concerning thought and ethics, which are still a part of the church's teaching today. It is clear, moreover, that in several stories these issues were worked out in reference to Judaism, and in these cases the latter is rather consistently portrayed as critical of the Christian movement and holding to positions from which the church departs.

The circumstances of history are that while initially the church was a minority, it has become dominant in places where Judaism and Christianity share a common life together (modern Israel being an exception), and Judaism has become a minority surrounded by the Christian majority. This very different situation makes it necessary for the interpreter to deal with these particular pericopes with sensitivity to the changed situation. It is a vice, not a virtue, to continue to portray Judaism in the negative terms of these stories, even when it is so portrayed in these segments of the Scriptures of the Christian church. Judaism itself has undergone changes from the first century of the common era, just as Christianity has, and the changed situation of majority and minority relationships makes it imperative for the Christian to see things in light of what has happened.

Perhaps an analogy is appropriate. As a child rises against its parent to assert its own independence, so the child (the church) rose up against its parent (Judaism) to work out its own way of life in relative freedom. It is important that such took place. For the church saw all things in a new way through Jesus Christ, and it was necessary for her to assert a new existence along the lines of her convictions rooted in the will of the risen Christ and in the characteristic freedom and inclusiveness of Jesus of Nazareth, as he was remembered in traditions about him.

But today the interpreter will ask, What is it in these particular stories that addresses issues of our times? The adversary is no longer Judaism or its representatives and adherents. To continue our analogy, the child has come of age, and if it is mature, it will rise up now and call its parent blessed. For it is precisely from our parent Israel that Jesus of Nazareth, crucified and risen, has come into our world and confirmed the promises to Abraham that he would be the father of many nations (Gen. 17:4-5). The adversary of today is any mind-set either in the Christian tradition or secular society which seeks to maintain positions, prejudices, or mores which will not allow the characteristic freedom witnessed to in these stories to have its way with us, opening us up to the free exercise of love toward neighbors whom many would consider "tax collectors and sinners"—persons of other religious, ethnic, racial, or cultural traditions.

We are faced then with a problem in hermeneutics. Knowing the circumstances out of which these stories were composed, we are compelled to re-present their stance, impact, and teaching over against the adversaries of our time. They call forth from the church the daring and shocking activities of declaring God's forgiveness, having fellowship with outcasts, doing good and saving life, rendering to God that service which is due him alone, attacking traditions which usurp the place of God's commandments, loving God with all one's powers and one's neighbor as oneself, and so on.

In our hermeneutical task we should also allow the realities of history to inform our thinking. Among the adversaries of God, his will, his righteousness and justice, and therefore the adversaries of Jesus himself, have been those who have persecuted the Jewish people. One wonders how much the conflict stories themselves—found in the Christian Scriptures—have contributed to anti-Judaism. If they have done such, they have been interpreted one hundred and eighty degrees in the wrong direction. Their intent is to work out in Christian thought and action a stance of embracing others—and particularly those (Jew or Gentile) who are despised within the larger social and cultural context. The adversaries of any people or persons are the adversaries of Jesus. The Christian church, and especially the interpreter of Scripture, must discern who these are on a day-to-day basis, rather than perpetuate a frozen mind-set, which is precisely what these stories challenge.

In our study and interpretation of the conflict stories we should remember that one of them contains two commandments which are binding upon Jew and Christian alike, and which from the Christian perspective are central to the task of hearing what Scripture says in all its parts: "You shall love the Lord your God with all your heart, and with all your soul, and with all your might" (Deut. 6:5; Matt. 22:37//Mark 12:30//Luke 10:27); and "You shall love your neighbor as yourself" (Lev. 19:18; Matt. 22:39//Mark 12:31//Luke 10:27). To this the evangelist Matthew adds, "on these two commandments depend all the law and the prophets" (22:40).

Appendix A: A Table of Conflict Story Classification

A Tabular View of the Material Admitted in the Works of Albertz and Bultmann (as controversy dialogues), Dibelius (as paradigms), and Taylor (as pronouncement stories). The letter "x" indicates that the pericope is admitted.

	Albertz	Bultmann	Dibelius	Taylor
Mark				
1:23-27, Healing the Demoniac			x	
2:1-12, Healing the Paralytic	x	x	x	x(2:3-12)
2:13-17, Eating with Tax Collectors and Sinners	x	x(2:15-17)	x	x(2:15-17)
2:18-22, Question about Fasting	x	x	x	x(2:18-20)
2:23-28, Plucking Grain on the Sabbath	x	x	x	x(2:23-26)
3:1-6, Healing on the Sabbath	x	x	x(3:1-5)	x(3:1-5)
3:20-21, 30-35, Jesus' True Kindred			x	x(3:31-35)
3:22-30, Beelzebul Controversy	x	x		x(3:22-26)
4:10-12, Reason for Parables				x
6:1-6a, Rejection at Nazareth			x	
7:1-23, Clean and Unclean	x	x		x(7:5-8)
8:11-12, Pharisees Seek Sign	x(8:11-13)			x

203

	Albertz	Bultmann	Dibelius	Taylor
9:38-39, Strange Exorcist				x
10:2-12, On Divorce	x	x		x(10:2-9)
10:13-16, Blessing the Children			x	x
10:17-27, Rich Young Man	x		x	x
10:34-50, Sons of Zebedee			x	x
10:46-52, Healing Blind Bartimaeus			x	
11:15-17, Cleansing the Temple			x	
11:27-33, Question of Authority	x	x		x
12:13-17, Paying Taxes to Caesar	x	x	x	x
12:18-27, On the Resurrection	x	x	x	x
12:28-34, The Greatest Commandment	x			x
12:35-40, Question about David's Son	x			x(12:35-37)
12:41-44, The Widow's Mite				x
13:1-2, Prediction of Temple Destruction				x
14:3-9, Anointing at Bethany			x	x

Q Material

	Albertz	Bultmann	Dibelius	Taylor
Matt. 4:1-11// Luke 4:1-13, The Temptation	x			
Matt. 8:19-22// Luke 9:57-62, Would-be Disciples				x
Matt. 11:2-6// Luke 7:18-23, Question of John	x			

	Albertz	Bultmann	Dibelius	Taylor
Matt. 12:22-37// Luke 11:14-23, Beelzebul Controversy		x		x
Matthew's Special Material				
17:24-27, Payment of Temple Tax				x
Luke's Special Material				
6:5 (Bezae), Man Working on Sabbath				x
7:36-50, The Sinful Woman in Simon's House	x			
9:51-56, Setting Out for Jerusalem			x	x(9:52b-56)
11:27-28, True Blessedness				x
12:13-14, Request to Divide an Inheritance				x
13:1-5, Exhortation to Repentance				x
13:10-17, Healing a Crippled Woman	x			x
14:1-6, Healing Man with Dropsy	x		x	x
17:11-19, Healing Ten Lepers				x
17:20-21, Question on Coming of Kingdom				x
23:27-31, Lament over Daughters of Jerusalem				x

Appendix B: Rabbinic Texts
Related to Chapter I

1. M. 'Abod. Zar. 4:7.[1]

They asked the elders in Rome, "If God has no pleasure in an idol why does he not make an end of it?" They answered, "If man worshipped a thing of which the world had no need he would make an end of it; but lo, they worship the sun and moon and the stars and the planets: shall God destroy his world because of fools?" They said to them, "If so, let him destroy that which the world does not need and leave that which the world needs." They answered, "We would but confirm them that worship them, for they would say, Know ye that these are [true] gods, for they have not been brought to an end."

2. *Midrash Bereshith Rabba*, Parascha 10 (on Gen. 2:1).[2]

The cursed Hadrian asked R. Joshua ben Chanina: How did God create his world? The rabbi shared with him the explanation of R. Chama bar Chanina. How then is that possible? continued the Caesar. The rabbi led him into a small house and told him: Stretch out your hand toward the east and toward the west, and toward the north and toward the south. Likewise it happened with the work of creation before God.

3. *Midrash Bereshith Rabba*, Parascha 28 (on Gen. 6:7).[3]

(Text of Gen. 6:7, "So the Lord said, 'I will blot out man whom I have created from the face of the ground.'")

Hadrian, may his bones be broken to pieces, asked R. Joshua ben Chanina: From whence will God let new life blossom forth for men? He gave for an answer: From the vertebrae of the spine.

How do you know that?

The rabbi continued: Bring one to me, and I shall convince you. They ground a vertebra in a grinder, but it was not ground up; they placed it in fire, but it did not burn; they put it in water, but it did not dissolve; they placed it on an anvil and began to strike it with a hammer, until the anvil cracked and the hammer split, but no change was to be noticed in the vertebrae. The word *'mhh* (lit., I will blot out) is interpreted: I destroy my creation, but it does not destroy me.

4. *Midrash Tehillim* on Psalm 10.[4]

Another comment on "Why standest Thou afar off, O Lord?" (Ps. 10:1). This verse is to be considered in the light of what Scripture says elsewhere: "With their flocks and with their herds they shall go to seek the Lord, but they shall not find him. He hath drawn off *(halas)* from them" (Hos. 5:6). A certain sophist asked Rabban Gamaliel: "Is it possible that you still say, 'We wait for the Lord who will deliver us?'" Rabban Gamaliel answered: "Yes." The sophist said: "You are uttering a lie. God will never return to you, for does not Scripture say, 'He hath drawn off *(halas)* from them' (Hos. 5:6)? Can a childless widow who, performing the ceremony of *Halisah*, draws the shoe off her brother-in-law's foot, expect to have her dead husband return to her? And therefore does it not follow that God will not return to you?" Whereupon Rabban Gamaliel asked the sophist: "In the ceremony of *Halisah*, who draws off the shoe, the woman or the man?" The sophist answered: "The woman draws the shoe off." Rabban Gamaliel then said: "God has drawn off from us, but we have not drawn off from Him. If the surviving brothers draw the shoe off the woman's foot, what validity would such an act have? Therefore does Scripture say, 'He hath allowed them to draw off from Him'? Not at all! It says only, 'He hath drawn off from them.' Thus also Scripture says, 'I opened to my Beloved; but my Beloved had drawn away, and was gone' (Song 5:6). Accordingly, the children of Israel cried: 'Why standest Thou afar off, O Lord?'" (Ps. 10:1).

5. *Midrash Qoh.* on Eccl. 5:10.[5]

A Samaritan asked R. Meir: Do the dead revive again? Yes. Concealed or publicly? How can you prove it to me? I shall present proof to you neither from the Scriptures, nor from the Mishnah, but from daily life. In our city a noble man lives, to whom all secretly confide their affairs, and he gives them back to them publicly. Now if a man committed to him things in the presence of people, will he present them in secret or publicly to him again? Publicly. Would that your ears might hear what your mouth speaks! said R. Meir. Men give to their wives a white drop to develop, and God gives it back to him as a fully developed creature; so how much more will the dead man, who is publicly brought to the grave, also return publicly and, what's more, even with louder voice?

6. *B. Sabb.* 31a.[6]

On another occasion it happened that a certain heathen came before Shammai and said to him, "Make me a proselyte, on condition that you teach me the whole Torah while I stand on one foot." Thereupon he repulsed him with the builder's cubit which was in his hand. When he went before Hillel, he said to him, "What is hateful to you, do not to your neighbor: that is the whole Torah, while the rest is the commentary thereof; go and learn it."

7. *B. Ros Has.* 176.

Bluria the proselyte put this question to Rabban Gamaliel: "It is written in your Law, [she said], 'who lifteth not up the countenance,' and it is also written, 'The Lord shall lift up his countenance upon thee.'" R. Jose the priest joined the conversation and said to her: "I will give you a parable which will illustrate the matter." (A parable follows, and then R. Akiba arrives and gives a teaching.)

8. *B. Hag.* 5b.

R. Joshua b. Hanania was [once] at the court of Caesar. A certain unbeliever showed him [by gestures]: A people whose Lord has turned His face from them. He showed him [in reply]: His hand is stretched over us. Said Caesar to R. Joshua: What did he show thee?—A people whose Lord has turned His face from them. And I showed him: His hand is stretched over us.

They [then] said to the heretic: What didst thou show him? —A people whose Lord has turned His face from them. And what did he show thee?—I do not know. Said they: A man who does not understand what he is being shown by gestures should hold converse in signs before the King! They led him forth and slew him.

9. *B. Yebam.* 102b.

A certain Min once said to R. Gamaliel: "You are a people with whom its God has performed *halizah*, for it is said in Scriptures, 'With their flocks and with their herds they shall go to seek the Lord, but they shall not find him; He hath drawn off [the shoe] from them.'" The other replied: "Fool, is it written: 'He hath drawn off [the shoe] for them?' It is written, 'He hath drawn off [the shoe] from them'; now in the case of a sister-in-law from whom the brother drew off [the shoe] could there be any validity in the act?"

10. *B. Sanh,* 90b.

[A Samaritan] asked R. Meir, "I know that the dead will revive, for it is written, And they [sc. the righteous] shall [in the distant future] blossom forth out of the city [Jerusalem] like the grass of the earth. But when they arise, shall they arise nude or in their garments?"—He replied, "Thou mayest deduce by an a fortiori argument [the answer] from a grain of wheat: if a grain of wheat, which is buried naked, sprouteth forth in many robes, how much more so the righteous, who are buried in their raiment!"

11. *B. Sanh.* 90b, 91a.

An emperor said to Rabban Gamaliel: "Ye maintain that the dead will revive; but they turn to dust, and can dust come to life?" Therefore his [the emperor's] daughter said to him [the Rabbi]: "Let me answer him: In our town there are two potters; one fashions [his products] from water, and the other from clay: who is the more praiseworthy?" "He who fashions them from water," he replied. "If he can fashion [man] from water, surely he can do so from clay!"

12. *B. Sanh.* 91a.

A sectarian [min] said to Gebiha b. Pesisa, "Woe to you, ye wicked, who maintain that the dead will not revive: if even the living die, shall the dead live!" He replied, "Woe to you, ye wicked, who maintain that the dead will not revive: if what was not, [now] lives, surely what has lived, will live again!"

13. *B. 'Abod.* Zar. 54b.

Our Rabbis taught: Philosophers asked the elders in Rome, "If your God has no desire for idolatry, why does he not abolish it?" They replied, "If it was something of which the world has not need that was worshipped, He would abolish it; but people worship the sun, moon, stars and planets; should He destroy the Universe on account of fools! The world pursues its natural course, and as for fools who act wrongly, they will have to render an account."

14. *B. Hul.* 27b.

He put to him this further question: One verse says, "And God said, Let the waters bring forth abundantly the moving creature that hath life, and let birds fly above the earth," from which it would appear that birds were created out of the water; but another verse says, "And the Lord God formed out of the ground every beast of the field and every bird of the air," from which it would appear that they were created out of the earth?—He replied, They were created out of the alluvial mud. He thereupon noticed his disciples looking at each other with surprise. "You are no doubt displeased," said he, "because I brushed aside my opponents with a straw. The truth is that they were created out of the water but they were brought before Adam only in order that he might name them." Others say that he replied to the [Roman] general in accordance with the latter view, but to his disciples he gave the first explanation, since they [birds] are mentioned in connection with the expression, And He formed.

15. *B. Hul.* 59b.

Another time the Emperor said to R. Joshua b. Hananiah, "I wish to see your God." He replied, "You cannot see him." "Indeed," said the Emperor, "I will see him." He went and placed the Emperor facing the sun during the summer solstice and said to him, "Look up at it." He replied, "I can not." Said R. Joshua, "If at the sun which is but one of the ministers that attend the Holy One, blessed be He, you can not look, how then can you presume to look upon the divine presence?"

16. *B. Bek.* 5a.

A Roman general Controcos questioned R. Johanan b. Zakkai. "In the detailed record of the numbering of the Levites, you find the total is twenty-two thousand three hundred, whereas in the sum total you only find twenty-two thousand. Where are the [remaining] three hundred?" He replied to him: "[The remaining] three hundred were [Levite] first-born, and a first-born can not cancel the holiness of a first-born." What is the reason? said Abaye: Because it is sufficient for a [Levite] first-born to cancel his own holiness.

17. *Pesikta Rabbati, Piska* 21.[7]

Hadrian . . . contrived a problem for R. Joshua ben Hananiah, saying to him: The Holy One, blessed be He, bestowed a great privilege upon the nations of the world when He gave five commandments to Israel and offered five to the nations of the world. In the first five commandments, which the Holy One, blessed be He, gave to Israel, His name is involved with the commandments, so that if Israel sin, God raises a cry against them; but in the second five commandments, which He offered to the nations of the earth, His name is not involved with the commandments, so that when the nations of the earth sin, He raises no cry against them.

R. Joshua replied: "Come and walk about the city's squares with me." And in each and every place where R. Joshua led him, Hadrian saw standing a statue of himself. R. Joshua asked: "This object—what is it?" The emperor replied: "It is a statue of me." "And this one here—what is it?" The emperor replied: "It is a statue of me." Finally R. Joshua drew him along and led him to a privy, where he said to him: "My lord king, I see that you are ruler everywhere in this city, but you are not ruler in this place." The emperor asked: "Why not?" R. Joshua replied: "Because in each and every place I saw standing a statue of you, but a statue of you is not standing in this place." Hadrian replied: "And you are a Sage among the Jews! Would such be the honor due to a king that a statue of him be set up in a place that is loathsome, in a place that is repulsive, in a place that is filthy?" R. Joshua replied: "Do not your ears hear what your mouth is saying? Would it redound to the glory of the Holy One, blessed be He, to have His name mentioned with murderers, with adulterers, with thieves?" The emperor dismissed R. Joshua, who went home.

18. *Exempla of the Rabbis*, Exemplum 12.[8]

The Emperor asks R. Gamaliel, "If there is a God in the world, why does He not show Himself and why does He not speak directly to His creatures so that they might respect Him the more?" He replied, "God is a consuming fire." The Emperor is not satisfied with the answer. The next morning, Gamaliel slaps the face of his servant in the presence of the Emperor, who is wroth and thinks that R. Gamaliel deserves punishment for acting so in his presence. R. Gamaliel replies: "He brought me some extraordinary news; a ship of mine lost for seven years has suddenly returned fully laden without sailors and without sails." The emperor declares that is impossible. R. Gamaliel replies, "If so how can a world created by God govern and feed itself alone, without the One who looks after it?" The whole assembly applauds.

19. *Exempla of the Rabbis*, Exemplum 18.

Kleopatra asks R. Meir whether the dead rise in their clothes. The reply was, "In their clothes. The wheat when sown, grows with the cover (husks) on, and how much more should the dead rise with their covers on?"

20. *Exempla of the Rabbis*, Exemplum 50.

A Min and Gaboha b. Pesisa disputed about the quickening

of the dead. The Min said, "Woe unto you ye living who say that
the dead rise again; you are sure to die; but how can those who
disappear come again?" The reply was, "Woe unto ye sinners who
say that the dead do not rise, for those who have not been before
come into existence (are born) and yet you do not believe that
those who have been before can come again." He replied: "You
call me a sinner, I will beat you until I get your hump off your
back." Gaboha replied: "Come and do so and I will call you a
skilful physician."

21. *Exempla of the Rabbis,* Exemplum 55.

The Emperor and R. Gamaliel dispute and the Emperor says,
"God is a thief, He threw Adam into a sleep and then stole a rib
from him!" The daughter of the Emperor replies, "He is a fine
thief. Would you call a man a thief who stole two earthern cups
from you and replaced them by golden ones?"

22. *Exempla of the Rabbis,* Exemplum 84.

Story of the man who tried Hillel's patience by asking him
irrelevant questions, in the hope of angering him and thereby
winning a wager of four hundred *zuzim.* The first question was:
"Why are not the heads of Babylonians round?" and the answer
was: "Because they have no clever midwives." The second question, put after an hour's delay, was: "Why are the eyes of the
inhabitants of Tadmor small?" The answer was: "Because they
live in caves." At the end of another hour the third question was
put, "Why are the feet of the inhabitants of Afriki flat?" and the
reply was: "Because they live in swamps." He did not lose
patience after all.

NOTES

1. Translation from *Mishnah* (H. Danby), 442-443.
2. Translated from the German text in *Der Midrasch Bereschit Rabba* (trans. into
   German by August Wünsche; Leipzig: Schulze, 1881) 40.
3. Ibid., 124.
4. Quoted from the *Midrash on Psalms* (2 vols.; trans. William G. Braude; New
   Haven: Yale University, 1959) 1. 157-158.
5. Trans. from the German text in *Der Midrasch Kohelet* (ed. August Wünsche;
   Leipzig: Schulze, 1880) 76.
6. This and subsequent quotations are from *The Babylonian Talmud* (I. Epstein).
7. Quoted from *Pesikta Rabbati* (2 vols.; trans. William G. Braude; New Haven:
   Yale University, 1968) 1. 415-416.
8. This and the subsequent quotations are taken from *The Exempla of the Rabbis*
   (ed. & trans. Moses Gaster; New York: KTAV, 1968) 54, 56, 63, 65, 72.

Appendix C: Hellenistic Texts Related to Chapter I

1. Diogenes Laertius, *Lives of Eminent Philosophers* 2.8.69.[1]

   (A chapter of sayings by Aristippus)

   When Dionysius inquired what was the reason that philosophers go to rich men's houses, while rich men no longer visit philosophers, his reply was that "the one know what they need while the other do not." When he was reproached by Plato for his extravagance, he inquired, "Do you think Dionysius a good man?" and the reply being in the affirmative, "and yet," said he, "he lives more extravagantly than I do. So that there is nothing to hinder a man living extravagantly and well." To the question how the educated differ from the uneducated, he replied, "Exactly as horses that have been trained differ from untrained horses."

2. Diogenes Laertius, *Lives of Eminent Philosophers* 5.1.19.[2]

   (A chapter of sayings by Aristotle)

   Being asked how much the educated differ from the uneducated, "As much," he said, "as the living from the dead." He used to declare education to be an ornament in prosperity and a refuge in adversity. Teachers who educated children deserved, he said, more honour than parents who merely gave them birth; for bare life is furnished by the one, the other ensures a good life. To one who boasted that he belonged to a great city his reply was, "This is not the point to consider, but who it is that is worthy of a great country."

3. Diogenes Laertius, *Lives of Eminent Philosophers* 6.2.59.[3]

   (A chapter of sayings by Diogenes)

   When someone expressed astonishment at the votive offerings in Samothrace, his comment was, "There would have been far more, if those who were not saved had set up offerings." But others attribute this remark to Diagoras of Melos. To a handsome youth, who was going out to dinner, he said, "You will come back a worse

man." When he came back and said next day, "I went and am none
the worse for it," Diogenes said, "Not Worse-man *(cheirōn,)* but
Lax-man *(Eurytiōn)*."

4. Xenophon, *Memorabilia* 3.13.1-3.[4]

On a man who was angry because his greeting was not returned:
"Ridiculous!" he exclaimed; "you would not have been angry if you
had met a man in worse health; and yet you are annoyed because
you have come across someone with ruder manners!"

On another who declared that he found no pleasure in eating:
"Acumenus," he said, "has a good prescription for that ailment."
And when asked "What?" he answered, "Stop eating; and you will
then find life pleasanter, cheaper, and healthier."

On yet another who complained that the drinking water at home
was warm: "Consequently," he said, "when you want warm water
to wash in, you will have it at hand."

5. Lucian, *Demonax* 21 and 43.[5]

(21) When Peregrinus Proteus rebuked him for laughing a great
deal and making sport of mankind saying: "Demonax, you're not at
all doggish!" he answered, "Peregrinus, you are not at all human."

(43) When someone asked him: "What do you think it is like in
Hades?" he replied: "Wait a bit, and I'll send you word from
there!"

6. Philostratus, *Lives of the Sophists* 1.19.[6]

(A collection of the sayings of Nicetes)

Though he was deemed worthy of the highest honour in Smyrna,
which left nothing unsaid in its loud praise of him as a marvellous
man and a great orator, he seldom came forward to speak in the
public assembly; and when the crowd accused him of being afraid:
"I am more afraid," said he, "of the public when they praise than
when they abuse me." And once when a tax-collector behaved
insolently to him in the law court, and said: "Stop barking at me,"
Nicetes replied with ready wit: "I will, by Zeus, if you too will
stop biting me."

NOTES

1. Translation by R. D. Hicks (LCL; 2 vols., London: Heinemann, 1925) 1. 199.
2. Ibid., 1. 463.
3. Ibid., 2. 61.
4. Translation by E. C. Marchant (LCL; Cambridge: Harvard University, 1923) 253, 255.
5. Translation by A. M. Harmon (LCL; 8 vols.; Cambridge: Harvard University, 1953) 1. 157, 165.
6. Translation by W. C. Wright (LCL; Cambridge: Harvard University, 1961) 65.

Index of Modern Authors

Index of Scripture References